Also by George Callaghan

Non Fiction
Artworks
George Callaghan Sketchbook
(How to be a Real Artist in 24 hours)

Children's
100 Chocolate Soldiers
(Illustrated by George Callaghan)
VILLEFRANCE
(Illustrated by George Callaghan)

callaghanprints.com
www.eakingallery.co.uk
www.gallerysalamanca.com.au
www.saddlerscourt.com

THE LAST MINSTREL

An Autobiography by George Callaghan
Artist, Craftsman, Musician.

Copyright © 2015 George Callaghan.

All rights reserved. No part of this book may be reproduced, stored, or transmitted by any means—whether auditory, graphic, mechanical, or electronic—without written permission of both publisher and author, except in the case of brief excerpts used in critical articles and reviews. Unauthorized reproduction of any part of this work is illegal and is punishable by law.

ISBN: 978-1-4834-2686-0 (sc)
ISBN: 978-1-4834-2685-3 (e)

Library of Congress Control Number: 2015902629

Because of the dynamic nature of the Internet, any web addresses or links contained in this book may have changed since publication and may no longer be valid. The views expressed in this work are solely those of the author and do not necessarily reflect the views of the publisher, and the publisher hereby disclaims any responsibility for them.

Any people depicted in stock imagery provided by Thinkstock are models, and such images are being used for illustrative purposes only.
Certain stock imagery © Thinkstock.

Lulu Publishing Services rev. date: 03/06/2015

To Sadie (my mum)

Forget me not

De gustibus non est disputandum

Dostoyevsky's *The Brothers Karamazov*

Contents

Foreword ix
Preface xi
Acknowledgments xiii
Introduction xv
Dramatis Personae... xix
Preamble.. xxi

Chapter 1   County Antrim 1
Chapter 2   South Africa 14
Chapter 3   Sydenham 34
Chapter 4   The Working Life 52
Chapter 5   Immigration 74
Chapter 6   Tasmania 113
Chapter 7   Hamilton 132
Chapter 8   Bruny Island 162
Chapter 9   Cygnet 181
Chapter 10 The Barge 205
Chapter 11 409 223
Chapter 12 Lherm.. 244
Chapter 13 Age of Enlightenment or things to ponder 268

Foreword

Six of us were having dinner at my home, and nuclear war was the frightening topic of conversation. Someone suggested that each of us should make a list of 10 people that they would invite into their survival shelter. George Callaghan was included on everyone's list. On four of those lists he was number one. When the shit hits the fan, and society fails, he would be one of the few who would be able to reinvent everything - from fishing to hunting, from farming to engineering. Not only did he have knowledge of how everything worked, but he could teach us all how to re-establish what was necessary. More than that, he would keep us all entertained - as not only was he a superb luthier, but an accomplished guitarist, harpist and singer.

He would also decorate our lives with sculpture and painting ... and now this book.

Maybe this artist *will* be let into Utopia!

Doctor John

Preface

I have never read, and probably never will read *Zen and the Art of Motorcycle Maintenance*. Apparently there is one type of individual, one who knows everything about how his motorcycle works on a road trip, and another who isn't particularly interested in how his machine works, just as long as he knows where it can be fixed.

Once I got a grasp of this concept, the philosophical motes were cast from my vision.

Stef, my partner, and I have been together for thousands of years. We are at opposite ends of the pragmatic stakes. Where I fail, she excels. Her innate ability keeps me out of all sorts of strife. Our differences in opinion keep us engaged in endless conversation for endless hours. Sometimes we argue, but rarely row.

Sherlock Holmes measured his problems as a two or three pipe problem. Our morning discussions are similarly measured: a three cup or four cup tea/coffee discussion, two to three hours every morning. As I am self-employed, I do not have to rush out of the door in the morning, so this routine has been nurtured for over 40 years.

Stef still hasn't a clue about how things work. But she is always patient or clever enough to feign interest while I explain. I am still like that guy who owns that first motorbike (a Vespa scooter); I still want to know what is wrong with it when it breaks down, but nowadays I pay someone to fix it.

Acknowledgments

Thanks to my best friend ever for her support as only she knows how.

Also to my editors, Fred Thornett and Lee Ann.

Introduction

The last Minstrel

Legend has it the Minstrel was charmed by the De Danann (the Celtic underground fairies) with the gift of the muses.

Hourly, nay, daily his talents were proclaimed through out the land. Healers, therapists, wizards, herbalists and soothsayers sought his council. It was said that his gifts of vision and music could cure all maladies of the heart and mind. The tranquillity of his images could transform the wildest beast to the meekest lamb. As his fame spread across the land his presence was eventually sought by the King himself.

Because the Minstrel had brought peace and wisdom to the Realm the King appointed him as ambassador and he was designated to travel the universe and share this kingdoms message of serenity.

Enlightened by his travels through out the cosmos the Minstrel eventually returned to his native land.

Alas! Alack! The grayness and dullness of his welcome by his fellow citizens discomforted him, he hurried himself to the King for some sort of explanation.

"Why the sadness in everyones eyes?" thought the Minstrel.

As he reached the outskirts of the city he became aware of advertising billboards and 48 sheet posters displaying all manners of promotions using his image to promote all sorts of horrible products, events and ideals.

His heart grew weary along the last miles to the Kings palace where he begged an audience with his friend the King.

"Why have you done this? " he sadly enquired of the King.

"What my Minstrel friend?"

"Used my image and persona to promote everything that all the citizens know that I deplore? Who has done this? Surely not your noble self?"

"My ministers have done this" the Kings conscience replied. " Send for my ministers!"

The Oligarchy arrived.

"Listen to my friend, the Minstrel and explain!" the King declared.

"Your Majesty, our ailing economy sought ways of enhancing our international status, and our parliament sought methods of promoting our wares throughout the world. Our department of industry and tourism thought of using our most positive and popular image to associate with our assets and that was HIM! " They declared pointing to the Minstrel.

"Who gave you permission to use the Minstrels persona and image?He belongs to no man!" roared the King.

"Well he did of course your Majesty"

"When and where did I give you that permission? " asked the Minstrel.

"We had numerous meetings with the Minstrel where he gave permission to use his persona and his ideals " replied the Oligarchy in unison ignoring the Minstrel.

"And exactly WHEN? " replied the King.

"Why, why, em……three months ago, your Majesty"

"Surely our Minstrel has been traveling the ether at my request for the past several years?"

"Oh…….. oh yes….. well we had our meetings over the telephone" squirmed the Ministers.

"And did he give you his permission to use his image and persona on all of those promotions?"

"Oh yes of course! not only did he give approval to them but he also declared how wonderful the photographs were and was particularly pleased with the sound quality of his music that we had recorded. He was delighted with the specific rose perfume that we used on the *scratch and smell* point of sale"

"Stop! Stop! Stop! " cried the King " Pageboy! Send for my Minister of Justice!"

"I am already here, my Liege."

"What thinks thee of these declarations by my Ministers?"

"This is all very well Sire, but the *sightings* of the photographs? The *sound* quality of the harp music. The *smell* of the flowers on the scratch and smell? *Approved* over the phone? Me thinks I smell a rat your Majesty, something is rotten in the state of Denmark!"

But his logic was drowned by the Oligarchies cries of "But! But! But.......he knew what we were doing your Majesty!"

But their lies and steamrolling overwhelmed the Minstrel and with a saddened heart he left the palace and eventually the streets of his homeland.

"Hypocrite!" strangers hissed as he wandered his crestfallen way " You said you despised de forestation, multinationals, logging, industrial pollution, global warming, weapons of mass destruction, institutionalized music, competitive sports!"

The Minstrels sadness deepened as he surrendered to the jeers of his fellow countrymen, his ideals fading with each step until he left the boundaries of his homeland, Transmania.

His fading steps echoed like the shattering of the petals falling from the last rose of summer.

Dramatis Personae

Sadie: My Mum
Jim: My Dad
Joan:Sister
Anne: My first wife.
Stef: My Constant Companion

My daughters
Sunita
Miche
Mea
Lena

My son
Fintan

Julian: My closest friend
Bill Mac: Surrogate Dad
Mike: One eyed friend

Preamble

Working Class Life in Belfast and the Harland and Wolff Shipyard

The modern era of shipbuilding in Belfast began in 1792 when William Ritchie launched the 300 ton "Hibernia" a year after his arrival from Ayrshire with ten men and materials from his ship yard at Saltcoats.

Shipbuilding rapidly expanded at the River Lagan and by 1838 the first iron built ship in Ireland was launched by Ritchie and McLaine. The shipbuilding industry gradually moved from the banks of the Lagan to Queens Island. In this decade Messrs Harland and Wolff, two young and skilled engineers, acquired an existing shipyard and rapidly expanded its output. This was in large part by innovation in ship design. Thus they increased the carrying capacity of their iron ships by greatly increasing their length without altering their beam. They also replaced the wooden upper decks of their iron ships with iron. This turned their ship hulls into something rather like the box girders that were becoming popular for bridge building in Victorian England.

By 1880 Harland and Wolff ceased towing their hulls to Scotland to have Clydeside engineers install the engines. Thereafter the company made its own engines and associated equipment.

By the turn of the 20th century the company was producing huge ships and was one of the world's leading shipyards. Its most famous vessel was the Titanic launched in 1911. During the First World War the ships yards were given over to naval construction. This recurred during the Second World War and over 130 naval vessels were launched. The shipyards were badly damaged by German bombing but recovered and were back in production within two years.

The shipyard still exists, but in recent decades most of the world's large-scale shipbuilding has moved from Europe to East Asia.

During the long growth of Harland and Wolff from the 1850s to its heyday in the early 20th century, large working class housing estates were erected to accommodate the many families whose men worked in the shipyards and associated industries. At its peak the shipyard employed more than 40,000 men. These men and their families lived mainly in terrace housing of limited comfort and much crowding. People were mostly poor and a "hardman" culture, so typical of the working class in the United Kingdom, was the lot of all boys who grew up in suburbs like East Belfast.

My father and grandfather worked in the shipyards most of their lives and their experiences greatly shaped my own life and worldview. Luckily I had some artistic and musical ability and I managed to escape the thrall of the shipyards and develop a career, firstly in advertising and later in painting. Alongside this my musical skills also matured and helped me to gain another range of experiences. Eventually I emigrated to Australia and after some time moved to Tasmania, the island state which sparkles as a jewel 250 kilometers south of the mainland. Tasmania is a large island. It is about three times the size of Switzerland or roughly the size of Ireland. Yet it has only half a million people. This makes, in combination with Tasmania's benign climate, its mountains, forests, beaches and exquisitely beautiful farmlands and towns provides an environment that has attracted many, craftsmen and lovers of nature. It attracted me and it has provided me with many adventures and some success, though I now divide my time between Ireland, Tasmania, England and France.

Chapter One

County Antrim

Where I learn to cheat the system, what courting meant, to sing Mum's songs, trust the police? Why I stuttered, how to build a caravan, make a trifle, what noise a gun makes, what bent nails are for, what is a coconut? And how to dot my "i's"!

Formby Park 44

The moss between the flagstones was gathered by my sister and covered the entire Delft plate. To this she added flowers so it became her fairy garden. Real girly stuff. We lads had better use for the cracks between the flag stones. It was between these cracks that we lodged our pierrys, Your whip was coiled around it, and with a firm jerk the pierry came to life, spinning at a great rate of knots.

Billy from over the road could whip his pierry the full width of the street in one lash. Sheer grace. Well not grace - that would be twee. You wouldn't want to be girly in our street, not with the Devlins over the road. These guys had attitude; they smashed windies with their pierrys. Their father, I'm sure, could beat my father. Billy's dad was a wimp - anybody's dad could beat his. He even did wimpy things like look at the stars through a telescope he had made himself. It was rumoured that he knew some of their names; Uranus. Even now I don't believe it.

The Devlins were always dressed in rags and caps. They always seemed to be bent over in the street gutter doing something dangerous - playing marlies perhaps. Tony, the youngest, had no fingers on one hand. His hand looked to be the result of Thalidomide - which it wasn't - that was years ahead. No, his two brothers had lifted a storm water grate. Have you ever tried to lift one of those buggers? They are weighed down with fear. Of course - that's the challenge. They lifted it – just. Tony put his fingers in the crack and off they came.

It was a time of rationing, and the children in the surrounding four houses all knew each other intimately – at least the boys did. The girl next door and my sister, well, why bother with them? But on rationing day, the four mothers and all the children would traipse on down to the ration centre and each mother would present her five or seven children to officials and acquire the allotted rationing. No one in the whole of Northern Ireland could have worked out how many children were in the average family, two to three maybe, although there were 17 in my mother's family -15 sisters. Anyway, each mother took their turn in owning and presenting all seven children.

Rogue

Northern Ireland was a nation of rogues in those days, except for those up the Malone Road and the Lisburn Road where all the toffs lived. Later I learnt that they were worse. But a rogue was someone you could deal with. You could rely on not trusting them - it was a pleasant way of saying you were a crook. My dad in those days was a pleasant crook. It was the smouldering days of the war. Being a tradesman and an emerging suppressed coward, he was not required for the war time machine. He was a fitter and turner with his chief's ticket, which allowed him to run, service and repair ships' engines. This gave him continual access to the dock areas and the decks of any ship in for repairs or re-stocking. Re-stocking for him meant not only filling up his pockets with sugar and tea, but the lining of his coat as well with the additional tin or crate of corned beef. He jovially passed the policeman at the end of the gang plank absolutely loaded. On one occasion he had wrapped himself in a beautiful runner carpet, and murmured "goodnight" to the policeman as he tried not to bend his legs too much. As usual the tram will be full, he thought, and no one will notice another standing passenger. Horror of horrors! The tram was empty! He couldn't sit down; he couldn't bend at the waist, so he stood on the empty tram for the entire journey.

My mum Sadie and he went courting. Never quite worked out what was meant by that - after you're married, what's the point? But courting they went, with an added ingredient – a saw. This was not for protection or anything kinky; Northern Irish people are not kinky. The saw was to cut down palings for the fire. After becoming a dab hand at the art, or perhaps because he had exhausted all the palings in the area, he removed every other roof beam instead - not only in his own home, but next door as well. I know the two houses are still standing, so if you live there - be careful Formby Park.

I've been told that my earliest recollections of Belfast might be false, but then there is always some git who wants to dash your childhood memories.

I always thought the flashing lights I saw at night, held up high in my father's arms, was Belfast being bombed during the war. Now I am told they were probably flashes made by the trams crossing the overhead points. But then the memory deceives; that's its job. I recall seeing a motor car accident. I gave witness, but was hounded by the insurance companies to review my statement. After four separate requests I got rid of them by explaining, 'the memory only recalls the memory of recalling the memory' - recalling the memory, I forget the rest.

Class

Our house was brick which was cement rendered. I told people it was pebble-dashed - it wasn't - that was a class above ours. There was a path that went past the front door to the back garden. I fell five times on this path and split my forehead wide open. Truly - three times in one day. Three trips to the hospital. I've just been to the mirror; the scars are all still there. Incidentally, I never was baptised - the church was bombed, so my soul is available.

The back garden faced onto an enormous, vacant field. In the middle of this was a rock as big as Ayers rock. Mum said that on St Patrick's Day, he rolled it around the field, and if it ended sunny-side-up we would have a glorious summer. Needless to say, it always ended up sunny-side-down.

Against the house at the back there leaned lots of planks of wood - off-cuts from my dad's caravan he was building. From these, most days I made buildings of every abstract description. I never did actually understand what these buildings were. One thing they had in common was that you got inside them – only one way in – which could then be secured against the perpetual enemy, and provide a peephole from prying mothers. This was a time when I had nothing to relate these buildings to; no TV, no cinema, no books - only songs my mother sang. I felt I was back in the womb and felt all fuzzy and well.

My mum often sang around the house, but her songs were not the songs that my dad sang. He sang popular songs of the day. My mum's songs were different. She sang songs that her mum had sung to her, or songs that she had learned on the streets of the Shankill Road. These were the folk songs of Belfast, and they have always stayed with me.

I think that my mum could have been a good cook; she used to make wonderful concoctions when she and my sister got together, but my dad's demands for 'meat and two veg' must have cramped her style. She would sit me on the bench with her as she baked, and I salvaged the crumbs. I once saw the kitchen bench covered in crumbs. I made these into a pile and shoveled them into my mouth. They turned out to be sawdust - as my dad was working on the kitchen cupboards!

My dad would often get a yearning for an ice cream, and off he would set. He would be gone for hours down the Old Park Road, and he would return with a large mixing bowl half-full of Fusco's ice cream. These journeys must have been in winter, as I recall that the ice cream was always solid when he got it home!

Come Little Leaves

Written by the American poet George Cooper (1838–1927), music by Thomas J. Crawford.
(I have used one verse only)

Come, little leaves,
Said the wind one day;
Come o'er the meadows
With me and play.
Put on your dresses
Of red and gold;
For summer is past,
And the days grow cold.'

Dobber

Mum claimed my dad was shy, as he would never venture into the back garden if any of the neighbours were about. I reckoned he was terrified of the cops. My granddad got arrested by the cops once. He was working in his shed when the local Bobby called in for a chat. He had always done so for years - for a fag and a cuppa. He noticed one of my granddad's spanners had Harland and Wolfe stamped on it - granddad was another rogue. He arrested my granddad there and then. Rumour had it that he was French, they were renowned as a nation of dobbers. I myself have been dobbed into the gendarme three times already; maybe I am a rogue. Neither my dad nor my granddad trusted a policeman from that day – don't think I do either! I don't know if my dad was shy, but he seemed to be given to fits of anger. Mum had made me a car. It was fantastic: blow-up tyres, steering wheel, front and rear suspension, rack and pinion, differentials, overhead twin cam shaft. I ran down the road to greet him, dragging it behind me, excitement bursting from every pore. 'Get that thing into the house. The neighbours will think I've made it!" he cried. A block of wood and four cotton reels, hmm … I think I will make one again.

Outside in the street were a row of bomb shelters. Concrete boxes with a flat roof. We were not allowed to play in them. In truth, I didn't want to, as they were full of dog doo. I looked in there and I never understood why a dog would want to do his doos in there. But there they were. The movie *Odd Man Out* features one of these fallout shelters; they were poorly built.

One day a massive crane arrived. It had a big iron ball which swung from one side of the road to the other. Us kids cheered and cheered as they smashed them to smithereens. We didn't like those shelters, and they got in the way of our guiders and billy carts. The Devlin's were kings at making billy carts. One piece of wood for the front axle, carved down at the ends to hammer on two ball bearing wheels - giving maximum ground clearance of half an inch. A stolen fence plank - if there were any left that my dad hadn't nicked - a back rest and two scrounged pram wheels, and you were off. If you were lucky, the Devlin's would let you ride behind. And if your mum didn't catch you, you'd be gone down the Old Park Road, through Belfast and on to Gilnahirk.

Bellevue

At Easter we always went to the zoo. Well, we went there once. Yellow gorse flowers were gathered earlier on in the week, and eggs were boiled in them until they turned yellow - too long and they turned brown. Mum said we were to roll them down the hills at the zoological gardens, at Bellevue. The hills had to be mown to a billiard board perfection, as no matter how steep the hill was, or how short the grass, the egg just sat there as still as a mushroom. They were supposed to crack open at the bottom of the hill when they collided with some religious icon - something to do with mangers, rabbits, three old men and a guy named Herod.

Religion never got a look in in those days. Even Christmas only happened because of the weather. My sister and I were in a Christmas club. We subscribed our pennies to a shop on the Old Park Road that we walked to. I recall seeing a dog approaching us with a string of sausages in his mouth; it disappeared through a hole in the fence just before it reached us. We looked behind the fence to find the dog feeding several puppies. No, no - that was just one of my father's stories - but we did collect our Christmas chocolate selection box from the shop. Mine was in a box that had the form of a lantern with Christmas scenes on all four sides. Mum hung it around the light in the living room. It was wonderful. The illuminated Christmas scenes were my ambition for the rest of my life. I have re-lived that Christmas lantern every year.

Dad had made me a massive train for Christmas. I came down the stairs late one night; saw it there in the living room. The engine was fired up with a full head of steam. Black acrid smoke filled the living room. Coal was being shovelled into the fire box. "Mum, mum!" I took off shouting. "There's the most incredible train in the living room - it's on the floor."

My mum cuddled me between her knees. "Now, now, you've just had a dream."

"What's a dream?" They'd been mentioned before, but what was a dream?

"Now quieten down, rest a while, and we'll go into the living room and have a look." We peeped around the door. "See, there you are, nothing," she said.

Well it wasn't a long-lived disappointment, as the train did appear on Christmas morning, along with a very confused understanding of what exactly a dream was. Of course the train was superb. I knew that my father would not have produced anything less than brilliant. But was that the remains of poo on one of the wheels? Had it been rushed out of the house to one of the air raid shelters? After all, I had searched the entire house – not a trace …

He made me a scooter the following year. I'm afraid it didn't go down well, as my sister got a bicycle. Ungrateful prat that I was, maybe I did deserve what was to follow years later.

My dad was making progress with his caravan. The frame was up on blocks. It must have been badly balanced, though, as it slipped forward on to him. Seemed dreadful at the time, but retrospectively, although I was watching when it happened, there was no weight in it, as a caravan frame is no more than an assembly of 18-inch squares of nothing held together with one-and-a-quarter-inch square laths. He didn't half make a fuss.

In later days, when I was fit, I had a Mini Minor roll backwards onto me, which I held off the ground. It had been bogged and the girl I was with couldn't drive. I put it in reverse and lifted, while she let out the clutch … idiot! Not her; me.

The Caravan

Our caravan was parked in a farmer's field, along with others. It always seemed to be winter when we visited - which was often. It was always raining, or else I was over my head in snow. Dad and I crossed the moonlit field with me disappearing at every step beneath the snow. I never recalled mum at the van.

Dad made hot, thick custard. 'Good custard is always slightly burnt with a pinch of salt' - he would claim with authority, while I fiddled with an old radio and a dead battery, trying to get it to work. Now I think about it, we did visit in summer, and of course it was raining … but snow? The trip on the train passed out of Sydenham and moonlit flooded fields, and as it approached Hollywood, I recall gypsy camp fires. That trip was definitely in summer, for there was a gloaming sky, and the evening was quite late. We had with us a rabbit hutch that my father had made for the boy in the caravan next to us. I don't recall him, but I do remember that he'd been to Borstal. That night my dad cooked spuds and a cabbage that he had stolen from the farmer's field next door.

19 Devon Parade

Going to my granny's was always a joy. Her house set values that have lasted forever. She seemed to be always whipping cream filling when we arrived. The sponge cakes had been baked, and sliced sideways on the table waiting for the cream filling to be spooned on. There was no strawberry jam, or jam of any description, to distract from her filling. Still, I haven't a clue how she made it - maybe it was pure butter. At this time people were still using banana essence in cold mashed potato as a dessert, but granny's cream-filled sponge I'd go back in time for.

Her Christmas fruit cake she laboured over for days, removing not only the stalks, but also the stones, from the raisins, sultanas and currants.

Butter was in every cupboard, bought from the country farm where many of my granddad's brothers lived. Eggs were stored in the potting shed at the back lean-to, in a crock filled with Isinglass - which preserved them. This was next to a huge machine full of gears, levers and rusted springs and a massive handle - a clothes mangle – and I wondered how granny could operate that thing without getting her bosoms mangled.

She had one of those buff-coloured bowls sitting at an angle in front of the fire; more butter was softening. What was she baking now?

Over the next few days - we always seemed to stay for several - granny would be making her trifle: the most complex of Fairisle knitting with jelly I have ever seen. It started with her bringing in from the front hall, the empty fish bowl - a fantastic item - a common glass fish bowl surrounded with a casting of a Tudor cottage in a cliché garden, and by a fence next to a stile sat a little boy; a Pears soap bubble boy with a fishing rod, the line of which dropped down into the bowl.

Granny had hundreds of jelly crystals, each one a different colour and flavour - there weren't that many flavours in the whole world! She divided each packet into two. Now she had 200 packets spread throughout the house! One half she dissolved in boiling water. When it had cooled this was added to the fish bowl. The other half of the jelly she dissolved, but when it had cooled she added whisked egg white to it - which turned it a pastel colour. This she added carefully to the first layer of jelly when it had set. She continued this process until the entire fish bowl was full. There were thousands of layers. Where was the sponge cake you ask? My granny didn't add that rubbish, not while my granny had her cream!

Skills

My dad and I must have inherited our skills from my granny. She was renowned for not only her cooking skills, but mum said she was also a superb seamstress. Someone mentioned that she had owned a shop with her sister in her youth.

Dad and I didn't inherit my granddad's skill. The cupboards in my granny's had been built by him and they were shocking. All doors were butt joints overlaid with plywood, painted cream with green trim, and warped. They swung open and none of the catches lined up or worked. There was a shoe rack behind the kitchen door, a rickety thing of dowels and the remains of two floorboards - it would never have made it to a first-year school project. This guy had built the Titanic, on his own.

My granny had varnished the entire elaborate wooden fireplace in the parlour, it never dried. She unknowingly had used engine oil. In 30 years it never dried. However, my granddad never noticed.
The front parlour also contained four elaborate Queen Anne chairs. These had been salvaged from one of the opera theatres in Belfast that had been bombed during the war.

The front hall - which led to the parlour - was tiled in an ornate way, maybe by those Italian tilers who tiled the Crown Bar in Belfast. Behind the front door hung their only really valuable possession - an oil painting - a seascape. In the foreground was a rowing boat - five or six people were in it. In the middle of the picture was a bigger boat, which I think was in peril. To the right was another row boat. Another four or five people were in that. The sky was stormy. The boat in the middle had a French flag. Isolated in a larger area at the front of the picture was a firkin – a small keg. I would stand in front of this painting for hours and think that however you did this - I wanted to be able to do it too.

In the parlour next door, behind a curtain, I found a wooden item. It had a long dowel, the thickness of a brush shaft, attached to some sort of handle. There was a small notched wheel on the side with a smaller handle. There was a thin piece of wood like a wooden ruler. This piece was spring-loaded into the notches of the wheel. I turned the small wheel – rat a tat, rat a tat, rat a tat – wow! My mum and granny came running through the door, and the machine gun was whisked away never to be seen again. I think Granddad had got it for me from a toy maker nearby, who lived and worked in Hillfoot Street. I went there with him once and saw all the toys unpainted under his work bench. I think it was there that I learnt that people actually made toys.

In the small back garden was a strange raised, oval flower bed Granddad had made from one-inch thick slate. There was a lawn surrounded by Granny's flower beds. Lilac trees grew in several parts of the garden. The white lilac flowers were never allowed in the house; it meant death. On top of the raised garden beds was a pile of wall frames and roofing frames for a cottage Granddad was going to build in Lower Ballinderry. I discovered later that they were held together by a collection of rusted, bent nails, perhaps he collected them, or maybe even swapped - them three bent for a straight. Was my grandfather's workmanship an example of the standard of workmanship that was accepted at Harland and Wolff? He was a turner - what other ship did he help to sink?

Orange lilies grew in one corner of the yard. Granddad was proud of these flowers, and I'm sure they held no sectarian value, for I never heard or felt any of these sentiments echoed in our house until years later.

The Arches

Going shopping with Gran was a treat. She was on first name terms with all the shop keepers around the arches, where the train went over on the way to Comber. Geordie Lemon, the green grocer would give her only the best of his veggies. At the bottom of the road, just up from the Paragon was, I waited anxiously for Granny to take us to the grocers. Here she always bought half a pound of broken biscuits, and two marshmallow chocolate covered biscuits for Joan and I, and for later - a packet of crisps, which came with its own little twist of salt in blue paper. Then back down the hill to the Paragon – that was a girly shop.

When we stayed with Granny and Granddad, both Dad and Granddad left the house together and came back home from the shipyard together in the evening. "I hope those kids are not still in my house!" Granddad would holler. "I'll skin them alive!" This was the cue for Joan and me to go and hide behind the coats that were hanging behind the door of the kitchen. He would lean into them and we'd giggle. I can still smell the Woodbine and the Park Drive on their breath.

Fright

That Christmas will forever remain in my mind of how never to behave. My sister and I were sitting on our mum and dad's bed. We had just unwrapped all of our presents. I don't recall ever having a Christmas tree.

Dad said, "Sadie, I'd love a cup of tea."

Of course it was still dark. It stayed dark forever in those days; it still does. "What will I do if the bogey man gets me coming up the stairs?" asked Mum.

"Don't worry about that," said dad, "George will save you."

Mum was gone for what seemed a long time, when she hollered from the stairs, "The bogey man has got me!"

I'm told that I didn't speak for two years after that, and when I did speak I spoke with a dreadful stammer which lasted until I was 18. It was the reason I failed my teacher's interview at Art College.

I slept with my Aunt when she came to stay – Aunt Dolly. The bedroom Dad had painted pink and had been daubed at regular intervals with a sponge dipped in red paint. When it was time to go to bed, I'd smuggle some broken pieces of bread in my pyjama pockets under the blankets. Granny had told me how, as a child, she had made her school friends jealous by taking a poke to school filled with broken bread, pretending that they were sweeties.

Somehow not all of the bread pieces were eaten, and ended up under the bed against the wall. Aunt Dolly told me that at night, when I was asleep, a slice of bread emerged from the ventilator above, crawled along the bottom of the bed, slithered under the sheets and down onto the floor. Have you any idea how a slithering, crawling, slice of bread looks? I can - I've been terrified of them ever since. I felt that I genuinely had a clean slate with my imagination; there were no books in my house to cloud it with preconceived images – all the images were my own.

Wolf was our last dog - an Alsatian of course. Dad had bred them for the war effort. There was a kennel, which I never saw, up in our loft. Dad had built it forgetting rule number one: it must fit through the glory hole. There were certificates of bravery hanging in the hall that the war effort had awarded my dad – which I thought was unfair, as it was the dogs that were brave, not him.

All Dressed Up

During one of our stays at Granny's place, a man visited and set up a load of photographer's lights in the front parlour. Mum dressed me up real girly like. Granddad, Granny, Mum, Dad, Joan and me were all dressed up like pork chops, and the photographer took our pictures. Mum looked really nice; Dad was going bald, while Granddad had kept all his hair. Granny's ample bosom was here, there and everywhere. Joan, well, she just looked twee!

There was a 12-inch square cardboard box on our kitchen bench and Mum un-wrapped it. It was a parcel from Dad, and inside were several items that I had never seen before, including a coconut and a jar of peanut butter! What swanks we had become!

Dad was in South Africa. I'd never even noticed that he had gone but it did give reason for my Granny's and Granddad's behavior. Granny had made me a brown velvet suit with satin piping - which I refused to wear once I was out of her sight.

Granddad taught me to sing *Hello Patsy Fagan* - a terrible song that I won't elaborate on! Or maybe I will! This I was to sing to Dad when we arrived at the quayside in Cape Town - whatever that was!

Then suddenly Mum, Joan and I were off to live in South Africa - which was beyond the moon. My school teacher could have told me where it was, but I was too preoccupied with dotting my 'i's'. Having learnt how to write, it seemed to be all important that i's should be dotted as interestingly as possible. Several of them were graded and shaded! Carrs Glen School would be proud of me when I reached Cape Town.

Chapter Two

South Africa

Where I learn to blow things up, not to tell my Dad everything, to be a racist, keep silk worms, make weapons of mass destruction, to hate, fire a Luger, build model aeroplanes, smoke Dagga, what sex looks like and why Mum got sick.

Cape Town 1946

My Granny had made me a superb, dark brown, velvet suit with satin piping for my arrival in Cape Town, I could wear it today with absolute confidence without feeling a Moffie and my Granda had taught me a song of arrival to sing to my dad on the quays of Kaapstad.

HELLO PATRICK FAGAN
Traditional Irish folk song collected from George Callaghan (senior) 1942 (I have used one verse only)

'Hello Patrick Fagan, you can hear the girls all cry,
Hello Patrick Fagan, you're the apple of my eye.
You're a decent man from Ireland,
As no one can deny.
You're a harum, scarum, divil may care 'em,

You're a decent Irish man!'

Jesus, I hate that song! Thank God the occasion never arose where I actually had to sing it. Although I did wear the brown velvet suit, exactly the same outfit that I have seen Oscar Wilde wearing in an old photograph. My Dad must have had the horrors! I was five years old.

Crossing the Line

The trip to South Africa was exciting at first, especially when we crossed the line and King Neptune and his entourage appeared over the side of the ship and went through their routine; the same routine that I have recently seen performed in Belfast by the local Mummers group. The play and characters were identical. There was a king who held court, a judge, and a surgeon who performed make believe operations on 'patients' selected randomly from the audience. The surgeon under the cover of a sheet would pretend to cut the person open with a huge saw, a butchers cleaver and large scissors. He would them produce for all the court to see an endless stream of sausages.

CA54919 was the registration plate of my dad's car. We owned a car. Wow! We drove along De Waal Drive at the bottom of the most incredibly flat mountain - as flat as a table top. Sometimes it had a layer of cloud on it. "That's the tablecloth," said dad. To the right was a bright, shiny thing in the sky. It had been seen many times before as we sailed towards the equator. Dad said it was a permanent fixture in our new home.

We drove along the bottom of this mountain to Plumstead, to a house called 'Dempsey'. This was to be our home for some time: one bedroom for all four of us; a kitchen – which vanished before I saw it, it was so small – and use of an unused garage. The lady owner had cooked pumpkin scones and pineapple fritters and introduced us to her alcoholic son, Alex, who was on the front stoop lying down in a state of DTs.

My dad went to South Africa with his friend, Walter Smith, from Sydenham - he was a saw doctor. They arrived with a shipload of tradesmen on a South African government assisted passage scheme - which was available only to tradesmen. On arrival, hundreds of men were sent back to the UK as their qualifications were from the British military force; these were unacceptable in South Africa.

Around the corner now lived the Smiths, the family who had migrated at the same time as us from Belfast. In front of their home was the highest Tarzan oak tree imaginable. Our Walter, our Bertie and our Geoffrey were already installed in the tree. Several rope swings allowed us to navigate the entire circumference of the tree. Their sister, Sadie, did girly stuff with Joan.

We lived there for a long time. Occasionally Mum and Dad locked us out of the bedroom for some unfathomable reason.

Cobble Joe

Local black children used to gather outside our house, just where there was a huge fig tree on the vacant lot next door. These children had leather whips about eight or 10 feet long, and at dusk the bats would fly between the fig tree and a pine tree on the other side of the road. For about half an hour the crack of these whips filled the air, as the children would whip those bats clean out of the sky.

We had been there for about a week, when a horse and cart driven by a black man and a woman stopped outside our house. He was shouting something, but we could not understand what he was saying. So my sister ran into the house to fetch Mum. Mum listened carefully, then with an air of understanding, she asked them to wait while she disappeared into the house. After some time she emerged with a tray on which there were two cups of tea, sugar and milk. By then I had worked out that they were actually saying - "Cobble Joe!" - the local fish! How my mother ever interpreted that as 'a cup of tea' …

I would play at Alex's feet and he bought me all sorts of building games, mostly Meccano. He challenged me daily to construct one of the items from the manual, while he wasted himself away drinking milk and brandy. Do they really mix? There were also colouring books and crayons. Was he a bit strange, or just a nice but sad man? He died in hospital after a particularly drunken hallucination. He asked Dad to chase 'the black children' out of the front garden; they were sunflowers! He supposedly left me his chicken farm - which I never saw.

It was here at Dempsey Street that I first encountered my father's raging temper. He lost his car keys in the garage. Of course, I had been building something there in the garage. He punched me around until he found them – they'd fallen into the motor car tyre beside his bench.

Boxing

A boy of my age lived across an empty field. His brother knew how to make gunpowder. We were going to blow up the entire field. Instead we just dropped heavy weights on a pile of the stuff. Although we did make a sort of pipe bomb using two half-inch bolts - both screwed into the same nut with gunpowder in between each bolt. We threw these onto the road and today I still suffer from that experience; I have tinnitus.

His big brother took us to a boxing club. Dad said I could go. I hated it. Dad asked when I was going again. I lied and said Brian wasn't going and wouldn't take me. "Okay" said dad, "I'll take you." At that exact moment I lost control of not only my childhood, but my teenage years as well. I hated boxing, but I had seen the violent side to Dad and I became terrified of displeasing him. I attended the Wynberg boxing club once a week, and later Claremont boxing club. Mum might have stepped in, but I could see she was also frightened of her Jim.

When we moved to Phillips Terrace in Wynberg, he bought every bit of boxing equipment, and to escape this intimidation was impossible. There was no alternative but to wait this one out. In the meantime, I snatched time to be a kid.

Wynberg

There were four corner shops in our area where we shopped every day. One specialised in fruit and vegetables. Another in bulk rice, sugar, beans, split peas, tea and broken biscuits. A third seemed to sell only tins of things. The fourth shop we never used, as my mother had an argument with the owner over a stick of liquorice. He had given me the root part, and my mother wanted the black, concentrated sort. But he reckoned that I had chewed on the root and would not take it back; my mother threw it at him and it hit him between the peepers.

I went every day to buy fresh milk. This I brought home in a white ceramic jug covered with a doily. The journey home was always tiring, holding out the jug in front of me for one-and-a-half miles. I could have carried it easily by my side in the Billy can, but I never saw Billy cans until I came to Australia. Every Saturday morning we went to 'The Van'. This was a van about the size of a very large removal lorry. It was there every weekend, parked below the huge pine trees. On week days Robert, my friend next door, and I would collect pine nuts, bringing them home to his mum - who included them in a toffee bar that she would make. On Saturdays, however, everyone in the area would line up at The Van for their week's supply of bread, sugar, potatoes and flour. Everything was sold in bulk at wholesale prices.

It happened that for two days my father went missing. My mother and Walter Smith searched unsuccessfully for him everywhere they could think he might have gone. Then he arrived at the house late one afternoon, with his chin in a mess of 25 stitches. He'd had a motor car accident and had been taken to the emergency department at Grootscoer Hospital. They had stitched him up and sent him home, but for two days he'd wandered about not knowing where he lived (I think I wished he would never come back.)

For a while we had lodgers who lived in our front spare room at Phillips Terrace. This couple were either Spanish or Italian, and they had a daughter called Brenda. I used to terrify her by showing her the finger I had from a dead man - this was a small cardboard box, slightly larger than a matchbox, with a hole in the bottom through which I poked my finger. It was surrounded by cotton wool and stained with red ink.

The Smiths also had a lodger. He was Greek, and every Saturday he made hundreds of doughnuts which he glazed in sugar and filled with fresh cream. He sold the doughnuts to the neighbours. Every now and again I get a craving for those doughnuts, so I get my friend and wife, Stef, to make me a pile just like them; cram-packed with full cream.

Little Lulu was my favourite comic book character and I had a dog named after her. She was a full-bred Alsatian, and my father had paid a lot of money for her. He was most upset that one of ears flopped over. This was the result of her running underneath our car just after my father had parked it, and Lulu had burnt her ear on the exhaust pipe. I used to delight in teasing her with a ball and in the height of her excitement replace the ball with an onion. She ended up in tears and howling.

My father bought home a budgie in a cage and set the cage high up on the kitchen cupboard. In the morning, Lulu was still sitting in the exact same spot we had left her in when we went to bed - staring at the budgie in a pool of saliva about three feet in diameter. The budgie only lasted a week on the back veranda before a butcher bird killed it.

This was about the same time that my sister cut her hair. Joan wanted short hair. This didn't just mean a trip to the hairdressers. No! An appointment was also made at the photographers, who took a photograph of Joan in her splendid plaits that reached down to her bottom. When the plaits were cut off, they were kept in a wooden bowl that my father had made especially for them as a shrine.

The Caravan II

Mr Smutts, the man who owned the building site opposite our house, knew that my father had made a caravan back in Ireland, so he offered him the use of any of the materials on the site. I knew that this did not include any materials that were locked away in the farm houses, or in the locked sheds on the property. This, however, did not stop my father from unscrewing a section of the corrugated roof and removing enough ash and teak to make the frame and the furniture for his entire caravan. I spent endless evenings standing at the back of his circular saw holding lengths of timber that he was ripping into smaller pieces. There was hell to pay if I did not hold the two pieces apart correctly. Too much and they would not travel parallel to the fence; too tight and the saw would jam.

I spent a lot of time in his workshop when he was not there, making all sorts of things that I got from plans in Popular Mechanics magazine. Every tool had to be returned to its rightful place, and there couldn't be any evidence that I had been there when he returned to his shed in the evening to work on his caravan.

Love

Silk worms were now all the rage, and I, like all the rest of the class at school, were learning how to get the worms to weave beautiful shapes of pure silk. When the time comes for a silk worm to start spinning a cocoon, it needs a corner of some sort to spin its cocoon into. If you deprive it of a corner, you can produce some interesting artifacts. One way is by cutting a piece of cardboard in the shape of a heart, diamond, oval or circle, about four inches wide. You then put a pin through the middle of it, and pin it firmly down onto a corked bottle and place the silk worm on top of the shape. The silk worm will wander over this shape looking for a corner to make its cocoon, leaving a continuous trail of silk behind. After two or three days of the worm searching the cardboard shape, it will be completely covered in fine silk. We would then remove the silk worm, and put it in a corner where it usually had enough silk left to make an adequate cocoon. This was then wrapped in cotton wool to await the reappearance in moth form - to lay eggs - which the next year would again hatch into silkworms.

The woven silk shape was removed from the cardboard template. We used these shapes as bookmarks. The silk worms ate mulberry leaves and it was high up in the middle of one of these trees where I first met Eunice Diedre Van Berk. Wow! Any girl that could climb that high into a tree gob-smacked me! It was love at first sight! She became a great friend, and I met her every day after school. Even when she later went to high school we kept our friendship going. She was one year older than me. She came to visit me when I was sick in bed, with a load of School Friend comics. I don't know how she ever got past my mum and dad - they were opposed to the sexual differences in the human race; maybe they weren't aware there were any. It was my last year at that school and I fell in love with her – I think. Only a little bit girly still.

The Lads

Our Walter, our Bertie, our Geoffrey and our Sadie had moved into one of the new corner houses on Phillips Terrace, and beside us was Nirvana, a builder's yard of about five acres of land cram-packed with planks scaffolding bricks, stones and steel things. Robert McAlpine was now my best friend. He lived next door. Every Saturday morning we'd all traipse off to the movies – Hop-along Cassidy, *Roy Rogers - girly* - but also Gene Autry, Johnny McBrown, King Arthur and Lancelot. The afternoon was spent with the rest of the guys re-living each frame and scene and building weapons of mass destruction: catapults, foot operated machines for firing bricks 50 yards, things that automatically set fire to other things, racing cars, bows, crossbows – it never stopped. Mum spent every weekend wrapping some kid's impaled foot – there were lots of four-inch nails about sticking out of planks.

We made a massive aeroplane with a 12-foot wingspan. This was powered with the twisted inner tubes of a motorcycle. We were never able to wind the rubber tight enough to get any more than a short shudder, though. It may also have been relevant that the propeller was heavier than the rest of the entire plane.

All of us had slug guns with which we shot turtle doves. We cooked these on a blow lamp. As I recall they tasted marvellous! In later years I kept pigeons with the intended purpose of cooking one to recall those moments, but now I do not like the taste of pigeon.

The Dam

Three fields away, and across the road that we were never allowed to cross, was a dam with a small island. We had built a boat that logically held three. Seven of us, at least, would attempt the crossing and it always sank. None of us could swim.

Two more boys, David Hendry and Andrew Zula, joined the melee, and they led the way when we went mountain climbing above Kirstenbosch Gardens - up through Skeleton Gorge. I've got my name carved on a tree up there, above the falls. We climbed all around the mountains until we were in view of Lion's Head. I can't believe we did that, as I am now terrified of heights. I would have been happier sitting on the edge of the well in Kirstenbosch Gardens. (At this well, Mr Trudeau, our teacher, demonstrated refraction with his cane, as it appeared to bend when it entered the water. I never saw him ever cane anyone.) Back we went along the mountain, past the gardens and above Wynberg, or somewhere near there, then we climbed back down a fire break of stones and managed to start a landslide - we were terrified the rocks would end up in Wynberg.

My sister and I were still walking to Plumstead School, and we had to travel through a shanty town of Cape-coloured people. I trembled at my sister's side, but she was a pillar of bravery beside me. She cheated, she was genuinely nice to people. Joan was three years older than me and not so easily manipulated. Her character was forming already.

The South African Education Department – bastards – got hold of me in time. They were succeeding in turning me into a little racist prick. From the earliest days at school, it was obvious that us white kids were totally a cut above the dark children. Not only were they black, but the goodies we were getting at morning break were superior to anything that was sold from the stores Joan and I passed every morning on the way to school.

When we got to John Graham Primary School, we were getting two handfuls of whatever fruit was in season for morning break. When fruit was out of season, we got dried fruit or a block of cheese. When winter arrived, it was hot soup or stew. I never found out if we paid for this. If not, I'm sure it was paid for by some collective apartheid racist gits. These days I truly feel guilty for enjoying my school days in Cape Town. Well … not all of them.

One year I had a teacher who was the most horrible person I have ever met; I knew he was everything bad in human psyche. He started every morning's lessons with a game played from the Bible. He would read out the name of the book, chapter and verse. The first person to call out the first line got a point. It didn't take Joseph Borington long to learn that an awful lot of those stories started, 'And the Lord said'. Problem was, the masochist had a solution to this: if any answer was called out with those lines and it wasn't the right story, the offender was caned – boy or girl.

Everyone had nicer hair than me: wavy, curly or springy. Mine just sat or fell flat. Ah ... so that's why Hitler was such a tyrant - it was his hair. Like Hitler, mine fell across my forehead. All the Brylcreem in the world wouldn't keep it up. Every time I leaned over to write or do my sums, down it fell.

"Boy, I've told you about that hair!" He then removed a clip from the ginger-haired girl's hair - everyone knew she had boos, and clipped my hair back. I had lost face in front of all my classmates. I removed the offending clip and fired it at the teacher. It hit him right between the eyes; must have inherited my good shot from my mum. He sent me from the class to wash my face and to return when I was calm. He then proceeded to give me six whacks with his quince stick across the bum. I spent the next three months avoiding my dad. If he had seen the bruises he would have beaten the shit out of this bastard, which oddly enough, I would have found embarrassing. That teacher taught us Scottish Nationalist songs – I hope that wasn't the reason I became a folk singer – reverse psychology maybe ...*in todays light, further punishment.*

Morris Minor

Mrs Thaall was the sort of teacher that all teachers should be. Teachers then taught everything. Of course, my favourite lesson was craft. The fly squat we made looked just like the real thing: a twisted piece of wire stitched onto a six-inch square of fly wire, and edged with bias binding. There wasn't a safe spot for a fly anywhere in Wynberg. The place mats we made from raffia, Mrs Thaall she saw my first one; I was her teacher's pet forever. I can still out-plait any kid on the street. Our whistle lanyards were to die for.

Three afternoons a week, Mrs Thall read to us - *Five go off on Kirin Island* - Julian, Dick, George and Timmy the dog. Gems of literature they were. Really Mrs Thall's favourite pupil was Raymond. While she read, Raymond always knitted. She drove a Morris Minor – British racing green and black.

Woodwork was my second favourite subject, but it was taught by a teacher who only came in one day a week. He taught the basics - which have stayed and made great sense: don't choke a hammer; what angle to hold a plane; how to sharpen a chisel, and all the different kinds of chisels.

After three years at John Graham's, the final class teacher was Mr Tredeau, another person born to teach. He always wore a brown suit, and he carried a cane - which he constantly held between his outstretched arms. He moved it up and down, stroking his private parts with it. I've been told that this was a sexual gesture. He also demonstrated the respiratory function by pointing and placing his cane on Sarah's ample chest. Mr Tredeau was fit, but rotund. He took us for PE too. Also he coached the football team which I played for. I was terrible, but oddly, the only time I didn't play we lost. I didn't play as I was in hospital having my appendix removed. I have a huge scar from that. It was not in the right location and they had to dig further. The scar is nine inches long. I know I shouldn't rave on about appendix scars, but three weeks later my dad had me boxing in the South African championships. A foul below the belt would have split me wide open.

An African Ghost Story

Mr Tredeau told us this ghost story:

'A land owner and his slave were returning home from a large town in the Transvaal. The rains had been falling continually, and several of the bridges had been washed away. They saw a distant light shining and the landowner headed towards it. The slave was too frightened to go with him and stayed behind. When the land owner eventually arrived at the home, the lights went out. He knocked for a long time at the door but there was no answer. He turned the front door handle and it opened. There was a long hallway before him, with numerous doors leading off to the left and the right. As he proceeded down the hallway, all the doors were locked. As he walked he was aware that someone or something was breathing down his neck. On his return down the hallway, he noticed that the first door that he had tried to open was now ajar. He entered and there was a key in the lock on the inside of the door.

This was a bedroom and no one was using it, so he locked the door and made himself comfortable in the bed, putting the key underneath his pillow. He was exhausted and was soon fast asleep.

Several hours later he was awakened by the noise of the bedroom door handle being turned. He reached under his pillow for the key, but it was gone. The door slowly began to open and two black hands emerged around the door. The hands were not attached to a body and they started floating towards him as he was lying in the bed. He did not know if he was dreaming or not, but he managed to shake himself into action. He grabbed his boots and clothing and fled from the house.

Later in life he discovered an article in a Johannesburg newspaper of a time years ago when a very nasty Boer boss master had lived in this same house, and had punished one of his black servants for stealing a cabbage by chopping off his hands with an axe. The slave died from this and the hands had been continually looking for the boss master for revenge.'

As a boy I tried hard to keep this story out of my head, as we often walked home at night past a graveyard.

I know two South African ghost stories. Here is the second:

'There is a mountain pass through the Drakensburg mountains. It is said that even today if you try to go through this pass at night, the figure of a lady dressed in the costume of the Voortekkers will run out in front of you trying to wave you down. If you swerve to avoid her, your only option is to turn to the right. This takes you over the edge of a 1000-foot drop. If you try to swerve to the left you will bounce of the rock face, and probably end up falling over the edge as well.

The correct procedure of course is to keep in the middle of the road and knock the lady down. I have been through this pass and have seen numerous cars at the bottom of this fall. They have collected over the years and are gradually rusting away. Very few travellers ever go over this pass at night time. It was claimed that in the early days of the Voortrekkers, oxen and a cart containing an entire family fell over the edge. All were killed, except for the oldest daughter who eventually died of exposure waiting to stop the next traveller in order to seek help for the rest of her family of nine.

So the tale goes that even to this day she tries to wave down passers-by to help.'

Not Pierrys

There was a lot more to be learnt at school that had nothing to do with teachers. Spinning tops were not like our pierrys back in Belfast. No, these were in the shape of a cone, tapering to the bottom with a metal point, wound with string and held in the hand, miles above your head. They were then hurled at a competitor's top that lay on the ground. David was the king of this. Usually a dent on the opponent's top met with cheers, but David smashed more tops to smithereens than anyone else. With great dexterity it was possible to lift the spinning top between two fingers into the palm of your hand, then continue to use it to knock your opponents top out of the target ring *I can still do this.*

Another lad was a whizz at charms: plastic bracelet-like charms thrown into a ring. Ah, boring. Almost everyone in our class was world famous for something: Eddie Hybner had a collection of tortoises older than Cape Town itself; Peter Cato had walked the full length of the underground storm drain from his house near Constantia to school; Oliver's dad had caught the biggest fish at Hout Bay; Francis was famous just because everyone wanted to be called Francis. Most famous of all was Alwyn Deagaar. He could hold the end of his foreskin closed while he did a piss. It swelled up like a balloon. He would then give it a mighty squeeze and squirted the pee as high up as the roof. I saw that myself and got covered in piss for my trouble.

I was always the smallest in the class at school, but never suffered because of it, as Joan was always there to bash shit out of anyone who tried it on - and it don't do to be bashed up by a girl. Joan was nothing but downright stupid. She had to be, my dad said so. She was held back in the special class at school, and although she was three years older than me, she was now three classes behind me. Even to me back then, something seemed amiss. There was always something sad about Joan. She certainly wasn't stupid, but there were times when she became a shadow of herself. Was this only happening around my dad? She certainly was popular with the boys at school.

Dad had completed his second caravan and was working on his third. Again most evenings I spent two hours behind a circular saw, always alert to keeping the timber apart behind the cut, tight against the fence and level; the same with the electric planer. This seemed to go on for years. I was never allowed to go out until I had helped him, followed by one hour's rigorous training also two nights a week at the club, and one night at the professional club in Claremont. There was never any interest in my pursuits. I got those fortunately from the family behind us – the Zulus.

I got to know Andrew because he was my sister's boyfriend. He had two older brothers. The father owned an old TF MG, which he raced. The older brother owned a proper racing car. The other brother had rifles and all sorts of guns. They all made model aircraft from kits they bought. Andrew gave me some of the plans from those kits, and from these plans I built planes from sheets of Balsa that I had bought from Jack Lemkus in Cape Town after saving up my pocket money.

On Sunday mornings we drove down Wetton Road with the Zulus to an abandoned airfield. Perhaps it was an abandoned rifle firing range, as a road called Range Road ran down to Lansdowne. The entire day was spent either flying or trying to fly model aircraft: engine power, free flight, control line planes, gliders, jet-ex and rubber powered.

The older brother and their dad were tuning their cars, and Andrew's other brother let me handle his German Lugar. I fired one round, which blew off my head and removed one arm from the shoulder – what a wimp!

Andrew had lots of model aircraft hanging from his ceiling. In one of those he had hidden his one and only French letter. Andrew was from a broadminded family. Their toilet bore the sign: 'Will all the men in the house please aim straight'.

Her Fault

One day I took a short cut to Andrew's over the back fence to the Zulus. It was a six-foot fence and when I stepped out onto a clothes line. It snapped. My chin went 'smash' onto the rock below. My bottom teeth went straight through my bottom lip, while my four new front teeth were smashed from their roots. Mum was distraught and there was hell to pay all over again for her when dad came home. Apparently it was her fault.

Did I ever actually do anything I wanted to do with my dad? Anything enjoyable? In later years Stef and I made a recording of 50 international lullabies. Most had one thing in common: be a good boy or girl, grow up and help Mum and Dad with their work. But whenever I wasn't needed by my dad to help him, he just wanted me out of his hair. And at the times when I wasn't needed he just got angry. One day in particular I recall. I had just made a mini pencil box with a sliding lid. When you slid the lid open, a wooden snake popped out and pricked you on the finger. The problem was I hadn't cut the pin off short yet. "What's this?" he asked. He lifted it, slid open the lid and the spring loaded wooden snake impaled itself on his finger. He smashed the box and killed me. He did the same when I mounted a button on a spring over a hole, behind which was a pin. There was what looked like a speaker above the button, and it bore the legend: 'don't press this button'. He did.

The days at John Graham School were coming to an end, and Eunice had moved to Wynberg High School. I was still training every night of the week, and helping dad finish his third caravan. The Smiths had moved to Johannesburg and Robert's dad was killed when a lift he was working on came down and squashed him.

The day Robert McAlpine and I became best friends was when we started swapping sandwiches. I can't remember what was in mine, but Robert's had peanut butter and apricot jam on brown bread - which is still my favourite sandwich. We spent long days in his cubby house reading comics. Robert read out loud to me, I was a terrible reader. Robert even read the small print under the pictures of Rupert the Bear. I've often wondered just what encouraged the imagination. Reading what was written there or imagining what was there? I had my own cubby house, but it was cursed hallowed ground, as 20 feet below were buried a metal train and a daisy rifle I'd broken. If Dad had known I'd broken them he would've have kill me. I often accompanied Robert's family into the country: Paarl, Elgin, Franschhoek and Hermannas.

Phillips Terrace

There was a particular pile of gravel where we selected the stones for our catapults. We had drawn the face of a giant on the barn door at the far end of the stone yard. After hours of practising with our sling shots, none of us could even hit the barn door, let alone the giant's head! That guy from the bible, I reckon, used a catapult ... hmmm ... I wonder where he found the rubber or the elastic?

I was bent over the pile of gravel when a shadow was cast over me from behind. I then felt something at my throat. I looked down, and at either side of my cheeks was three inches of bright shining steel! I knew that if I moved the knife would slice its way into my neck. A face came into view, as black as black as black, with purple, blue and pink reflecting on his shining skin*. He started grinning from ear to ear as he removed the knife, showing how he had used the blunt, back edge of the knife. Instead of stuttering, there was an endless silence! Then I returned to my stammering.

We became very good friends. He was our new caretaker down at the builders' yard. He and his wife had just moved into a ten-foot by ten-foot corrugated iron shed, directly opposite our house. They were a wonderful, cliché'd couple. They recycled all their cooking utensils, and made pots and pans from empty oil, petrol and paraffin containers. The smell of their golden, plump, sausage-shaped bread being deep fried is a lasting memory.

One time the husband dug a grave-shaped hole and lit a fire in the bottom of it. Towards evening a lot of his friends arrived; they filled the hole with vegetation, draped 10 lengths of hosepipe, six-foot long out of the hole, and covered the entire ensemble with sheets of corrugated iron. The rest of the evening they spent in silence inhaling the smoke through those hose pipes. Seems a very peaceful pastime, I remember thinking, might try that outside my front door! That was dakka - or marihuana.

An incredible man arrived one day, dressed in traditional Zulu regalia, including shield and spears, bow and arrows. He banged and banged and banged on the caretaker's door, but they were not at home. He eventually stopped and proceeded to dig a small hole just in front of their door. He then continued to do what looked like a war dance that lasted for hours. I watched this all from the safety of our front stoop, 30 feet away. Dad forbade Joan and I to go anywhere near that spot.

Dad told us of a notebook that he had found up the Ormeau Road in Belfast. His father made him take it back to the exact spot where he had found it - it was a book of spells!

Eventually they left, for they were now a family; she had the baby tied on her bum, and a singer sewing machine balanced on her head! She was magnificent.

I once saw a man painting Negro faces on polished slices of stinkwood at the Jan Van Riebeeck Festival. He used those colours, and he was brilliant.

Grunts

Around this time Robert from next door and I were scrumping figs from over the fence behind the big barn. We were quietly walking along the roof when we heard grunts and groans coming from the undergrowth below. We watched in awe as a naked black man and a naked black woman were engaged in each other's embrace, oblivious to us. A burnt umber entanglement with flashes of pink … What on earth were they doing? Robert and I stared at each other in total confusion, stunned and unable to move! I think we're still there.

Towards the last days at Phillips Terrace I was in Robert's bedroom. Jean, Robert's sister, (who was best friends with my sister and the same age), was sitting on the edge of her bed in an immaculate white sweater. Her tits were massive. I approached her in slow motion, and before I knew where I was, I was groping them in an exploring, fondling fashion. I re-gained consciousness, turned and fled. Out of breath I hid in my bedroom, terrified, until it dawned on me she hadn't really tried to stop me. Wow! And I was only 12!

Robin Island

We lived in a really nice house in Phillips Terrace. Why on earth were we moving to Range Road in Lansdowne? I wondered. This was an older, smaller house backing onto a railway line. Someone had died in our bedroom … were they still there?

We had been to Lansdowne many times. Two doors down the road lived Mrs Waterson, and her three daughters. We had known and visited this family for eight years. Vera was married to an Irish man, Joy had an illegitimate son, and Maggie was just single, free and beautiful. For years we went on summer holidays with this lot, including the Smiths and many more, including the wee Spanish man who became a murderer. So why were we moving next door to these people? Joan and I were still attending John Graham School, but now travelling by bicycle down the Wetton Road backward and forward to Lansdowne. We passed the graveyard where we always said the Lord's Prayer when we walked past at midnight with Mum and Dad when we stayed out late.

We weren't poor. So why were we living in such a horrible house in what seemed to be a rather dodgy area? Dad had always had a good job. At Globe Engineering he had his own crew. His chief's ticket allowed him to take repaired boats on sea trials around Robin Island, and his second job was a tool and die maker at the United Tobacco Company - a highly skilled position - so why were we living in this dump?

Wee

Wee Paddy - as he was referred to by every one of his friends, and was called so because he was wee and his name was Patrick. I once had a wee hole in one of my teeth drilled and filled by a dentist at Dundonald - during one of my trips back home to Northern Ireland - and as I ventured down the dentist's pathway, I closed my teeth to feel the new repair and the tooth crumble.

I immediately turned round and confronted the dentist. "You said I had a wee hole in this tooth! The tooth has crumbled to dust!" I cried.

"Ah," she said in defiance of my expression, "sure … it was a *gigantic* wee hole."

I'd forgotten about that enduring way the Belfast people used the term 'wee'.

Wee Paddy's wife was Vera, the only one of the Waterson's three daughters to be married. Vera and Paddy had two sons. Vera hated Paddy's records; they were all Irish. He asked could he perhaps play them at our house on Saturday mornings. Somehow the news of these record playing sessions made their way to the Christian Brothers' Retreat at Landsdowne, and soon the record playing session turned into six or eight moaning, whinging, grieving, homesick Irishmen. As a consequence of this, I know nearly every crap Irish song that was ever written. I enjoyed these sessions, as the priests all gave me so much attention. Why? So if anyone asks at any pub session for the most obscure American-Irish rubbish song, I know it, even the sort of the thing that Daniel O'Donnell might sing. Stef is still amazed at the junk that is in my brain.

Mum changed. The house was often empty when we came home from school. On those days there was always money on the table for the pictures: she was there, and we would go and join her. She was always on her own. Then she took to wearing a vinegar bandage around her head as she always had a headache, and I often caught her crying. That terrible Christmas when Lulu, our Alsatian dog, ate the Christmas turkey, I found her in the outside toilet in tears. She stayed there all that day. Everything that goes wrong is always a mother's fault.

When I enrolled at Lansdowne High School, I was terribly out of favour in the community because I'd represented Wynnberg Boxing Club against Lansdowne School in their annual boxing tournament. One evening, not only did I win against Dougie my newest best friend, but I also received a special cup - awarded to the most 'scientific' boxer of the year. I had to be scientific; at this time, I couldn't punch my way out of a wet paper bag.

During one year's Western Provinces championships, during the preliminary fights, I came up against a boy whom I hit twice. Then he ran and cowered in the corner, just like I always wanted to do when someone hit me. I stood back and refused to hit him again and the fight was wisely stopped. Wow, did my father see red! What a golden opportunity thrown away to make my first knockout! I cried after his abuse, and for weeks I had turned into a moffie (South African slang for 'gay'). For nine years I'd dreaded those two nights of the week and the one-and-a-half hours of training every night. I did however become a good rope skipper, and on several occasions unofficially broke the world record for the maximum number of turns of the rope per minute!

Mum was proud of my silver cups and they had pride of place alongside the mini Brylcreem jars and mini Coca Cola bottles that she got at the Jan Van Riebeeck Tri-Centenary Festival. If you are reading this Robert, I apologise: I am sorry; I cheated on you.

Mrs Thaall was selecting work from the best artists in the class for the Jan Van Riebeeck Tri-Centenary Festival. Her choice came down to Robert's entries and mine. She chose mine. They were slightly better examples of cliché after cliché of predictable tourist junk. Mrs Thaall had set the rules. All work was to be original. I had copied mine. In all honesty I hadn't known those rules, as I must have been in hospital when she had set them. The outcome was that my work was shown at the festival, along with John Cobb's land speed car, the plastic ruler from the Mutual Insurance offices, and I think I do recall a demonstration of a colour TV, and the man who painted Negro faces on slices of stinkwood. A truly forgettable occasion.

Kommetjie

Mum had made us egg and onion sandwiches; one of her best recipes. Dad was at home when Joan and I came back from school. We were off to my second favourite swimming pool - Kommetjie -my first being Strandfontein, where there was a natural swimming pool. This was where I also saw my first whale washed ashore. We used to catch octopus in the rocks; we killed them by turning the body inside-out. It was at Strandfontein where I saw Dad and Maggie Waterson in each other's arms, beyond the breakers, where grown-ups went for a swim. Surfing hadn't reached South Africa then. Dad said he had a cramp and Maggie was saving his life. Well bully for her. Back to Kommetjie and Mum and Dad – they had news to tell us: we were off back to Ireland. What the fuck was Ireland? The last I known of it was the dark, miserable night aboard the Liverpool steamer waving goodbye to my granny and granddad, and singing Vera Lynn's, *Wish me Luck as you Wave me Goodbye.*

Chapter Three

Sydenham

Where I learn to live without sunshine. Where I learn censorship and bigotry, what religion is, what girls are for, how small I was, to do art, make friends, play music, smoke, not quite to have sex, how my father owned me, love country life, take a beating and how to belong.

Spam 1953

The introduction to the culinary cuisine of the northern hemisphere followed the exclamation from Dad of: "Wow! Spam and chips. Haven't had that since the war!" That was in Liverpool - the heart of Ireland - then on by boat to Belfast.

From the quay side we got a taxi to my granny's at Sydenham. The bright, shiny thing that we took so much for granted back in Cape Town was gone from our lives for what was to be an eternity.

Although dark, the first day was well underway. The shops we passed were lit up. The gas lights burning away. Trolley buses, diesel buses and trams were all vying for attention. Bicycles, bicycles and more bicycles and dark grey little men were rushing around all over the place.

Down the Newtownards Road passed crossroads. Were there pubs on all four corners? Pipes, cigarettes, cigars hung out of every face.

Everyone was coughing, spitting and hawking great hunks of phlegm that choked the gutters. Above us, as we went under the Hollywood arches passed a train, choking the sky on its way, looking for a dream all oblivious of wee me.

The taxi went under the arch and turned left down Consbrook Avenue. In the distance, I was told, there was a high hill to the north, Cave Hill, but this was confused behind the smell of smoke, and yet more smoke, the taste of smoke and the sound of smoke, past the dimly lit houses, making sandwiches for lunch while breakfasting on porridge and fags. And then there were more people on bicycles; women with headscarves. Dad said it got worse in the rain. Mum was whimpering and powdering her face at the same time. We turned left at Devon Parade. Mum said it would get light within the hour. This was a red brick jungle, smoke belching from very crevice, exhausted garden gates looking for attention, barely illuminated windows, and now our new home.

While Mum and Dad did family things, Joan and I wanted to get out and explore. It eventually got light, but it was now starting to get dark again. A lot of boys were kicking a ball at the end of a row of houses. There were goal posts painted on the brick wall. As I stood around as only a lost moron can, I was invited to join – no fuss there.

That evening a boy from over the road called. Could I go with him to the movies? They were showing a French movie, *Wages of Fear*, at the New Princess down the Newtownards Road. "No," said Granny. "Yes," said Granddad. The admission fee was paid in jam jars, pegs or rubber bands I think.

In later years I found I had seen one of the better movies ever made, but this was now being shown because of the risqué scenes like the pissing on the rock scene. During elicit sequences, the house lights were turned on: censorship. Granddad had given me the money for an ice cream sold from a stall just below the screen. Was that really pee shimmering on the floor?

It was after that first football game that I ran into the house shouting, "Mum, Gran, Granddad, Dad!" They were all sitting round the fire. "'Fuck' is not a South African word!" I declared. I kissed everyone goodnight and headed straight for bed.

Too Obvious

The first major problem was school. I had just missed the 11+ exams, the results of which decided what sort of school you would go to, grammar school or other. I had to report to the Education Department near St. Anne's Cathedral to be individually assessed. Here, I encountered the second arse-hole in my life. I was shown books of design and patterns and asked to complete the sequence. I stared and stared at them.

"Can't you see the right one, you stupid boy?" he cried. Now I knew how my sister felt when my father called her stupid. He went on pressuring and pressuring. "There! There! Can't you see it, you idiot? You fool!"

To me it was all too obvious - of course I could see it, but by then I was in tears. I'm afraid I failed that little man's test. I was placed with the lowest of the low in Ashfield Secondary Intermediate school, just one step lower than the gypsy encampment along the road to Hollywood.

The news got around the girls of Sydenham that there was a rather exotic catch to be had - just arrived from foreign parts. This appealed to Jacqueline Thornton's vanity (one such girl). She had more parts than Jean McAlpine (another such girl), but she dismissed me instantly when she encountered my dimensions. I was always tiny. Dad tried all remedies to make me grow. I was the smallest in our family. Mum was four-foot seven-inches. I had to wait until I was 16 for a final stint of growth which shot me to five-foot six-and-a-half inches.

Sydenham

Sydenham is a village separated from the rest of East Belfast. There were times when I thought it had seceded, perhaps even had its own border controls. Did we carry our own passports? Conswater and Victoria Park were to the north, the prefabricated houses to the east, across the Hollywood Road were foreign parts; the rest of Belfast was a jungle.

There were three ways of identifying the locals: what church you went to - *there were eight of them, all in a half square mile*; the size of your garden, and what illnesses you had. The whole psyche of the area started in Sunday school. The goody-two-shoes of the class would eventually become the next lot of Sunday school teachers, where spiders immediately spun their webs in their sub-conscious and between their knees. They handed out tracks from the bible - which you were supposed to take home to Mum and become lovely little boys.

The Boys Brigade was a militant extension of Sunday school and I became a member. Dad had been a member; consequently I had to be one. Of course they had their own Sunday school, every Sunday morning. The Boys Brigade wasn't all bad. I made all my friends there, learnt to play the bagpipes and tenor drum, and set fire to a church meeting.

I can't recall how I ever managed to save enough money to go to Boys Brigade summer camps at Ballywalter and Portrush. I was given sixpence on Sunday mornings to put towards going to camp, but I always bought fags with that. I have a faint recollection of seeing the Boys Brigade saving card blank for weeks before we were to go off to camp, mine was blank. Maybe the Brigade had a slush fund for fallen lads like myself! BB camp was great fun, those anal, military-type sergeants finally relaxed and we all had a great time. The advanced party had already pitched all the bell-shaped tents and the huge marquee. On our arrival we were sent straight to the nearby farmer to fill our palliases (mattresses) with straw. The food was great: continual Ulster fries! A trip into town resulted in the ruination of the ghost train by two friends and me. I remember leaving with a particular monster's hand stuffed up my jumper. All outings with the Boys Brigade ended in song:

'There is a BB camp far, far away,
Were we get bread and jam three times a day
Ham and eggs we never see
Get no sugar in our tea
Come and see us gradually
Fading away ...'

They were usually cleaned-up versions of military songs.

The Girl Guides were the BB in skirts. The Scouts? The only thing I learnt from that lot was: to be prepared. Luckily all this goody-two-shoes crap was complemented by the billiard hall. Here a bloke could learn to sit with his knees apart, stare and spit on the floor, and eventually - when you got that right - you could learn to smoke and perhaps even learn to play snooker.

I had made friends with a lad down the street called Eawarty. My granny became enraged when I brought him into the house. He was called a Catholic, and my granny showed me some old newspaper clippings in her china cabinet which told of some people poking pitchforks into pregnant women, and how this Eawarty's parents were to blame. Somehow I think that my mum had planned to protect me from the usual Irish bigotry. And I thought that apartheid was bad.

Meanwhile things were not going well in my granny' s house. My mum was getting sick. She had a continual pain in her right hand - the result of an operation that she'd had back in South Africa. She had even visited an African witch doctor, but nothing worked.

Beliefs

By this time I was starting to ask myself questions about beliefs. I remember the exact occasion when doubt first entered my mind. I had been saving hard to buy a box of paints from Littlewoods. There were 100 colours in the box, and I had planned in my mind the picture that I would paint with them that coming Sunday. Saturday morning, first thing, I was on the bus into town and went straight to Littlewoods. I paid for the paints, got straight back to the bus, sat in the front seat upstairs, and opened the box and started planning the whole picture over again. Now I lived at the end of the bus route in Sydenham, and I knew only to get off the bus when the engine of the bus had stopped. When the engine of the bus did stop, I hadn't looked up from my box of paints once, and when I did I did not recognise any of my surroundings. I had got on the wrong bus! Now I'd had total faith that I was on the right bus, and if - as I had been taught in bible school - faith moves mountains, why the hell was I not in Sydenham?!

Size

In Sydenham the size of your garden was important. But no one was interested in growing anything. Most of them had been concreted over. It was a social status. Those houses closest to the shipyard and nearer to the Newtownards Road had no gardens, just backyards and service entries. Nearer Consbrook Avenue, they had front gardens as well as back enclosed yards and entries. Closer to the Hollywood Road it was reported there were houses with both front and back gardens. Those houses put their bins out on the street.

Trying to work your way through this social minefield was simplified by the illness cue. When trying to identify exactly who you were talking about, a gentle prompt as to the illness in the family pointed to them immediately. "Och, you know, not Jimmy with the swollen ankles. No, no, I mean the one with the wee hole in his heart. The one who is dying with consumption."

Consumption. Sydenham had its quota. It was lit by gas street lamps one every 100 feet. On a good smoggy night you couldn't see from one to the next. There were special skills required that every man, woman and child had to learn before they were let loose on the streets of Belfast. First: how to accost a passer-by to hoist your rope up a lamp for your swing. Secondly: how to swing around the lamp without getting higher and higher, faster and faster, until wallop! – you slammed against the post's cast iron. Lastly: judging the exact length of the rope – too long and your arse scraped the flagstones, or hit the house close by. The post was rarely used as a cricket stump as it was next to the kerb, and the width of the road was too narrow for a pitch, and oh yes, we didn't play cricket - too churchy - although a cricket ball was good for breaking windows. If you hadn't matches, you could shimmy up a lamp, open the window and light your fag off the mantle. Often when I walked a girl home and was dollying her up outside her house, I would give the lamp a sharp kick, just above the heavy butt at the bottom, and that would cause the mantle to shatter. How cool was that?

I thought I was seeing the last of the lamp lighters but no, they had gone by my time, it was the clock winder with his ladder, climbing up to wind the seven day mechanism that switched the gas on and off. Five of us on the way to the Astoria Cinema at Ballyhackmore one winter, smashed every gas lamp with snowballs along the road from Belmont Avenue to the Newtownards road.

No Threat

I never had trouble making friends. I was small; a threat to no one. All the girls liked me. I think they all wanted to mother me; I was their exotic foreign pet. Things were not quite the same at school. My father had introduced me to Mr Stanley, the headmaster, as a South African champion boxer. The headmaster in turn introduced me to the class by telling them to leave me alone, as I was a champion boxer. By lunchtime they were lining up to beat the shit out of me. One bloke kneed me in the balls and I was violently ill for two weeks. I was terrified of my father asking me what was wrong. But because of my diminutive size I got sympathy from the rest of the class - who weren't into fighting.

After the first few months at Ashfield Secondary Intermediate, it somehow became obvious to the headmaster that the git at the Education Department had made an error; I wasn't stupid. They moved me to the new Advanced Technical section of the school to study for my Junior Certificate. I had missed the first all important lessons in algebra, though, and never really found out what all that shit was about. English – well, that hadn't been invented at John Graham Primary School in Kaapstad.

Desmond Kinney was the art teacher, and although I didn't know it, was barely six years older than me. In the last year at school he called a meeting of my father, the headmaster and me. Would it be possible for me to be the first student from a technical school to go to Art College? He had one year to prepare me. Could I drop all unnecessary subjects and study art instead with him and the other art teacher and craft teacher? I dropped science, geography, metalwork, woodwork, PT, religious instruction and English - 23 periods in all. I sat my Junior Certificate at the end of the year and got nine distinctions -the highest number in Great Britain - but failed the exam. Why? I failed the compulsory class of English. This sent the Education Department into meltdown, as I received a special award for the highest number of distinctions in Great Britain. Then the Education Department juggled their books and I got my Junior Certificate. At the time I didn't know that Mr Smith, the metalwork teacher had lined me up with a job at Shorts, the aircraft factory. And that Mr Atkins, the woodwork teacher, had organised a job at a Conswater carpentry factory. Desmond Kinney had also put me up for a job at Nicholson and Bass, should my application fail to get into Art College.

Help

There was a huge guy in our metal work class, not the brightest tool in the shed. He was having trouble draw-filing the edge of his project. He asked for my help. I saw it was in the wrong position in the vice. I couldn't undo his vice, but wasn't going to let him know that, so I brought my left hand down with a mighty thump on the handle to try to loosen it. I don't know what happened, and years later still don't, but I looked down blood was saturating the dick area of my short trousers. I collapsed from fear! I woke up in the staff room surrounded by staff members and a doctor, with my dick totally wrapped in bandages (how do you bandage a limp dick?)!

There was no lasting damage - except to my pride. And all the girls from the girl's school lined up along the Hollywood Road to view the boy who had caught his dick in the vice! (There should be a song about that!)

The Sydenham Gang

Margaret, who lived across the road from me, was a beautiful looking girl. She had a slight bend in one of her ankles that threw her leg sharply forward. I *courted* Julia Brown for what seemed a long time. Her mother initially adored me, but she would not let me near the house when, after a party, I'd first felt her tits. Julia told her mother and asked her if this was okay. Julia had a lovely friend called Sheila, who wore glasses and was almost blind! She was entranced by Billy McCune, but rarely got to see him as his parents never let him out in the evenings. He was made to stay in and study.

Two girls, who came from a different area, often appeared as if from nowhere. They were Norma Boyd and Dorothy Thompson. Billy Longridge and I always fancied these two. They were smashing and we would follow them anywhere in Belfast. We had to walk them home at nights - they lived miles away - but we were always rewarded by a feel up!

Angel Face was the prettiest of all the girls. She always seemed to wear a wide open, gaping blouse and you were guaranteed a good eye-full when she leaned towards you. None of the guys ever went with Angela. She towered above us all. She was about six-foot tall, but she was a beautiful person and ended up marrying a millionaire. Davey Patterson, Terry Plackitt, Dennis Boyde, Dessie White and myself were the main nucleus of this group. Dessie had a bread run. He used to help the man who delivered bread from the Ormo bakery van all day Saturday. Dessie was a lovely guy, and not only because he always had money - which he earned from his bread round - but also because he always had fags. He was a diabetic and took insulin every day. He was the only one of us who ever got sick during this time. He ended up in hospital with a tumour on the brain; we all visited him. He recovered and eventually went to live in Canada.

Davy Patterson was 'alive, alive oh!' He was fired with enthusiasm for everything. He and I were thrown out of the Boys Brigade at the same moment for disobeying an order: turning left when everyone turned right. I also taught him to smoke, for which he was forever grateful. A distant cousin who came from a street further away than most, was famous throughout the area for organising a show in which one of the girls in his street lay on her bed and he charged all the lads in his street six pence or two fags to feel her tits and have a look at her t**t. He was great at organising things.

Billy Longridge was the Clark Gable of the group. This guy got all the girls. He had the best chat-up lines, and a lazy eye which made him totally irresistible to any girl. He was a brilliant football player; he even tried out for Glentoran, the local league team. He went to grammar school. He had a top-model push bike with 10 gears. Hanging around this guy instantly put you in with the 'in' group. I think the feeling was mutual, as he thought that I was the cleverest thing around. We did have one altercation though, when a difference of opinion was to be decided by a boxing match. I had the boxing gloves. I also had a head protection unit. Billy insisted on wearing this unit, and refused to fight me if I was going to hit him in the face - so the whole thing became a none event!

Billy's father and my father did some sort of deal, as Billy's father worked in the aircraft factory and my father needed aluminium for his caravan. Lots of our fathers had sidelines involving material 'liberated' from their places of employment. Lots of men who owned cars had brackets welded underneath for stealing steel from the shipyard. My own father made a bit of money on the side by making roof racks for motor cars; he would drive in to work in the morning with no roof rack, and drive out at night with a newly made rack adorning his car.

On rainy nights we assembled, sorry, *every* night we assembled in the bakery doorway. It had a vantage point in all directions. Anyone arriving up or down Consbrook Avenue on the bus could be seen. It was also an early warning place to view prowling parents. We were mostly preoccupied with smoking. Various techniques had been tried and adapted by all. Always short of cash, there was always enough for fags. Sydenham didn't have a pub, so drinking never entered our imagination. We stood around, shuffled, and stood around some more. I had taken on a spurt of growth, but was still leaving the house in short pants. I found a dress-suit at the back of the wardrobe. It was Granddad's - which he must have worn to the Masons. I pinched this and would change into it in the toilet out in the back yard. I also nicked his white satin scarf. I wore a donkey jacket for years and I suspect cut a dashing figure – five-foot six-and-a-half-inches now, black satin flashing down the side of my dress-suit trousers. In these I blended into family, and father never noticed, don't think he ever realised I had grown or cared.

Assembled at the bakery there were major decisions to be made: What are we doing tonight? Shall we venture out beyond the village? We were quite a crowd of boys and girls - six or seven of us. If it was summer - we'd venture down to Victoria Park where the swimming pool was. A long distance swimmer trained there most times when we weren't using it. Billy Longridge was very impressed when I fell into the pool accidentally, clothes and all, but upon surfacing, the first thing I did was suck the water out of my watch. Motivated by brilliance, Billy thought. Motivated by the fear of my father, more like.

Eric Cairns had us in stitches with his various mimes. Eric, Davy Patterson and Billy Longridge and I formed a skiffle group. Wee Dougie was our drummer. We entered a competition at the Empire, the site of Victoria Square. We won … a crate of beer. We gave them all to Dougie to drink with his friend - who'd been to borstal.

Diagonally across from the bakery was a sign that advertised what was showing at the Strand Cinema: Christopher Lee, the new Dracula. We all went that night - there were 19 of us - us the guys racing ahead down the hill towards home to jump out on the girls and frighten the bejaysus out of them.

The other direction we ventured on a Sunday afternoon was south up the Cairnburn Road, and onto the Old Hollywood Road, where an old man lived in a picturesque stone cottage. He always allowed us to drink from his well; there was always a clean glass. Then it was back home along the Old Hollywood Road. These were usually uneventful days, as we were wearing our Sunday best. On the final leg home I'd nip into peoples' gardens and pinch flowers for mum.

Usual Rules

Of course we hadn't been long in Belfast before my father found a boxing club. Usual rules applied: I wasn't allowed out until I'd completed one hour of training; then onto the club once a week; then monthly tournaments. He wasn't learning. These Belfast guys were hammering the shit out of me regularly. I had learnt how to look after myself in the street. The formula was brutal but simple: when cornered, plan to land three fast punches very hard onto your opponent. Don't stop to gauge the reactions. If you'd done it right the troublemaker should be flat on his back. I once did this to three guys who stepped out on me at the bottom of Consbrook Avenue. One claimed I had made a pass at his girlfriend, which I had. This was going nowhere but grief, and it was cold, calculated and fast. I looked back from 50 yards – sorry I still don't know what a metre looks like – the three of them were still on the ground. I think I'd be capable of doing the same today - hoping my adrenalin would take care of my pain.

Terry

Terry became my best friend. He wasn't in the BB nor went to Sunday school or bible class. He lived in the street next to ours - Oakdene Parade. His parents were the loveliest of people. His mum was jolly and his dad was just the way dads should be. I know now they must have been underground, secret atheists - which was totally against the law in Belfast. I myself was an atheist, but just didn't know it yet. You could never let anyone know - they'd have had the RSPCA excavating your land for signs of the dead chickens you'd used in your voodoo offerings.

I was supposed to be at BB bible class on Sunday mornings or Sunday school. But I was in Terry's house. I'd make his mum and dad and Terry a cup of tea in bed. It was a regular thing now. Terry's dad worked at Shorts and had made Terry a guitar out of plastic scraps from the aeroplanes. It was dreadful. My guitar was a Gibson Kalamazoo - an excellent guitar - except for the bent neck which made it impossible to play.

The ABC Minors Cinema Club held a colouring competition and I won a bike - a new one - but one of those old fashioned things with rigid articulated brakes, not the cool cable types, like the ones on my own bike. I sold the bike that I had won and bought my own guitar. My bike had belonged to my dead uncle, Dad's brother, who died at 13 years old when he jumped into the Lagan river, straight after playing football. His lungs had collapsed. His ghost lived in my box room, along with his records and pink basket-weave chair. I travelled miles for guitar lessons, through the jungle areas of east Belfast, past families arguing out in the streets, screaming at each other. Past squinty-eyed children, drunken men, plates flying out of windows, children with callipered legs, bottle-bottomed glasses, one-eye-patched-glasses, gentian-violet-dyed-necks, onwards to a man who wanted to teach me how to play the Hawaiian guitar, not skiffle. Yes, my dad had lined this up.

Ballinderry

Granddad died shortly after our return from South Africa. It didn't affect me much, but it sure knocked my dad about; he went to bits. Mum had said something to Granny and we were kicked out of the house.

The bungalow that Granddad had built in Lower Ballinderry was to be our home, miles from nowhere into the country, past the most horrid smelling glue factory. After stopping in Lisburn to buy a cheap brown Bakelite razor for my dad, we arrived in Lower Ballinderry. The front door of the bungalow wouldn't budge. The back door had been nailed up. We entered by smashing the front door in. The reason it wouldn't open became obvious. The bungalow had been constructed on five 44-gallon drums filled with concrete, one in each corner, and one in the middle. All four near the outside had sunk into the wet ground. The one in the middle that was kept dry didn't sink. I kept thinking of the Titanic, and men like my Granddad.

I learnt about country living cycling back and forth to Achalee: how to use a scythe; how to sharpen it as well as bill hooks; how to sharpen hay cutters; catch a pig; milk a chicken and collect eggs from a cow … and of course, I still wasn't allowed out before I had completed my training.

I was now shooting my first successful ash longbow, and had the living daylights frightened out of me when I went hunting with my sister Joan and an actual hare popped up in front of me.

Dad wasn't working, so he must have been collecting the dole. He would head into Belfast in his best suit and his Anthony Eden hat. Wherever money was concerned, my dad always dressed up. When time came for me to go to college, and I'd got my scholarship funding, he would dress up like a shiny Marley and head off to the bank to cash *my* cheque.

We lived in Ballinderry all through that summer. I had missed out on schooling. I had with me a crystal radio set I'd made at school, and I used to sit on the roof of the 'shack' and listen to it while I painted a view of Lough Neagh. It was a shack, not a bungalow. I myself had built better in South Africa.

Dad eventually got a job in the gas works in Belfast and travelling was impossibly expensive. Mum was then forced to apologise to Granny for something she'd said, and we moved back in with her. I had my box room again. Joan slept with Granny, although everyone knew that an older person sleeping with a younger person sucked the vitality out of them. In Belfast they believed that shit - like you could have your blood group changed if your mother didn't like it. Mum and Dad slept in the back room. After eight months of living with Granny, my mum had a nervous breakdown. I think the last straw was when she spilled a cup of tea over the freshly wallpapered living room. She tried to wipe the tea off and removed the pattern instead. Gran was in England visiting Aunt Dora, dad's sister. I stayed up the whole night painting the pattern back on before Granny returned in the morning. Mum was in hospital for months, wasting away. When she eventually recovered we moved out to East Sydenham, near the pre-fabs.

The Field

The field in Sydenham was the only vacant green bit of grass and it was ours. The grass was long with a flattened area, where we lolled about on long summer evenings. Us guys would cycle down the entry that went behind our local chipper, peddle onto the grass, step off the bikes and light up a fag in one smooth action; real cool!

The girls would arrive and we would chat there for hours. Later we would head off down to Victoria Park. In that field there were six huge concrete blocks with large metal hoops embedded in them. They were anchor points for barrage balloons from the Second World War. Later a church was built on our field.

Desmond Kinney, my art teacher from Ashfield School, designed the mural for that church on which I assisted with the mosaic tiling. When the mural was finished, critics claimed that it was sacrilegious, as it portrayed Christ at the end of the table, and not at the centre of the table as in Da Vinci's Last Supper. Unlike Da Vinci's depiction, our mural was portrait-shaped, not the tradition landscape. God blew that church down in a storm. The only thing left standing was the wall with the mural on it. People actually claimed that the mural was the cause of the church blowing down. It always amused me that the painting of the last supper by Leonardo Da Vinci has Christ and all the lads sitting on ONE side of the table, all facing the camera as in a table setting for a television sitcom.

Silver Cups

I was sitting in the billiard room, knees apart, and had just spat very accurately on a fresh piece of chewing gum squashed on the floor. And I had a Woodbine in one hand. Through the main door came my father. I looked upwards to the heavens. Fuck. The silver images of the silver paper cups above my head flashed. "Out!" he hollered. For the three-quarter-mile walk home he punched me. He bounced me off fences. He pushed me through hedges. He would have banned me from leaving the house ever again, but I was starting work that week. Those silver things above my head? If and when you could afford Players or Senior Service cigarettes back then, the silver paper was rolled around your finger, and then twisted and flattened at one end to form a silver cup. You then spat on the flat end and hurled it at the ceiling. With luck it stayed up there forever.

My father was now a terror to the family. He was abusive and violent towards us all. Once he hit my sister when she was about 19. She was two years older than me. I stepped in between them and for the first time challenged him to stop his bad behaviour. He knocked me down three times. Each time I returned to my feet. This was a Saturday morning, and it happened just before my father and I were to set off for our usual morning trip together into the city. When we walked along the lonely lane that was a short cut to the bus stop, my father cried. Like many abusive fathers, he would lose control and then be full of remorse; remorse which was more embarrassing than a comfort.

Town with Dad

When my father was in a good mood I adored him. Maybe it was a comparative thing.

On Saturday morning we'd always go into Belfast town together on the bus. We'd get off the bus at Alfred Street and walk along Upper Arthur Street, past the arts supply shop where I'd be allowed just enough time to admire the latest work by Vernon Ward, Maurice Wilkes or Kenneth Webb. Then it was on to Woolworths for hot salted peanuts for Mum, along with the trashiest selections of perfumes I had ever encountered.

Dad had a school friend who owned a tool shop. The pair of us drooled over the goodies. Hugh McMasters demonstrated a bobby dazzler of a fine-toothed tenon saw that had just arrived, which he bent back completely on itself, and squinted along the cutting edge; as straight as a die. Later that morning we passed an old busker playing a similar saw with a violin bow. "It's got to have a double bend. It's the closest thing to the human voice!" he said; he was right - just like Yma Sumac - the Inca singer who had a range of four octaves. After checking the time of the Albert clock, we crossed over Royal Avenue towards Smithfield. The Angelus was just ringing. A team of Guinness draught horses were passing. One of them slipped on the cobblestones and was in the act of falling to the ground. Out of the passers-by, four men stepped forward - including my dad - and in minutes the horse was hoisted to its feet. Jeesus, I was chuffed. Each and every one of these men knew exactly where to stand and how to lift that horse. Apparently this was a regular occurrence.

Down the street and into the Land of Oz, a tapestry of the most amazing clinking, clanking collection of caliginous junk: Smithfield. Three alleyways through layer upon layer of Neolithic deposits which had never seen the light of day since Napoleon deposited his nose on Cave Hill. All this was covered over by a transparent roof. If you stood still in Smithfield for ten minutes, everyone you'd ever meet in Belfast would pass by. Dad knew every item there and proudly accepted my challenges: what's that for? And what would you do with that? He knew everything did my dad.

We never spent long enough at Smithfield, as we needed to get to the cart. There were several of these carts; they were set up on a vacant bomb site because of the War. Here we'd stand and listen to the most amazing collection of priceless jewels on offer: priceless antiques and priceless household time saving devices, all for under three shillings. You'd have to be a mug to miss out on these gems. Dad was that mug, as he always brought home some load of junk. Mum loved it, though, and had a cupboard full of the stuff. Poor Joan was going to inherit the lot.

The bomb site was next to St. Anne's Cathedral which was one of the ugliest buildings in Belfast. (The thought of the Celtic cross on the side facing Cave Hill is embarrassing, and the recent spike makes it look like one of those buildings that God rejected. The powers to be in Belfast literally missed the point of the spire in Dublin.) Here Dad excelled in explaining just how these showman achieved their powers: "Now ladies and gentlemen," he said, "I am going to bend, not only one, but two six-inch nails with my teeth. You don't mind if I wrap them in this little piece of canvas to protect the enamel on my teeth do you?" With a roll forward onto his back and a leap to his feet, he would reveal two nails, both bent almost in half. "Now my brother will put this massive rope around his neck, and you 10 men will pull on that side, and you 10 men on the other, and just with the muscles of his neck he will defy you to strangle him!" My God.

To thunderous applause, one of them was rolled in a sheet of canvas and two members of the audience bound him in a long length of thick heavy chain, as tight as possible. With a staggering silence from the audience, he began vigorously rolling around on the spread out tarpaulin, and as if by magic, the chains fell off - truly amazing. "And as an added bonus, ladies and gentleman, for one shilling we will give you this pen. Look, here inside is the winner of this afternoon's horse race at 4:30!" Thunderous applause - especially for those in the audience who confirmed a win from last Saturday. I could barely contain myself till we were on the bus home.

We'd walk back to the bus station outside City Hall. There were flower sellers all along the front of it. I don't recall him ever buying any for Mum. Perhaps that was really girly, or poofy, or of course – a moffie!

While waiting for the bus, Dad would explain the significance of the Masonic cherubs surrounding the lamp posts outside the City Hall. Dad was a Mason, but never asked me to join. Apparently that was against the rules. I could ask him if I could join, but he couldn't ask me. When Dad died, I found a few strange things in his wallet, including some Masonic cards in code; about as clever as how Robert McAlpine and I used to communicate with each other when we were nine-years-old.

When we were on the bus home, Dad explained: "Nails are drawn hard. Thicker wire is drawn, pulled through a smaller hole. This not only creates the head, but work hardens the metal. These performers have simply heated up the nails to red hot and let them cool - which returns them to softer mild steel. The guy took two six-inch nails and overlapped them one-and-a-half inches. These he bound together tightly by that piece of canvas - there is no stretch in that canvas - making it one length of steel about nine inches long. His teeth were only used to keep the canvas from coming unwound. He then had a nine-inch, mild steel rod in his mouth. You could bend that!" he exclaimed. "The rope around the neck: look how thick the rope was - it was huge. It was a tug boat rope. Tie a knot in that and all the guys in the shipyard couldn't pull the hole left in the centre closed. The brother wrapped in chains: well, you can't tie anything irregular like a soft, floppy human being in chains. As you have seen, you just roll around and they will just fall off."

"Yeah, Dad," I replied, "but what about the right name of the winning horse in the pen?"

"Idiot. Work that out for yourself," he said.

He didn't tell me till we were sitting down to lunch. The name of each different horse was in each pen; somebody was bound to win! Lunch was always the same on Saturday: an Ulster fry.

Chapter Four

The Working Life

Where I learn to handle art materials, all about cardboard boxes, to enjoy purving and adore factory girls, live in fear of milk bottles, what Rhododendron bushes are for, that there are more chords on the guitar than 'D', to dismantle and rebuild a Vespa before breakfast, that some people have nicer parents, waste my time, be beaten up, have a love affair with opera, fall in love, shed my apron strings and make very bad choices.

Haunted 1957

The first part of the factory was the printer's, run and owned by Mr Nicholson - who I never met (although I did work there for one month) - on loan from Mr Bass. There I first met Peter Stone, who was to haunt me all my life. Further down the street in the direction of the Ormeau Baths, was the box making factory, owned and administered by Mr Bass. Between them was the tiny building of the brew (the-employment office). I had been interviewed by Mr Bass, an incredibly stern, angry-looking man, dressed in an impeccable, expensive, navy-blue pinstripe suit. I think he owned Belfast. If I behaved myself he would make me a 'proper apprentice to a proper artist upstairs on the first floor', he'd said, until such times as I went on to Art College. I had come highly recommended by Desmond Kinney, and my school report was amazing - even our class teacher Mr Malone couldn't believe it. Mr Bass advised me to report to his secretary that Monday.

I passed the entrance exam to the Art College. I was 15 years old, and was rejected at the enrolment. No one had mentioned the fees. There was no way our family could pay for anything like that. Fees? Fees? No way. Then the word 'scholarship' was mentioned. Wow - big words were coming thick and fast: 'Rejection', 'enrolment', 'fees' and now '*scholarship*'. What on earth was that?

The beatings my father had given me had had an effect, and took me years to sort out - in fact I'm still sorting it out. I did notice that I had stopped spitting in the street, and the buds of ideas were dawning; things I had learnt at school I could actually use. Nothing was going to stop me from smoking, though - much, much too enjoyable. Love to take it up again, but my wife won't let me die.

No, my father's domination was a thing of the past, I decided. I would look after my own application for a scholarship next near. In the meantime, I would work at Nicholson and Bass.

Robin's office was 12 feet by 10 feet. He sat at the window where the light was best. I sat at a typical office desk, drawers on either side. Robin looked anything but an artist. He wore a chemist's overcoat. He had fair hair and gold rimmed glasses. From the moment I entered his office, the learning began. On that first day I learned how to make a paper folding tray to mix background colours, and how to mix background colours. You mustn't lay a colour down with the same brush you used to mix it, he explained. He taught me what colours bled, and what colours were nightmares to use – carthamus pink, fallow blue - disaster. He showed me the different board and paper, from rough to smooth - that was impossible to lay a background colour on. I had started working on a series of acetate handkerchief boxes, all with windows to show off the embroidery on the handkerchief. There was a label on them that claimed they were Irish linen, hand-woven in Ireland. When Mum was a little girl it was her job to stick these labels on the hankies. These acetate lids had three bells, three bows, three arches, three doilies, three posies and three stars. All of this before lunch.

Staff Member

At this time I wasn't considered to be on the staff, although I did wear a tie. There were other men around the factory. Outside our office door were possibly 80 women, from magnificent to older magnificent. They all sat in front of a metal 18-inch square table which was heated underneath by an electric element. To their forward right was a heated pot of glue - rabbit glue. To their left was a pile of pretty printed pictures. Behind was a pile of strawboard boxes. To their immediate right was a vacant spot. With the aid of the paintbrush that stood in the glue, the table was painted with a fine film of glue. With dexterity, a pretty picture was allowed to fall onto this glued table, picture side up. This was then removed, covered with glue, and allowed to fall into one of the strawboard cardboard boxes that was now beside her, and then folded around the sides. Who wouldn't want to marry a woman with that skill?

It was rumoured that these women would grab any unsuspecting young boy, pull down his trousers, and slip a milk bottle over his dick. Then one of the more well-endowed beautiful girls would flash her tits at him. It was supposed to take hours to go back down. I was living in terror of this happening to me; retrospectively I think I was living in fear that it would never happen to me. Damn that tie - it set me apart as a member of staff. There was one of those rare, beautiful, freckled-faced, freckled-titted, large-bosomed birds who seemed to get into the goods lift with me every time I used it. She was amazing, and I hoped and prayed she'd do something dreadful to me - but she never did!

Once the women did grab me, and I thought my luck was in! But no, they threw me down the rubbish shaft from three stories above the ground floor. I panicked in fear, but the girls had been working on a new type of box that had a thin layer of sponge between the box and the picture-sheet, giving the box a cushion effect. The waste chute was full of sponge off-cuts.

On the floor above us the heavy machines, guillotines, scorers and corner punchers were operated by men who always seemed to be grumbling about the approaching visit of the safety inspectors, who slowed down the operation of their machines. They had to replace all the safety guards and mechanisms on news of their impending visit, and remove them as soon as they left. The top floor had a huge automatic machine that covered handkerchief boxes eight-inches square. This machine was constantly breaking down, and there was a permanent maintenance mechanic in charge. The canteen was also on this floor, and on long summer days I'd buy an Irish home-grown tomato and lettuce roll, and go up on the roof to watch the Lagan go by behind the gasworks wall and the clock tower.

In winter I'd be down in the basement having my toasted barmbrack in the boiler room with the men who really made Nicholson and Bass work. The store men also stoked the boiler. Several of these men worked on the second floor, so did the company delivery truck driver who taught me how to play guitar. Then I only knew 'D'. He knew them all. But my father was still trying to control me; he forbade me to take my guitar to work.

Off to the Plaza

On Friday night all the girls, almost without exception, would sit sideways on their chairs. Their hair would be out of their scarves, their curlers were gone, and half would be facing the window doing up each other's faces. Then they'd all face away from the window to do up each other's hair. At knock-off time they removed their white overcoats and Belfast here we come! I felt the Plaza Ballroom shudder at the thought.

NICHOLSON & BASS ANTHEM
Written by George Callaghan 1956
(I have written this song myself based on what the girls sang)

Feck 'em all, Feck 'em all
The cardboard scoreres and all
Bless the pay clerks and office staff too
If they had their way we'd be out on the brew
'Cos we're saying me girls Feck em all, as back to our benches we crawl
We get no enjoyment from Bass's employment,
So cheer up my girls, Feck 'em all

They say if you work hard you'll get better pay
We've heard all that crap before
Clean up your glue pots and polish your tools
Sweep up the factory floor
There's many an apprentice has taken it in, hook line and sinker an 'all
We get no enjoyment from Bass's employment,
So cheer up my girls Feck 'em all

Feck 'em all, Feck 'em all, the fitters, guillotiners and all
Bless all the cutters and the folders as well
Bless Abernethey, he cuts such a swell
'Cos we're saying Feck you! to them all, as back to our benches we crawl
We get no enjoyment from Bass's employment,
So cheer my up girls, Feck 'em all

Now they say that the foreman's a very nice chap
Oh what a tale, please do tell
Ask him for leave on a Saturday night
And he'll pay your fare home as well
There's men up above have spoken their minds by writing rude words on the wall
We get no enjoyment from Bass's employment,
So cheer up my girls, feck'em all

Feck 'em all, feck 'em all, at the Plaza we'll have such a ball
Feck all the store men, the van drivers too
Bless all the management, we love them its true
'Cos we're saying goodbye to them all, as back to their benches they crawl
We get no enjoyment from Bass's employment,
So cheer up my girls, **fuck 'em all!***'*

Vespa

The boiler room became out of bounds when I was given a pay rise and put on the staff. I was earning £9 a week - £2 a week less than my father. Mum and Dad were keeping £5 from me, but with the balance I was just able to save enough to pay for a Vespa 125 scooter. This I wasn't allowed to take out of the street until the body was scraped back to bare metal and two coats of primer and three top coats were applied - rubbing back between coats. I had to know the ignition backwards, the electrical system - which I never really understood - how to de-carbonise the piston and barrel, and how to split the crank, replace the big end, the gudgeon pin, the kitchen beater mixer, the whirling blender, replace the automatic toasters filliments and mend a puncture ... Even then I was not supposed to leave Sydenham.

Petrol was a problem with the scooter; rarely could I afford it. I would travel with Terry to the outskirts of Belfast and run the Vespa into a ditch. We would then wave down a small truck or van and con him into giving us a lift home - a fictitious destination - the scooter had enough petrol for the return trip. Our ploy was to chat up local country girls, saying that we were university students doing a study of castles in the area. Once I got chatting to an older couple of 65 or so, and their daughter, who was about 35-years-old, while Terry waited. She climbed onto the back of my scooter to show me a particularly interesting castle on her property. Under a Rhododendron bush I lost my virginity, but never found the castle.

JustAs the Tide was Flowing (Traditional)

Collected Portaferry Northern Ireland from Sarah McClurg 1943
(I have used one verse only)

And as she lay upon the grass
Her colours they kept changing
Then she cried out and said alas!
Never let your mind be ranging
Here is twenty pounds I have in store
com back when you will for there's plenty more
For my jolly sailor I adore
Just as the tide is flowing

Terry and I had a run-in with the police down the Newtonards Road. We were down a lane having a piss, when two policemen grabbed us by our collars and spun us round. They were very rough and Terry was rather flustered. At the moment when they were showing us their badges, he kneed one of them straight in the balls and he went down like a lump of lead. Terry then took off in the confusion. The other cop let go of me, so I made my escape as well.

We visited a lady who owned a mansion up the Cairnburn road, and all the surrounding lands with the secret garden at the bottom of the woods. We were smartly dressed and were wearing the hats we had got for Christmas. We sought permission to build a small shack in the woods above the gully, and much to our surprise, she allowed us - with the condition that it must not be visible from the house or her grounds.

I had drawn up a plan at Art College, and soon Terry and I would have our secret retreat. The man who lived in the gardener's cottage showed us how to build a chimney. He also agreed to advise us on how to make a sod roof. The project never was finished, although we did complete two walls, the stone floor and the fire place. The major problem was Terry; he was dangerous with his carelessness and incompetent handling of tools. The first hint of this came when I watched him chop down a branch that he was sitting on. I had left him in an area where there was a particular tree we had selected for an upright post. I returned half an hour later, hoping that he had cleared away some of the larger branches. I looked up just in time to shout at him about the branch that he was sitting on - the one that he was actually cutting down. At that moment the branch broke, and he flung the axe in the air. It fell and hit my head near my right eye. My eye turned black and my cheek was cut directly below the eye.

We worked every weekend through the winter. I have a vivid memory of Terry and I with no shirts on, with a two-man cross-cut saw between us, cutting through an 18-inch thick log with the entire surroundings deep in snow. The project came to a halt after the incident with the large bread knife. I was following close behind Terry, who was clearing the way through the thicket with the large knife. He hit me accidentally across the front of my left hand, slicing three of my fingers. The arteries in two of the fingers were severed, and blood squirted everywhere. The scars on my left hand are a memory of those days! I also have an 'L' tattooed on my finger - which not only recalls Linda, but Terry, who fancied her as well. Terry, however, had other fish to fry. There was a new flame on the scene; a real redhead - Hilary.

Linda

When my father had finished his caravan, Terry and I decided to try it out before it was towed away the next day to Milisle. We lay awake that night in the caravan fantasizing about two girls we fancied. Norma Boyde was on my mind, a girl with great everything, and she had just consented 'to go' with me. She was a distant cousin, the same branch of the family I'm told as William Boyde of *Hop-a-long Cassidy* fame. Terry was drooling about the girl called Linda Knowles. She had been hanging around for some months now with a guy who I truly disliked because he was so horrid and cruel to her. She had just split with him and was on the loose. Terry and I were groaning and moaning under the blankets about these two chicks and what we were going to do to them; actually we were both having a wank.

The next night I was first at the post office were the gang usually met. It was pouring with rain, and standing next to the phone box with an umbrella was Linda. I got in under the umbrella with her and started chatting. I had the impression that she fancied me. I sure as hell fancied her, but never let on, as her boyfriend - the one that I disliked - was a real hard man from Templemore Avenue. I asked Linda to the movies that coming Friday, putting Terry completely out of my mind. Not only did she say yes, but actually she fronted up at the Astoria where we went to see Charlie Chaplin's *Modern Times*.

Body Builders

When we first got our first TV, Dad watched body-building, boxing and the wrestling with enthusiasm. He would 'ooh' and 'aah' at the physical prowess of a specific individual. He would ask my opinion on a particular pair of biceps, and expect the same 'oohs' and 'aahs' from me. He was uninterested by my rising curiosity in sex. I frequently aroused his ire by going into raptures over a great figure, or a set of tits on a beauty queen. Once when I commented on Sandra Dee's great arse, his irascibility reached new heights. For a while I thought that he would ban me from watching TV. He cornered me once to show his disapproval of me sitting in the parlour holding Linda's hand and having my arm around her. "We'll have no nonsense like that in this house, you'll embarrass your mother!" he roared.

My father realised things were changing. I had a steady girlfriend – Linda - and I wasn't playing with him anymore. He asked me to help him lift the engine out of the car. I apologised - I couldn't as I was going out with Linda. When I came home at lunchtime, he was standing on the two mudguards of the Austin, a rope around his neck, and the engine swinging in mid-air. I don't know how long he had been there. His face sure was red.

I was building a double bass for the skiffle group. It was much too big, but I kept working on it every Saturday morning. I'd knock off around 10 o'clock and go and have a cup of tea with Granny. She hadn't called me that morning, so I went to investigate. The door was locked. I climbed onto the roof of the lean-to at the back of the house and then through the bathroom window. I went into Granny's room; she was totally still. Without thinking, I slid my hands under the bedclothes and felt her skin. Ice cold. She was dead.

Dad was adjusting our first TV, trying to get a picture. He froze to the spot with my news and eventually collapsed into his chair, barely moving out of it until Granny was buried. Mum asked me to take over, as she'd never seen 'her Jim' reduced to such a useless heap. With my girlfriend Linda beside me, I took charge of the entire funeral arrangements, everything – flowers, church, grave digging, visits to relatives, choice of coffin, booking of passage for Dora, births and deaths notices, etc., etc. - boy did I grow up as Dad grew down. He was a blethering jellyfish. Someone would eventually suffer for this, and it wasn't going to be me.

Within the safety of our teenage years, Linda and I enjoyed the security of each other: groping, fondling, feeling, poking, counting - but never quite fucking. We travelled for endless miles through Sydenham entwined, under rhododendron bushes, in railway stations, in endless entries, shop doorways and back seats in cinemas, and it only came to an end when she buggered off to Australia, with barely a goodbye or a by your leave.

With my granny gone, and Linda going off to Oz, Mum recovering from a nervous breakdown and my father on the prowl, I decided that I was getting out of there. Whilst going with Linda I had severed relationships with most of my friends. I would go to Oz and find Linda one day.

Art College

By the time I'd started Art College, I had painlessly left the girly stage, drifted in and out of the bigger bit stage, and was just about at the I know bugger all stage. There were two classes of us in the first year, 20 of us in each class, and we were going to spend one month on each discipline of art. What? I came here to draw pictures, not to breed with them! Stained glass, lithography, silver-smithing, lettering, etching, pottery, textile design and sculpture … at the end of eight months we were to make a choice. I chose lithography and lettering. After one year I had learnt nothing that I had not learnt in Nicholson & Bass. I went into second year; same thing. The only thing I learnt was that more than three-quarters of the class were girls who'd been sent there by Mummy and Daddy as a sort of finishing school. I also learnt how to spell and use the word 'subtle'.

Because of my size and age I was no threat to the many beautiful female students. Several of them cast me in the role of a junior 'agony uncle', and I regularly had lovely, buxom art students hold me to their knockers while they cried their hearts out about the current guy who was mistreating them. One of these beauties was Dorothy White. She was my best friend at college. Dorothy was an adoring acolyte of one of the lecturers. He was a lucky man indeed. I - and as I have since discovered - all the other lads in my year were also lusting after her!

Once Dorothy was absent from college for a week and I missed her terribly. She reappeared with her entire face bruised and scratched, both eyes were bloodshot and both hands were in bandages. She had been shopping and had tripped. But because she had not let go of the two bags in her hands, she had fallen flat on her face.

Dorothy was a great singer. She and a friend called Sheila, sang wonderful harmonies to all the calypso songs of Nina and Frederick. This seemed to mainly happen in life drawing classes, when the lecturer was out of the room.

This was the time of Rag Week and us art students joined the parade and collected money for charity. But we pinched half of it for more close-to-home uses!

Subtle

It was in second year that I plucked up enough courage to talk to Joe McWilliams about my overwhelming feelings of inferiority and inadequacy. I explained to him, for example, that although I knew how to use the word 'subtle' - which I had often heard used by my fellow students - I had no idea what it meant. All attempts to look it up in a dictionary had failed because I assumed that it was spelled 'suttle'!

Joe took time to explain many things. He even taught me how to name drop. All in all - how to become a real wanker! Joe and his friends were an incredible bunch. Once, when a Russian satellite was sent into space with a dog inside it, these lads collected a lot of old radio parts, together with pieces of aluminium. They took up to the Cave Hill in the middle of the night. There they let off an explosion - which blew a small crater in the side of the hill. Into this hole they put the broken aluminium pieces, along with the radio parts. To this they tied a dog. They then telephoned the newspapers and police telling them about a flash in the sky, and indicated where something had fallen from heaven! 'Sputnik Lands In Ireland' was the headline the next morning!

Then there was the creation of the Cusendall ghost. In the summer holidays, Joe and his friends had as usual gone to work as waiters at one of the holiday resorts. One of them started spreading a rumour of a ghost that had been seen in the local graveyard. Joe disappeared from the scene that day, shamming a visit to Belfast for two days. But instead of leaving, he acquired a sheet from the hotel where he was working, and had gone to sit in wait in the local graveyard. In the meantime, his friends had been arousing interest amongst the holiday makers in order to persuade them to visit the local graveyard and view the resident ghost. But Joe, who was rather bored by then, started to make ready his costume behind the tombstones. They were expecting about eight or 12 people to arrive from their hotel. The cue for him to appear was that his mate would be whistling *Colonel Bogey* as he approached with his entourage. As Joe sat there he realised that this cue was stupid and would not work - why would any fool be whistling *Colonel Bogey* as he approached a graveyard? Especially at midnight! By now Joe could hear the footsteps and the whispers of the approaching skeptics. He was not one to miss his cue, though, and he stood up behind the gravestone and let out one mighty holler. He then panicked - as immediately in front of him stood 80 or more terrified viewers! Joe instantly dropped the sheet, and vanished into the night, as one hero shouted - "It's the ghost - get the bastard!"

One day Joe and I went sketching with the rest of our second-year class in the railway yards. Joe drew my attention to two men working on the engine of one of the numerous diesel engines in the yard. In those days, Joe always wore a suit - a rather drab, charcoal-grey one that had probably been bought for him, or passed down to him in the hope that he would enter the priesthood. "Watch," he said, and off he went with his sketch book under his arm.

I couldn't hear what was being said, but first there was a lot of waving of arms in the air and pointing to another engine in the distance. The two men then began packing up their tools, and by the time Joe had made his way back to me, the two guys were walking towards the other engine. "What was that all about?" I asked.

He replied, "I blew them out for working on the wrong engine and sent them over there to work on that one!"

Once Joes friend took a small blue vase into a shop in Smithfield and sold it for three pounds. Four days later, another friend went into the shop and bought the vase for six pounds. He asked the shopkeeper if he had the matching vase to it. "Sorry, but no," was the shopkeeper's reply.

"Well, if you come across a matching vase. I would be prepared to pay up to 25 pounds for it," the friend said.

Joe's friend left the phone number of the city hall with the shopkeeper. Two weeks later, another friend of Joe sold the original vase back to the shopkeeper for 15 pounds!

Joe could never leave well enough alone! Wandering down the road passing the University one day, on the way back to college from sketching at Shaw's bridge, he wandered into a small park where several old aged pensioners were playing dominoes in the summer shade of a Sycamore. "Have you heard about the three elephants that have escaped from the travelling circus?" he asked them. "They are wreaking havoc in the grounds of city hall!"

Off tottered the pensioners to check it out!

Bass Holiday

The same summer holiday that Joe was creating the Cusendall ghost, I had gone to Mr. Bass at Nicholson and Bass and got a job for the summer period. I worked for one week designing boxes, then the company shut down for its annual summer holidays for which I got two full weeks' pay! After the holidays I returned to Nicholson and Bass, to find that Mr. Bass was still away, he was in Switzerland and would be there for another month and a half. He had left me no work to do, but I was still on full pay. I sat around bored off my arse for days. Then I decided to put a ship in a bottle. In the second week I put two ships in a bottle. Just before I left, I put an entire fleet in a bottle. I also made a picture frame entirely from cardboard for a painting of a Tudor house that I had painted before I went to college. My Mother and Father hated the work that I did at college. The walls at home were covered with numerous paintings of mine, but all from before I went to college.

Third year

The year below us held a party in our studio across the road from the college. It was gate crashed by Queens University students. A massive second year student - a farmer with farmer's boots - stood at the top of the stairs barring their way, and proceeded to kick the shit out of them.

That weekend two mates from college and I went to the dance at Queens University. I was fumbling in my pocket for the entrance fee when I heard, "There's one of the fuckers! Get him!" One friend came to my assistance. One friend took off. I woke up in hospital, my friend beside me. He had a broken nose and I had two broken ribs and a split hand. I didn't chat anyone up that night.

Being totally uncultured, and not really in tune with all the varieties of music, Lonnie Donegan was the big breakthrough in Sydenham. Rock and Roll echoed from every Teddy Boy; their blue suede shoes turned them into mumbling Elvis's, complete with swivel hips. By the time I got to Art College it was jazz, or so everyone told me, because it wasn't so. While everyone was talking about Chris Barber, Humphrey Littleton, Thelonius Monk and Dave Brubeck, when it actually came to morning break, we'd all shuffle across the road to the coffee house where there was a juke box. It took me a year to learn that I was being played for a sucker. Older students were putting money into my hand, asking me to play the latest hit by Buddy Holly or the Everly Brothers - not the jazz they professed to love so much!

Then along came the opera. When principal opera singers came to Belfast, us students all volunteered as extras. Having a beard and being of the right height, I was selected as one of the standard bearers for Aida. The stage director miss-cued and we soldiers did not march onto the stage. But the next aria was a rave about the soldiers - who weren't even there. I was shoved on, and stood alone amongst these massive voices. I was terrified, but my stutter left.

Around the corner from that coffee shop five of us had a studio in a garret on the top floor. It belonged to a real artist who never charged us any rent. We spent most of our final year there, none of us bothered going to college, it was boring; I think it was supposed to be.

The artist who owned our studio ran a class of blue-rinse lady students who went painting at weekends to the west coast. There he would teach them to paint exactly in his own style. At the end of the weekend, he'd buy their paintings from them – what flattery. He would then join the paintings together with his unique black line. Voila!

Another 12 paintings. He also worked on 12 landscapes at a time, in a production line fashion.

By the time I'd got to the end of the second year, I knew that Robin Holmes had taught me more than these craft teachers knew, for that's what they were: craft teachers. It was only when I got to third year, and was under the influence of not only Tom Carr, Romeo Toogood and John Luke, but also from my fellow students, Oliver McLaren, Dennis McBride, Joe McWilliams and John Vallely, that there was even the slightest hint of something extra, something added: art.

The last year at college was spent learning, then unlearning to be a wanker - getting drunk, parties, getting beaten up, getting ribs and noses broken, breaking into the boiler room - where the steam engine heated the entire building - to gain entrance to the dance on Saturday night in the grand hall of the Art College's technical building.

South to Dublin 1960

Along with another lad from college, Billy McCunne and I set off for Dublin where there were 20 advertising agencies. We wanted to get work in the art department of one of them. I had my commercial samples of work from Nicholson and Bass - excellent for soliciting work. I also had my Vespa. We loaded it up. Mum pleaded with me not to mention to the neighbours just where I was going, and Dad told me not to discuss politics, religion or sport with *anyone*.

The first agency I went to was Kenny's in Baggott Street, Dublin, and I was interviewed by Eamond Gerrity, the managing director. He didn't have a position for me, but was very impressed with my sample folder. I was in a dream of approval. He got on the phone to a certain Pat Ryan.

"What's your name?" he asked me.

"Oh, Callaghan," I replied.

"You're to go straight round to see Pat Ryan," he said when he hung up.

My second interview landed me a job. Pat asked could I speak Gaelic, and my reply was, "No, but I speak Afrikaans." My salary always came in an envelope marked 'George O'Callaghan'.

Billy wasn't having success finding a job, and Billy was good. Problem was his samples were from Art College. In later years I wouldn't give anyone a job who'd been to Art College. My art samples were from Nicholson and Bass. "For your next interview use these samples," I advised, and gave him mine. He did, and we both started work the next week.

On my first day I learnt to use the grant projector for enlarging and reducing images, how to produce photo contacts, bleach with potassium ferricyanide ... and I set fire to the waste paper basket. In the studio in one corner was an amazing drafting table, which had more drawing arms on it than Shiva. This was there awaiting the new art director, Gerret van Geldrin, a Dutch man, an artist, and one of the world's leading authorities on migratory birds.

Tom was a finished assembly artist. Tom and I had lunch at The Capital in O'Connell Street, where he told me of his wife - who I later met. They had no children, and their marriage had been arranged by their priest as Tom was infertile, and he had to wait until the church found a woman who was also infertile before they would sanction a marriage.

Next door worked Billy Bolger, an incredible designer and illustrator. He worked with a writer, Bernard Share, who'd been to Australia and had written a book *The Moon is Upside Down*. On the floor below worked the most guilt-ridden Englishman I'd ever met. Guilty mostly because he was English - Peter Stone - understandably so. Yes the same Peter Stone from Nicholson & Bass.

I seemed to be doing most of the work in that studio. It was mostly finished art or assembly, so when an opportunity to apply for Kenny's in Baggott Street - who were looking for a designer - came up, I grabbed the chance. I asked Pat Ryan for a raise, but he turned me down, so I handed in my notice and took up the position with Kenny's.

Balls in the Air

I must explain here that as an advertising artist, especially a creative one, you are given a huge amount of someone else's money to spend in the most enjoyable way possible. You are paid whacks to sit around and think, getting it wrong nine times out of 10, but when you get it right you are the king of the agency - until you fall flat on your arse again. But as you have so many balls in the air, there's always one up there.

I was now average size, in fact, a typical Celt from Ulster: dark hair, swarthy skin, blue eyes that had been put in by sooty thumbs.

On the eve before I started work at Kennys, I was arrested by the Dublin Garda, and taken down to Police Headquarters and interrogated - especially about my Northern Irish accent. Apparently I had been reported suspiciously loitering outside a jeweller's shop, where I was waiting for a bus, and as timing would have it, I was growing a beard. No, no one could vouch for me. I knew no one in Dublin. Then I recalled Kenny's. I told them I was starting at Kenny's Advertising Agency tomorrow, the next day, and one of the policemen disappeared to return half an hour later with apologies. Not only did Mr Kenny vouch for me, but his brother had done likewise - and he was Lord Chief Justice of Dublin.

Contraceptives

The only place to pull a bird was at a dance, and none of my mates could dance - although they were dying to go to dances. They were too shy, or they could not afford dancing lessons. I had learnt to dance when Linda and I were together; we went to ballroom dancing classes and both got our bronze medals. We had to teach ourselves to jive, but then so did everyone else.

My father had been an excellent ballroom dancer, and his partner has ended up rating eighth in the British championships. He told me the story of a girl whom he had asked to dance, but she told him he was lousy. He took offence at this and spent the next year studying all he could about dancing. Then he went on a search for this girl and invited her once again onto the floor. He made a fool of her with his newly-acquired dancing skills and went on to declare that she was the worst dancer he had ever taken to the floor.

The logical thing to do was for me to teach myself to dance the role of the lady, and that way I could teach the guys to dance. This worked and we all started to go to dances together.

The first girl that I started dating in Dublin was a really nice girl who I had to give up, because she wanted to ride side-saddle on my Vespa! I took her home one night from a dance. When we arrived, her sister was in the living room with two Garda and they were singing. They had been singing for some time, and the song that they were singing as we entered was about a soldier and a sailor who were in a chapel praying for a number of rather interesting improvements on their appendages - along with some other things as well. They came to the beginning of the last verse and stopped; they had heard my Northern Irish accent.

"Do you love the Queen?" one asked

"Don't give a stuff about her!" I replied.

"Good!" came the response, and they continued to sing.

The last thing they sang was the chorus:

'A prayer for the Queen
The greatest old whore that you've ever seen
And if she has one child may she also have ten
May she have a fucking regiment
Hallelujah! amen!'

(source unknown possibly army recruiting song)

My next girlfriend in Dublin was a disaster. This girl, whose name I cannot remember, wore pancake-style make-up, and my shirts became covered in the mess of her greasy cosmetics. She just had to go. We moved out of the YMCA, where we were staying. We were discovered peeing out of our bedroom windows in the middle of the night and were asked to leave. We moved into a flat in a house by the Grand Canal. It had a holy statue of Christ bearing his bleeding heart on every landing on the staircase in the four-storey building. We lads lived in the top flat.

Billy and Pete had been to a car race meeting up north and they returned late one Sunday night - drunk. They had brought back with them a handful of British Union Jack flags. When I came down the stairs on Monday morning to rush off to work, each of the Christ statues on each landing was holding a Union Jack in each hand. At one of the windows - which was open - he was actually waving it! That night we were all asked to leave and were given a week's notice. As we were in a fully-equipped flat, this meant that we finally had to wash our bed linen. This was the first time we had washed it, though we had been living in the flat for a few months. God, the linen was disgusting! We used the grape squashing technique: we trampled them in the bath until they turned a lighter grey!

We all moved into a flat in Rathmines Road. By now we were going to dances regularly. Pete was yearning for a girl called Maria, but she would have nothing to do with him. She was about three years older than him. Pete was 16, and like many extremely clever people, he was socially inept. Pete used to read a novel in an evening. He completed a two-year accounting course in four months. The Irish airline, Aer Lingus - where he worked - were introducing computers into their office systems. The airline held a competition to select the top three employees to go to America for tuition. Pete came top, but management decided that he was too young at 16 to come back and teach the entire Aer Lingus staff how to use computers. Pete was highly intelligent in formal learning, but quite simple in some ways. Once he carved a very large 'M' for Maria on the back of his hand. He then spent hours, evening after evening, throwing a knife at a target in the shape of an 'M' which he had drawn on the floor.

Billy was dating a girl in Belfast whom he had met at college. She came from Newtownards and drove an Austin Healey. One day whilst driving, she failed to brake at the traffic lights at the Arches and drove under the truck that had stopped in front of her. Unfortunately she was permanently blinded in the crash.

I had never been a keen fan of heavy Rock and Roll. Unfortunately, though, most of the dances in Dublin were mainly concerned with Rock and Roll. So I attended a lot of the church dances - which offered mostly conventional ballroom dancing and easier music.

I used a plastic bristled brush with a slide on pseudo turtle shell handle. The cavity below the bristles was used for smuggling contraceptives across the border from Northern Ireland to Eire for friends. To my horror I noticed there were more than the usual hairs in my brush. Fuck, I was going bald like my Dad! Granddad died with all his hair, but Dad went completely bald at 22. My entire life flashed by. Linda had got out just in time! I had *days* to find a wife and get married - and I did. No time was wasted in finding what I thought was a suitable partner. Anne was always running away from home seeking refuge in religious communities. However, we hit it off, and planned to get married within the year. Three months later we were married and moved to London - where we applied to Australia House for the £10 passage to Australia.

I had written to numerous advertising agencies and after settling into a bedsit in Wood Green, I went searching the advertising agencies in London. I got a job on the first day as a visualiser with Butler and Gardner in Carlos Place near Berkeley Square.

The bedsit in Wood Green didn't work out. Anne and I were asked to leave after I connected an aerial to my radio - which was a piece of wire with one end connected to the aerial outlet of the radio - the other end hung out of the window. The cantankerous landlady accused me of upsetting the whole wiring system in the house.

One evening when making my way from the tube station in High Gate to my flat, I was harassed by two girls on motorbikes. They were all leather and studs. They probably picked on me because I must have looked a right Charlie: I was wearing the same sort of clobber that Desmond Kinney, my old art teacher, always wore. The costume was completed with an umbrella that I had learnt to point in true English gentlemen fashion. These two girls rode up on to the footpath. They blocked my passage in front and to the rear. They then proceeded to punch me and shove me against the wall. They quickly became bored, though, because they soon rode off.

The following reflected my thoughts of my relationship with women at the time. I later sang the song on The Dave Allen show

THE WOMEN ARE WORSE THAN THE MEN

Traditional collected from James Callaghan, 1952

Now there was an old man, he lived with his wife
And she was the bane and torment of his life
Riffle, riffle, tiddly foll day

The divil he came to the man at the plough,
Saying, "One of your family I must take now."
Riffle, riffle, tiddly foll day

Says he, "Me good man, I've come for your wife,
For I hear she's the plague and torment of your life,"
Riffle, riffle, tiddly foll day

So the divil he hoisted her up on his back,
And down below he hurried the pack,
Riffle, riffle, tiddly foll day

There were two little divils a playing with chains,
She upp'd with her stick, and knocked out their brains.
Riffle, riffle, tiddly foll day

There were two other divils looked over the wall
They said, "Take her away or she'll murder us all."
Riffle, riffle, tiddly foll day

So the divil he hoisted her up on his hump,
And back to the old man hurried the lump.
Riffle, riffle, tiddly foll day

Said he, "Me good man, here's your wife back again,

For she wouldn't be kept, not even in Hell!
Riffle, riffle, tiddly foll day

Now, I've been a divil the most of my life,
But I ne'er was in Hell till I met with your wife,"
Riffle, riffle, tiddly foll day

So it's true that the women are worse than the men,
For they went down to Hell and were flung out again.
Riffle, riffle, tiddly foll day

Chapter Five

Immigration

Where I learn just how bad things can get, to kill a good idea, why there are leprechauns at the bottom of the garden, about the best job in the world, how to live with giants, there is more to food than an Ulster fry, there is more to acetylene than welding, there is a free ticket out of here, that things go from bad to worse, about impotency, things starting to become untangled and I am out of here!

AUSTRALIA

We were called by the Australian immigration authorities to go to Australia sooner than expected, and our departure date was imminent. During the time in London, Anne had started to disappear out of my life for hours at a time, visiting friends she had made in the building.

When we arrived in Melbourne, we rented a flat in Richmond. We both began working. Anne's job was in a clothes shop opposite Flinders Street Station. My dilemma was that I did not want to let my folks back in Ireland know that I had failed as a husband.

Billy Longridge and George Shaw, his friend from the library in Belfast, had just arrived in Sydney. They called me one day at work to suggest that I try things out in Sydney. My decision was instant: fuck it! I'd had enough of the endless trials and dissatisfactions of living with Anne. I packed up my Triumph Spitfire sports car with a few possessions, including my art folder, and headed for Sydney. I had only recently learned to drive, and after 11 hours on the road, the cops pulled me over just outside Sydney for driving too slowly.

"Do you know how fast you were going, sir?"

"Um, about 75?"

"Try 25...!"

Anne followed me to Sydney and moved into my flat, insisting that her behaviour was the natural desire for a child. To this I conceded, and nine months later we had a baby.

JOCKSTRAP

My first job in Sydney was at Hanson, Rubenstein, McCann and Erikson – or as we called them – Hanson, Rubenstein, McSwine and Jockstrap. They had a design and packaging division where I designed numerous packages, which were approved, and after endless research, ended up looking nothing like the package that had been approved.

One day during the first week that I had joined Hansen, Rubenstein, McCann, and Erikson, I was directed into an office and the door was locked behind me. I was led to a cupboard that was also locked. Darrell, the high priest and head of the department, unlocked this shrine-like cupboard and removed a large, black book. This was the HRMcE bible. I was then locked in the room and left to read this book titled *Factor Analysis*. It had page after page of advertisements, mostly variations of the same ad, and mostly advertising Volkswagen. There were all sorts of percentage variations on readership loss or rise, should the headlines be above or below the photograph, should the photograph size be larger, also where the product name should be positioned, what point size the headline should be, etc. etc. It was like reading the Irish manual on sex; totally boring, and I had forgotten every "factor" before Darrell returned to unlock the door.

We landed the project of designing all the merchandising, including point of sale, play sculptures, menus, and sales features for Roselands

Shopping Centre. Ron Stannard and I were in charge. The highlight was the restaurant court, where I designed 10 different restaurants – Chinese, seafood, London Roast, Whistling Oyster, Indian, Asian, Japanese, Moroccan, French – all with their own merchandising. This was all at Roselands. The most hideous feature of Roselands was a kitsch copper rose fountain made by Peter Stone; yes, that man from Nicholson and Bass, Belfast. Later he was the out-of-place Englishman at Janus in Dublin, and now here he was, an out-of-place Englishman working on his out-of-place copper rose fountain.

LEPRECHAUNS

At this same time, when I first moved to Sydney from Melbourne, Billy Longridge and George Shaw had just arrived from Belfast. We were spending the evening in Manly, the major seaside town along the north shore. We'd wandered into a coffee bar called the El Toledo. Frank Clark was the resident folk singer. He was singing Bob Dylan's "Hard Rains are Gonna Fall" when he heard our accents. "Do you sing?"

"Does the pope wear a funny hat?" Without any rehearsal we sang for half an hour without batting an eyelid, and we brought the house down. Within a couple of weeks we were singing at an audition for Dave Allen, who had his own show on TV. They built an entire set for us, and it went to air. We were signed up by an agent who had seen the show. He promoted and booked us around every folk club and leagues club in New South Wales. We then went on tour with the Shamrock and Heather group, which was created to appeal to every plastic Paddy in Australia. There were numerous TV shows, and we were offered a recording contract with Festival Records for two LPs and two EPs. One album was banned in Northern Ireland because of the track "Kevin Barry." Looking back, they were naïve, but the recording companies then were cutthroat. Thirty tracks recorded in two days, no double tracking, no added effects, no pitch correction, no bass; in fact, no bloody good.

THE AD AGENCY

Retrospectively the most talented people I have ever met.
(This section is about the creative fourth floor)

On the rebound after being conned by two fly-by-night bastards who absconded with 25 textile designs which I'd done as a freelance artist, I had wandered into the directors office of the best advertising agency in Oz for an appointed interview. There was an accountant's executive in his office in a terrible flap. The art director who was to produce his layout designs had not turned up. He didn't ask to see my folder of samples. "Are these really yours?"

"Yes."

"OK, well, you'll do the job."

I had just landed the best job I could ever have wished for. Supposedly I was freelance; $4 weekly rent to them, free use of all equipment and facilities, and I could work for anyone outside the agency. In 16 years, except for a stint in Ireland, I worked for no other agency. Not only were there regular advertising campaigns but I also worked on all the food-related products in the agency.

During my days at college, did I learn to draw? Answer? No. The mighty dollar taught me how to draw. TV storyboards (this is a comic strip version of the proposed TV commercial) paid ten dollars per frame, and some storyboards needed up to thirty-five frames to explain the sequence of events. I ended up not only being able to draw well, but fast. I worked for myself, and for all the other art directors as well. I could do a storyboard of thirty-five frames in a day. Most of the ideas for TV commercials were conceived by the writer and the art director, and when weeks were lean, I would just add additional pictures to explain the concept.

There were six other art directors, all working on their own accounts. I was able to cross over onto all their accounts when it was discovered that I could produce and record advertising jingles, and had a complete understanding of 3-D display. I was working at home in sterling silver at the time. The list was endless making all the unusual props for photography. Silk Fashion Silver Award, the Helena Rubenstein Silk

Fashion set of silver buttons, the conversion of a fruit machine to look like the cockpit of a Qantas plane with a 20-foot wing span, a model of a baby jumbo jet as a birthday celebration campaign, Cottees rafts and robots for photography, point of sale for Ice Cream, etc...

At the same time that we were making a submission to the Esso petrol account, the executive directors got very upset by us plebeian art directors using their parking spots, so they installed a metal post that came straight up out of the ground, secured by a lock. These steel poles were painted with yellow and black stripes. So us art directors stayed behind one night and produced eight life-size Esso tigers, all sitting on their bums astride of the steel poles. They looked as if they were having a wank!

A similar prank happened when the company got rid of the well-loved tea lady and installed an automatic machine. One art director made a full-size cut-out of a tea lady whose legs went either side of the water spout. I found that one a bit crude.

Management installed thirty show boards covered in blue velvet, about one meter by one meter. These were eventually to have current advertising campaigns displayed on them. Three weeks had gone by, and still they had not been used. One morning when we came to work there was a notice pinned up in the fourth floor foyer advertising a current art exhibition, all proceeds to charity. I wandered around, enjoying all the exhibits. They were the same blue boards, but they now all had titles and prices: Blue Moon, The Blue Beyond, Blue Street, My dog Blue, I get the blues when it rains, Blue suede shoes, etc.

We art directors had in our possession a set of slides of a now very famous TV star. We had been on a TV shoot in the outback when this particular chappie picked up a goanna (a large, stumpy lizard) and stuffed it down the front of his trousers, which he then produced at tea-break by unzipping his fly in front of all the ladies. The photographer kept on shooting. I still have the slides which prove it!

Doing that first job was difficult, not because of the job; it was the constant ringing of the telephone. "What have you done with my pills? Is that you,?" It was an art directors office I was using and he had left his home, apparently without telling his wife what he had done with her pills. She was going frantic searching the house for them. She'd call his office every five minutes. "Is he back yet?". He eventually turned up. I never judge men anymore as being good looking or not; not since my wife told me that she fancied Anthony Quinn from *Zorba the Greek* fame. I thought this guy to be extremely handsome, and later saw him in a TV commercial playing the part of a Russian patrol guard. He designed all their packaging, and was one of the better colourists in the agency. One time he knocked his wife out with a rolled-up newspaper, hitting her on the head when a Huntsman spider landed on it.

Although being upset that I was working on his job and would probably steal his account, we did become extremely good friends when we discovered our mutual love of opera and a passion for Jussi Björling and Benjamino Gigli (I didn't know of Carlo Buti at this time; now my favourite singer since hearing him sing "La Paloma"). This was also the time of James Bond. We compared notes. I continued to work on that account, Channel 10 and he left to work in Melbourne.

In the same week that I joined the agency, a new English migrant started work as well. Although a traditionally sworn enemy of the Irish, this Englishman and I hit it off straight away, and have enjoyed the clichéd side of our nationalities ever since. We had a continual banter in the form of cartoons that we'd leave on each other's desks.

He has to be the most creative art director I have ever met, both in successful and unsuccessful advertising campaigns. There were too many art materials going missing from the supply cabinet, so one of the managing directors was put in charge of the key to the cupboard. Such power can corrupt, and it went to this director's head. This did not sit well with our new art director, who would often go straight into the managing director's office and take the key without asking for it. This led to the managing director chasing him around the agency shouting: "You're fired!" This happened regularly, once or twice a month.

That art director was responsible for the submissions we made to an American Agency. As a friendly gesture, we were to submit to them, and they to us, a slide presentation of all staff members. For our submission we dressed up all our staff in black suits, braces, shirts, home-made guns and machine guns – gangsters incorporated. When we received the presentation slides from their staff there was no attempt at humour; these guys really *were* gangsters, where were their guns?

Any obscure ideas he had, which included props, he'd call on me to make. One that was a waste of time was a house made entirely of glass for our fly spray account. This would be filled with flies, then one squirt down the chimney. "We'll kill flies in houses, not glass jars."

"Come on," said the creative director, "that," pointing to the glass house, "is just another glass jar."

On the day when the Englishman bought his Lotus Europa, we all awaited his arrival outside work. The pavement was lined with about 20 of us when he arrived in his flashy new red sports car. His little face was beaming from ear to ear as he pulled up beside us. He pulled the handle of the car door, but the door only moved six inches, and no more. The car was so low that from now on he had to park three feet from the curb.

Cars, of course, reflect what us guys thought of our own dicks. One art directors's car was a brand-new Alpha Romeo. He was a frustrated racing driver. After leaving it in for its first service, he was traveling back to work over the harbour bridge when the engine seized. The service agent had not replaced the sump oil. Of course it was under warranty, and they eventually replaced the damaged engine with a new one.

As for my car? I always worked on the idea that the daggier the car, the less likely the chances that it would be stolen. At this time I had a Land Rover.

The Englishman and I are still in contact. He's preoccupied with keeping fit and being a drain on the Health Service. His wife, collects things with an owl bent, which I occasionally send her. Hopefully she sends me dried peaches.

One Art director continually called the other a Horse Guard. To him this was some sort of insult. It never occurred to him that he thought this was flattering, as those guys cut a very fine figure. This guy looked like the bad knight in all the *King Arthur* movies; massive in stature. His desk looked tiny. He was a great layout artist. As an art director he was cool and always in control. We mostly used felt-tipped pens, which we referred to as "squeakers" because of the noise they made. Most drawings would eventually be interpreted as a photograph in some way or another. Any three-dimensional work he'd pass on to me.

He had a swimming pool, and his dream was to build a chunky bar; but he was having no luck with the actual bar top itself. The carpenter he was using wasn't getting it right, he kept saying that the top would move, expanding and warping all the time, being so close to the moisture of the swimming pool. "OK," I said. "I'll make that." I used 3" x 8" Oregon planks, three at 10 feet long. I drilled five holes at equal intervals through the 3-inch sides, threaded them onto 24-inch threaded bars, with counter-sunk heads and nuts. "There you go, mate, if they move, tighten or loosen up the nuts on the inside of the bar top."

His wife, welcomed me to Australia with a special dinner party which all the artists came to. What a meal everyone got. Superb cuisine. Me? I got boiled spuds, spuds in jackets, mash and chips. This was all whisked away after everyone had had a good laugh.

Beautiful Phil, as we called him, was an art director who was so handsome he had fallen in love with himself in the cradle. He dressed accordingly, and kept the company of like-minded souls. He never kept the company of us low-lifes. He worked for his own clients, and rarely for anyone within the agency. He was small, short-legged, and large-headed in every direction, but in his mind he was beautiful. The most unusual thing about this man was that we all liked him, without exception. He was popular among all the secretaries on the floors below. Secretaries from the floors below were forbidden to come onto our floor. It was not a rule made by us. I think their mothers had all approached management, knowing that their daughters would be corrupted if they came onto our floor.

All art directors were responsible for the art direction of any photography that was required, which included casting. Phil, always cast himself in his own work.

He never sat down. He was never even seen sitting down in a restaurant, choosing to stand at the bar and have a counter meal. He travelled back and forth to Bangkok – no one knew why. Perhaps it was to sit down.

In the next studio was Johnny. He was one of those artists from the old school. He had a great foundation in all the disciplines required for the period before the war. He had been what they termed a "commercial artist" and had been a flyer for the Australian Royal Air Force. Truly a gentle man.

He listened to a rehearsal recording of The Leprechauns once. I knew he was a muso as he played in a jazz band. "There's no vibrato!" he went on to explain. "All your singing is on the beat. Each syllable is given the same value. There's no sex. It's just like your Irish priests would have everyone sound; sexless!"

One art director was the epitome of scruffiness. He was scruffy even before he put on his smock. He was a walking art supply dispenser; squeakers, brushes and rulers protruding from every pocket. His pockets bulged with tubes of paint. In his top pocket he kept a Lucid scope which he attached to the edge of his bench. His face was covered in daubs of paint. His mouth held his current three brushes, and bleed-proof white was on his tongue. That stuff was foul. It removed all traces of saliva like eating a kaki fruit before the frost has got to it.

We'd chat about his daughter, who was heavily into folk music. She loaned me a copy of a recording of the "The Fair Flower of Northumberland" which I sing often.

A man and wife team had fled London when they discovered the man above them had been perving on them through a hole in their ceiling. How do you discover something like that? I must admit that these days I scan the hotel room I'm staying in for hidden cameras. Once I was watching TV in a hotel my wife and I were staying in and I'm sure I got a flash of our naked bodies on the screen.

Alan did all the TV storyboards and was actually *on* the staff of the agency. He was going home at lunch to nail some palings on his fence. His wife had just rung up to say they had just arrived.

"Don't forget to dovetail the nails," I said in passing.

"What? What's that?"

"Two nails go in at an angle, tapering outwards from each other. Then the kids can't pull them off to use as guiders, or they can't be stolen by my dad."

After that, Alan consulted me on all his home improvement projects.

One definition of art is choice; at this, Jules was superb. He gained a position at the agency purely on the weight of a book of photographs he had cropped. The book was called *Cowboy Kate*. He couldn't draw, he couldn't do lettering and he was useless with a brush; but he was superb with a pair of scissors or a Stanley knife.

Normally an art director would start with an idea, illustrate this with a squeaker or pastel pen or a brush, and eventually a photograph. This guy started with a photograph, then spent hours, sometimes days, experimenting and cropping. Maybe he'd cut a piece of type from a magazine, arrange this with a bit of body type and a cut-out logo. Off he'd go in search of a copywriter to write a headline the length of his cut-out piece of type, and write for him some body copy relating to his photos. Weeks later, voila!

One of our copywriters, collected his own and somebody else's child from kindergarten, and on the way home the back door of his car flew open and the children were flung out onto the road. He came to a halt, and ran round to the rear of the car. The child at the bottom of the pile was crying, and his legs were twisted in all directions, he rushed them to emergency; the copywriter couldn't bear to look.

"You may come in now, everything's all right," said the doctor.

"Doctor, what did you do?"

"It's OK, he had his shoes on the wrong feet."

Our floor was out of bounds; the creative floor. Copywriters and art directors. Tin gods. We got away with murder; but then, we were always working under extreme pressure. We didn't save lives or do anything worthwhile, but there were times when all of us worked right around the clock, several days in a row, to meet a deadline.

Once I was sent down to Adelaide on a job with a writer. We didn't sleep nor see the outside of the hotel for five days. That was a job for Simpson washing machines, fridges and cookers. I designed, among other jobs, nine brochures for their appliances, each with a different kitchen. These kitchens were left in the hands of a kitchen maker, to be completed for photography. They were delaying on finishing the first kitchen, and I had to return to Adelaide to sort out the problem.

"No, no, no!"

There before me was one superbly built kitchen, with cupboard, drawers, and doors all working perfectly.

"Nothing has to work; it just has to *look* as if it does," I said. "A sheet of Laminex, a few pencil lines, stuck-on handles in the right place, and *voila*! One kitchen! Shouldn't take you longer than two weeks for the whole nine kitchens."

The art director in the studio next door dressed superbly, and had immaculately manicured hands and a ramrod straight back. He had come from England via Hong Kong and displayed a most fantastic watch, which he was extremely proud of. I asked him the time regularly. It took him a long time to realise I was taking the mickey, as not only did he have to stop what he was doing, it also took two hands to tell the time!

I had been to his house many times, and had seen his display of model royal sailing ships that he had made himself. The quality was the best I'd ever seen. He showed me newspaper clippings from back home in England, of how he and a friend had built a model submarine and used it at an international model boat show to torpedo and sink a competitor's boat, the *Queen Mary*, who had come "Best in Show" one time too many.

This dapper man was a really nice guy, mild and gentle, until the day he came into his office one morning.

"Come into my office, boy, and have a look at this."

I went round the pillar, and there he stood, his back arched ramrod straight. He stood absolutely to attention, his arms presenting on his shoulders, an ancient military-looking rifle. He spun it sideways and presented it to me for inspection. This guy was serious, and in a military voice he explained how he had restored the woodwork on the butt of the rifle. It took months using hot irons and water, soaking and removing every dent. There wasn't a blemish on it.

It was his bearing that defies description. Then I recalled how he'd told me when we first met that he had been in the Horse Guards. He's military. So that's what was meant when yer man insulted the other by calling him a Horse Guard.

A friend who owned a small agency around the corner had owed me money for over a year for some drawings I had done, and it was getting time to move to Tasmania – he still hadn't paid up. At the last minute I left a message with his secretary, that I still hadn't been paid. An hour later I received a very angry phone call from Terry. "Call round here this instant; there's a cheque sitting here for you on my desk. Now!"

Terry and I were pretty good friends. He was a kind and gentle guy; whatever had gotten into him? I needed the money and I went straight round to his office. I opened the door and fell immediately into a heap on the floor, belly laughing and rolling around. He sat behind his office desk in a uniform of an 18-star general. Beside him stood two subordinates, also dressed in military uniform. Against the wall leaned three military rifles. It was that time of year when the military reserves go off on their military training. It's the uniform, or the presence of a rifle; it warps the mind. When the screaming hordes come over the hills to rape our women and children, I want those guys on our side. I recalled what he had meant at Sofala (which you'll read about in a later chapter): "We'll show off our firepower!"

Recently Stef and I were having a very pleasant evening with friends we had just met. They seemed rather harmless, and he had behaved like rather a bumbling fool. In fact, he was a bumbling, blethering idiot. I mentioned how the presence of a gun or the donning of a uniform can alter the person's character. "No it doesn't! Of course it can't!" he immediately declared. I thought he was about to get off his chair and beat the shit out of me. "I'm afraid we shall never be friends, George." His wife declared that of course he changed, completely, just as soon as he put on his uniform. "Well, that's why I fell for you." she has said.

I hadn't known that he was military. He was the leader of "The Charge of the Light Brigade."

A creative team usually consists of an art director and a writer. Most of my accounts were food-related. The agent's writer on food was Mitch. She was my senior by 10 years or so. We became extremely good friends after I had spent many hours consoling her when her boyfriend was killed in a helicopter accident. He was a cameraman, and had worked on numerous superb Australian movies. She occasionally lunched with us art directors, traveling to and from restaurants on the back of my motorbike. She and her (late) boyfriend, always travelled in the outback of Australia during their annual holidays, taking photographs.

One of her lasting stories I often tell and re-tell, it is so contrary to Western thinking. They had met with a family of Aborigines going walkabout. This is a term used when an Aboriginal family, for no reasons us Westerners can fathom, just decide to drop all their possessions and take off to the horizon. They encountered one such family. One aged grandparent, mother and father, a teenage son and two young children. The father asked them for water. Mitch filled their water container. The father took the container and gave it to…? At this stage Mitch stopped the story and gloated as I questioned her with a look.

"Go on, what did he do with the water? He gave it to the teenager, who gulped the lot."

They gave them more water, which they then shared around. The elder of the family explained, in response to their quisling looks, that if they really got into trouble, their only hope would lie with the youngest and fittest member of the group – pointing to the young teenager. It's a long way from our attitude of women and children first.

That lovely lady was the first of my advertising friends to snuff it. I mean her no disrespect, but I will always remember her for saying, "There's nothing that can shatter the tranquillity of the bush like a woman pissing."

While a submission was being made to a new client, it was usual for several art directors to be working on it at one time. Sometimes secrecy was of the essence, and we would be held up for weeks on end in hotels. In the agency we worked regularly through lunch, but at times lunch could be a ridiculous affair. Each art director had his favourite photographer, and depending at whose studio you were working at the time, the photographer would join you for lunch. Some of these lunches got completely out of hand. It was often at the Taiping, beside Paddy's market, when that happened. This at the time was the best Chinese restaurant in Australasia. Usually there was a queue up the stairs to get in. The police detectives would be there before us with brown paper bags on the tables. There were no tablecloths; they would just slow down the turnover. The restaurant didn't have a liquor license, and each bottle of alcohol was in a brown paper bag with the name of one of the waiters on it. Officially it belonged to the waiter. At times there were 18-20 of us at three tables joined together. I have stood on these tables and had the entire restaurant singing for hours. We were into all kinds of food, and not one of us just ate to live.

One o'clock brought on instant decisions; where to have lunch? One restaurant was as good as another. The Indian at Crow's Nest was our communal choice, although individually we preferred our own favourite closer to home, or occasionally my favourite, The Bombay, up the bloodykingscross (all one word).

You could get Nasi Goreng at the new restaurant in North Sydney, or a New York-cut steak with blue vein cheese. Of course there was Italian or Greek, but all the secretaries ate at these. Weekly we'd go to the 729 Club, named after Channel 7, Channel 2 and Channel 9 – there was no Channel 10 represented there. You'd get the most conventional food superbly prepared. You could also lose your earnings on the pokies, a part-time occupational hazard with most Aussies. The rugby league clubs all around Sydney were for top-grade pub grub, especially steaks; but again the poker machines ate into your appetite.

There was always the standby – the counter lunch. The first counter lunch I ever encountered was in Melbourne, where I had just started work at Brown and Bruce. My fellow artists suggested a counter lunch. This meant looking at a menu written on a blackboard. If you chose to eat in the bar, it would cost you half price for the same meal. You'd eat it standing it up, like Beautiful Phil fashion. Usually it would be some form of stew accompanied by three veggies and chips cooked in oil, not lard as in UK fashion. There was a hot pudding for dessert. Most pubs also had a barbecue grill outside where you could choose from a varied selection of cuts of steak and have it cooked for you. There was also a mixed grill on most menus comprised of steak, lamb chops, sausages, bacon, eggs, and chips, and always too much salad. The best way of holding up any bar is with a freshly baked roll, pastrami and New Zealand epicure cheese, or a length of cabanossi or kabana from the delicatessen next door. When I was too busy I'd send out for a couple of salmon fishcakes. I have tried in vain for years to duplicate these, but no luck!

Occasionally we'd try a new restaurant, of which there were so many: Mexican, Spanish, Japanese, African, (a long way from JANUS the agency in Dublin, where I had bought four pancakes, half an ounce of butter, and heated the pancakes under one of the photographic lights.) There was even a French restaurant but we never went there, as the secretaries went there too. All those French waiters with their French accents had never been further afield than the food strip in Manly.

Preparing work for photography could be very involved. Finding the correct Eskimo pie for Peters Ice Cream could involve opening cartons and cartons to find the perfect one. Creating a stew meant making a gravy first, cooking all the vegetables and meat separately – undercooked, and placing them three-quarters buried in the gravy. A layered cake involved numerous cakes individually sliced to give several layers all perfectly equal, then removing a wedge for internal exposure. Each layer was then creamed, and the wedge creamed separately. When assembled, the home economist would tickle and prepare all the exposed cake.

Perhaps the most involved prop for photography was the flip-top pack of cigarettes. Open any flip-top to pull out some cigarettes, and the crest of Rothmans or Stuyvesant is hidden by the cigarettes. The lid needs to be lifted higher and tilted forward. All the cigarettes are too low in the open position, and you cannot see the brand name or crest on each cigarette. They all have to be elevated. Once the entire pack is photographed, a block of wood, cut a half-inch larger, will be made of the pack, including the new angled and elevated lid. A male model with very small hands – a model for cigarette advertising, had to be 26 or older, nothing immoral about this bunch – holds the larger block in the exact angle as the pack has been photographed. The two images are assembled – result. Larger-than-life packet of fags.

Ice cream was straightforward – coloured mashed potato. Real ice cream would melt under the photographer's lights. The next step was the re-touching of any minor blemishes. I recall trying to pass onto charity the rejected ice creams. They all refused.

For Qantas group travel, I had this idea of marking out a large map of Australia in a drive-in cinema, and place groups of people together, hopefully in their uniforms. I pictured a bowls club, a tennis club, and a darts club. For that added Australian touch, we would locate, right in the foreground, a group that represented the manliness of Australia, the Australian Life Saving Club. We were to take the photograph from high up in a cherry picker. After wasting half the morning, we eventually had to relocate the bowls club to the fore and the lifesaving club to the rear of our map, up near the Northern Territory and out of focus; those bastards couldn't keep their hands off each other! Everything in the photographs would have been a blur as they continually played around grabbing each other's balls.

One of my favourite photographers was incredibly creative, knew all the tricks, was totally disrespectful and bloody funny. He was known throughout Australia for not joining the RSL – the Return Soldiers' League. He had passed all the enrollment interviews and for his final inauguration it was essential that all his documentation should be cited, so he brought all his papers in for presentation. He was a Nazi. I suppose in today's era of political correctness he should have gained admission.

He was of the opinion that we should be very good friends, both of us having a common enemy – the British. Me, being from Northern Ireland, went straight over his head. At my going-away party he made his arrival in his Hitler youth uniform and proceeded to award us all with cardboard cut-out replicas of German iron crosses.

This man was wild, and he would go off his head at times. I saw him throw a Hasselblad out of a second-story window, and I was with him when he lost one in the surf at Manly while shooting a job for me. The shot required a gentleman in a dress suit riding a surf board. This was one in a series of marvellous photos done for the "way-out world of Peters Ice Cream." Some of the shots were ridiculous; 30 people bursting out of a telephone booth, Skippy the Bush Kangaroo eating ice cream, 17 in a Mini, dancing the Go-Go on ice cream. The shot that I loved was of a now-famous TV star. She was in the nude, and entirely painted with body paints; I did the body painting. It tickles my fancy when I think back to how I had to suck her nipples to make them sit out for the painting!

I had another unusual experience with a photographer. This was caused by the imprecision of the English language. The shoot concerned involved seven models. Andrew left a message to ask me to postpone the shoot and bring the session two hours forward. The shoot was originally scheduled for 11:00 am. so I fronted up at 1:00 P.M. I was four hours late for the shoot that had started at nine o'clock! Boy were they delighted with me! All seven models had to be paid for the extra four hours that they had been sitting around. Since then I have always insisted on precise times being specified for all appointments. So if I am asked to bring a time forward or backward, etc., I always ask, "Exactly what is the new starting time, please?"

We were all at an exclusive Italian restaurant. The guy at the next table, who was with his lady, came over to us and asked us to keep the noise level down a bit, as he was trying to have a romantic meal with his girl. There were eight of us, all from the agency; we had just come from a boxing tournament where Lionel Rose encountered the Fighting Harada from Japan, so we were probably hyper, and much too bloody noisy. After ten minutes we hadn't let up in the slightest, and he came over again.

"Gentlemen, I asked you politely to ease up a little."

"Fuck off!" said our bravest.

The stranger stood erect, pulled back his coat and removed a gun from its holster. He then blew a hole in the roof. We shut up! ...Lionel Rose won.

I thought I had dispelled boxing from my psyche, then someone pointed out to me a health food store along the north shore at Collaroy owned by a famous boxer, Jimmy Carruthers. At ten years old I had stayed up in Cape Town to listen to him fight Vic Toweel, undefeated world champion from South Africa. Bantamweight is the most popular weight in boxing. The entire world waited anxiously for this fight. It lasted four seconds. Jimmy Carruthers won.

Our same crowd were having lunch at the 729 Club one really, really hot summer's day. All the girls from the fourth floor of the agency were there as well. We were all pretty well pissed by three o'clock. With the girls' help and the aid of taxis, we all made it back to work, except we did not return to our studios. Instead we ended up in the test kitchen, where the fridges were well stocked with alcohol and ice cubes. We managed to get the place in a total mess with the ice cubes from the fridge. The test kitchen cook was putting ice down someones trousers, yer man was putting ice down Julie's knickers, someone else was trying to retrieve his trousers that had been thrown out of the window, I was lying on the ground being rubbed with ice on my bare chest. This was all on the ground floor, where all the secretaries lived. They were taking turns at looking through the glass window in the kitchen door. Someone had now taken off his trousers to dry them over the cooking stove. At this moment, in through the door came Anne, my wife, looking for her maintenance money.

The 729 club used up too much of our bloody money. Not that the food was expensive, it was the poker machines; we would all throw money into a kitty, and of course lose the lot.

The food at the club was great, but the entire place was too comfortable. We drank far too much and spent far too much money gambling on the slot machines. Alcohol had always been a problem with me. I have at times kept pace with my fellow Irishmen, as well as with my fellow Australians. The problem has been, and always will be…I just don't like alcohol. Neither did my father, nor my grandfather, also, when I force the stuff into me and I do get drunk, I seem to do very stupid things. During the time when I owned my first Land Rover, I pushed a six-foot-high wall over in order to get from one street to another. This happened when a crowd of us had gone to the horse races. My car had been hemmed in by other parked cars, and the only way out was from the next street. Between me and the exit was this six-foot wall.

Another time I was parked down a driveway and someone had parked over it. I used my Land Rover to push his shiny new Holden out of the way. I then continued stupidly down the pavement to avoid the traffic lights.

No advertising award ever sold a product, but it does add to an agency's prestige. I had won several awards for the agency, including a full-page advertisement, awarded by the Australian newspaper for "Beat This!" This drew attention to the poor way in which the NSPCC were operating in Australia. I was asked to defend the advertisement on an interview at the ABC. There was also a representative from the child welfare department to defend their position. They immediately launched straight into the attack, wanting to know where I had acquired the photograph of the beaten child. Of course it was all makeup, the overstuffed cheeks were of my associate's son eating too many lollies. I cut their attack to pieces when I declared that most child abuse occurs in the hours between six in the evening and twelve at night, and their office closed at five.

We were off to Lazenby in England to spend winter near Penrith to be near the archery club, which reminded me of the time when the islanders north of Oz were wrapped in the James Bond movie starring George Lazenby. He made a TV commercial for a brand of cigarette. George on board a yacht, he lights a fag, girl jumps into the water, George looks as shark appears, dives into water, kills shark, climbs out of the water, fag still burning, takes a drag. How cool is that?

They had no still photographs for magazine promotion, we had to shoot some down at Botany Bay. We arrived on site, models, photographer and myself. The catamaran that we had hired was already there and in the water, but there was too much wind to move offshore, so we held the boat in place, the owner and I, while we set up for the photographer. We were shooting for about 20 minutes when a crab bit my toe and I lifted my feet off the sand. The boat swung round, the sail caught the wind and the boat took off, me being dragged along underwater on the bow. When I clambered aboard we were at least a mile out to sea; two models and I who knew nothing about sailing or boats. We were alone until I caught sight of the owner; he'd been dragged along too, and he was now clambering on board. Now that was cool.

ITALY

Our Sunita was a wonderful baby, and I poured myself into her. She was always happy. When Sunita was six months old we decided to return to Ireland. We did this because our compulsory two-year stay in Aussie had expired, and there was some dopey attitude that we had served penance and could now return to the homeland. We travelled back to Ireland on the *Fair Sky*, an Italian ship. At this time I was working for the Jackson and Wain advertising agency. They had used the *Fair Sky* for a Peter Stuyvesant advertisement. When the ship's social staff became aware of this, they asked me to redesign all their function area, as the ship was about to undergo a refit. Because of this I was given first-class treatment. This was most welcome, as I found the standard of everything on the ship to be very poor.

There was one other, and underlying reason for returning home to Ireland. I had uprooted Anne from Dublin, and I had always felt guilty about this. If I returned her home, perhaps we could start afresh. I was living in hope as I was enjoying being a dad, and Sunita was a joy.

In Australia I had paid for a right-hand drive Fiat 850, which I was to pick up in Naples where the *Fair Sky* was to dock. My plan was to motor home to Ireland; but on our arrival in Naples, a motor car registration strike broke out, I couldn't leave the country without the proper registration plates. We were forced to stay in Italy for three months, and our money was running out. Neither of us could speak Italian, but with pretty Sunita's blond hair she was a passport from our ignorance. One night when we were camped in a field outside a large Italian village, we were approached by a crowd of rather rowdy-looking hooligans. I reached underneath the blanket that we were sitting on and slipped my hand around the small axe that I had been using to chop kindling for the fire. Second thoughts forced me to my feet and I approached the lads saying *bambino* and signing to indicate that the baby was asleep. They quieted down immediately, and without exception they all crept up to the car window and stared in amazement to see such a small person with golden-blonde hair. Then they saw my guitar and we spent the evening singing Rolling Stones and Beatles songs. They knew all the words in English, and the guitar chords are the same in any language. The next morning they came around and invited me to have a game of football with them. I played goalie.

ACETYLENE

One morning, after a very bad night camping by the sea front, Sunita had been coughing all night. The sun was just rising as I walked along the water's edge with Sunita in my arms; she just would not stop coughing. Wading in the water were several fishermen with carbide lights. Earlier that night one of them had borrowed some soap from me to fix a leak in a gas line. Now one of these fishermen was walking towards me, raving away about something I should have been aware of if I wasn't such a fool! He raved and raved in Italian until he exhausted his patience. He stepped forward and with the air of a confident grandfather, removed Sunita from my arms, and gestured for me to follow. We stepped over a fence and walked into the middle of a pine forest. He stopped, put Sunita back into my arms, gestured towards the pine trees, and indicated that I was to stay put. Then he wandered back to his fishing. Sunita stopped coughing after about three minutes. The fumes of the resinous pine had done the trick! Now, that's alternative medicine!

Our suitcases and luggage from Australia never arrived in Ireland. Worst of all, my art folder, which I needed to get a job, had vanished as well. I had no option but to go to Kenny's Advertising Agency and ask Eamon Gerarty or Adrian if I could use them as a reference to any agencies that I approached for a job. This was going to be difficult, as I had no money and only the clothes that I stood up in; jeans and a French sailor's shirt. As it happened, Kenny's was searching for a senior designer. Actually when I first called at the front reception I was shown into the office of the owner, Michael Kenny. He had his office decked out like the cockpit of a Boeing 747. He had a microphone and an intercom to every room in the building. I don't know if he ever realised it, but the speakers in all the offices had been disconnected.

Michael Kenny had a brother who was the Lord Chief Justice of Dublin. On the death of their father, Michael had inherited the advertising agency. He knew fuck all about anything except being there on time and leaving on time. He arrived at work every morning at nine o'clock exactly, went straight to his office, placed his briefcase on his desk, opened it and took out the latest Donald Duck and Mickey Mouse comics. He left the office at 10 o'clock when the cinemas were open and stayed there until four o'clock in the afternoon. He would return to work, read his comics for an hour and leave work promptly at five o'clock. Strangely enough, he owned and could drive a car.

Adrian was the art director, and we had been very close friends years before. He invited Anne, Sunita and me to stay with them while we looked for a house.

We rented a house close to them in Glenageary, but Anne took off with Sunita and rented a place of her own along the Grand Canal. For a short time I felt free, though I really did miss Sunita.

I moved into Adrian's home and got on extremely well with Adrian and his wife, Mary. Mary still has a model of a wooden boat on her mantelpiece that I built while I lived with them.

The fun at Kenny's Art Studio was that we all loved to sing. Sandra and her friend Maureen were always asking Adrian and me to start a folk group with them, most of the day was spent working on our repertoire. Every second weekend I would drive home to my folks' place in Belfast. On the return to Dublin on Monday morning I would meet Sandra at about seven o'clock at Drogheda, where she lived. Sandra drove a souped-up Mini Cooper. I, at this time, owned a Fiat 850, the one that I had brought back from Italy. We would race through the back roads to Kenny's in Bagot Street. Sandra always won!

The art department of Kenny's consisted of Adrian, the art director; myself, a senior designer; Sandra, the junior designer, and Maureen, who was the assembly artist. After the pressure I had worked under in Australia, I could have run the entire show myself.

STUCK

One day at work I got a long-distance call from, the creative director of the agency, "When was I returning to Australia?"

"At the rate I'm earning here, two years at least!" I replied.

"Never mind that. We have restructured the place and have appointed six art directors and we need you here tomorrow!"

"Bloody oath," I replied. "I can be there if you pay the fare!"

When I came to work the next morning there was an air ticket to Australia waiting for me. The plane was leaving three days later from Belfast. Having said my thanks and made my apologies to management, I went to the studio to say farewell and my thanks to Adrian and the girls. Sandra was not there; she was sitting outside in her Mini Cooper which was parked behind my car. I opened the door and climbed into the passenger seat to say my farewells. Sandra was a large girl, very pretty; she wore the shortest miniskirts that I had ever seen, and she had no tits at all! I always knew that she liked me a lot. She was in hysterical tears. I still don't know how she managed it, but she climbed onto my knee, put her head into my shoulder and cried and cried and cried. It was the best feeling that I had about myself for years. Sandra and I wrote to each other for quite some time until she went to Canada, where she met some guy and got married. Soon afterwards she was divorced. She then emigrated to Melbourne, where she met a Croatian. I caught up with her to say hello a few years later. Because of her divorce and being remarried, her father refused to talk to her.

On a trip to Ireland many years later, Stef and I called in to see Sandra's mum in Drogheda. She was delighted to see us, and I spoke of Sandra to her. She was especially delighted that we had called through the day, as Sandra's father was away at work. He would not have her name spoken in the house. I don't really know how the conversation came around to campanology, but Sandra's mum took Stef and me to see her husband's bell-ringing book in his study. He had filled an entire one-inch-thick book in the most exacting copper plate writing with information about churches, that he had visited, together with the details of the tone and pitch of each bell, also the duration of the ringing. A picture is worth a thousand words; misdirected energy is the basis of a thousand absolutes. This foolish man absolutely refused to talk to his daughter Sandra.

MY FOLKS

Then came a phone call from my father, when was I sending the money for my wife and daughter to return to Australia? It was now three months that Anne and Sunita have been living in their house. I had thought Anne was living in her own flat in Dublin where she had a job. Apparently, however, she had left that flat the week I had left Dublin and moved back in with her mother, then on to my parents. I felt that I had to bring Anne and Sunita back out to Australia. My folks had accepted a fantasy that I was in Australia earning money for the fare to bring them back out to Australia. I was regularly sending maintenance money to Anne.

RED BACKS

Shortly after joining The Agency, I bought a building block of land on the edge of a cliff above Narrabeen Lake, where I was having a house built. I had read about red back spiders, along with the funnel web spider. I was breaking up a huge rock, twice the size of a car, with steel wedges and a sledge hammer, and consequently was dressed in shorts, no shirt. Or as they say in England, naked, or dressed like a gypsy. For a breather I knocked off work to carry agricultural pipes, used to drain water away from the rear of the house. There was a pile of these 18-inch long by 4-inch piled behind the house. With digital dexterity I lifted the next load and placed them carefully on the fragile pile. My hands were covered in red backs. I flicked them off, looking down at my solar plexus. It was covered in squashed red backs. I died instantly.

I was having a Swiss-style chalet built for me on the cliffs above Narrabeen Lake. It was furnished by furniture I had made myself, along with the kitchen cupboards and spiral staircase.

I was playing folk music at the Shack in Narrabeen regularly. There was also the concertina that had just been restored, and field archery along the Wakehurst Parkway.

Looking back I think I was doing all that stuff to take my mind off what a nightmare my marriage seemed to have been.

BILL MAC

I rented a house in Taiyul Road in North Narrabeen. It was suitable for the entire family, and we moved in and began to attempt to live as a family.

I had swapped my 12-string guitar for an MG TF that had no engine. It had been modified to take a Holden engine. My next-door neighbour introduced himself when he saw me working on the car. He was Bill Mackintosh. He turned out to be a whiz at motor cars. Bill was about 20 years my senior, and we became great friends. Bill lived and breathed cars and would work for hour after hour charging nothing for his time, but insisting on me paying for the smallest O-ring if he had to buy it himself. He even produced receipts. He was generous to a fault, as long as he did not have to dip into his own pocket. Well, he was Scotsman after all!

Anne got on famously with Peggy, Bill's wife. I was very anxious to make this new attempt at living with Anne work. I was really involved in my new interest in the land that I had just bought, and I was now doing the ultimate that was expected of any husband; building a house! What with Anne's new ways and her promise that if Sunita had a brother our family would be complete, it was the recipe for a perfect family. I had even acquired a couple of Labrador dogs. I wanted to believe this new dream we shared. So, I accepted the role of the perfect husband, and we proceeded to produce child number two.

I had cleared the five acres. This included using a forest devil to remove some twenty large trees on the block to provide space for a building site. A forest devil is a block and tackle operated by a lever on a ratchet. The steel cable from it was three-quarters of an inch thick. One end of the cable went to the base of any strong tree. The other end was attached about eight feet up the trunk of the tree to be removed. The forest devil pulled the tree down, roots and all. In the pool of water below the roots of one that I had removed there was an animal the size and appearance of a small crayfish. This, I was to learn, was a yabbie. It had apparently made its way from Narrabeen Lake half a mile away, and up a cliff 100 feet high.

I had made a cardboard model of the house that I wanted to have built. This I gave to a draughtsman, who used it to draw up proper building plans. I then found a local builder to build it for me.

Bill was the postmaster at North Narrabeen post office. He and his father had been held up at gunpoint and tied up. His dad had hand-built his own car and installed the first electric light in his country village. Bill had been a radio operator during the war, and had flown a Sunderland. He helped me complete many projects, and was always there to encourage me. He had a farm out at Hoxton Park at Parramatta. Parramatta amused me, as their budget was larger than that for the whole Parliament of Tasmania, yet the Parramatta Council worked for free. I went there often, and Bill taught me that the skills required for any trade were always at an average human level. Consequently, everyone is capable of transferring similar skills from one trade to another.

Bill taught me to lay bricks as well as Churchill. How to wire a house. How to cope with drainage. How to use plumbing, and to use all farm tools. He tried to teach me how to fly. I went up several times. I think maybe I could do that now, but not then.

Bill's two daughters' as usual, wanted horses. It is the responsibility of all fathers to fall victim to this twist. You buy them a horse after their pleading, and then they're terrified of the bloody thing. You then feel cornered to climbing on it to show that there's nothing to be frightened of, although you yourself only spent two lessons on a horse 30 years ago. Bill fell victim to one of his daughter's horses which had gotten caught up in a wire fence, and during the untangling the horse bit Bill's arm and broke it in eight places. When it healed, his arm was four inches shorter.

Bill always knew exactly at what time his wayward daughters would come home at night, and yet he slept soundly. In the centre of his living room there was a seven-day barometer that recorded the week's weather. It also recorded each vibration on the floor, easily read from the smooth line drawn through the hours of the night, so he knew exactly at what time the girls came home. Although I moved to Tasmania, we kept in contact regularly through the mail. Perhaps I was the son Bill had never had.

One item he had that I thought I might have inherited was a brand-new 1900 Holden, garaged at the bottom of his drive. He took it for a run every weekend, once around the block, to keep the oil around the engine.

His passion was the Mini, and his back garden was cram-packed with spare panels and engines. At the post office he would search for Minis for sale. He would travel with his trailer and bring them home, but before he set off he would have sold every panel and engine to clients, searching for what he was about to own. His challenge in life was to out-smart the time motor mechanics allowed for repairing breakdowns in the repair manuals.

Bills wife was Peggy. She was my first encounter with a really, true alternate. This was long before the hippy, trippy dipstick. She knew everything that was alternate, if I met her today I wouldn't give her house room and then I would miss out on the honest side of weirdo.

She knew all about companion planting, animal husbandry, astral ploughing and Medieval herbal torture, she was a walking encyclopedia of terrestrial sub culture and boy! How she could sing!

But like a lot of really good singers she gave it no importance what so ever, her harmonies were wonderful.

She dressed like a scarecrow.

When the time came to split New South Wales for Tasmania Peggy asked if she could travel with me as far south as Canberra in my Landrover to attend an official engagement at Government House.

I dropped her off at her hotel and collected her that evening. Boy did she scrub up well, it was the first time I had ever seen her out of jeans. We were off to Government House where she was one of several guest of honour of the Governor General who was a good friend of Peggy's. They were both air craft pilots and had learnt to fly together, or so she said. It was a grand moment when I drove up to Government House in the Landrover, hopped out and ran around to open the door for Peggy to alight.

I drove off to the entrance gates and parked on the nature strip to await 12 o'clock when I was to return to collect Peggy. I was contently strumming my guitar in the rear of the Landrover when there was a knocking on the side of it.

"Oh. oh, the cops!" I thought " I'm trespassing"

I was waiting for the " Move along you can't park here!"

I climbed into the front of the Landrover and looked out of the window. White gloves, black bow tie and tails! It was the admirable Crichton, a butler, bearing a silver tray, upon which was spread a complete selection of the goodies that were being partaken of up at the manor.

"With the compliments of the Governor and will sir kindly return the tray and utensils to the house? Bon Appetit!"

In the meantime Bill who was at their farm, was caught up in a roll of barbed wire fencing, he had been trying to free his daughters horse that had become entangled in it. The horse attacked him and broke his arm in eight separate places, impossibly his daughter knocked the horse out with her fist.

When Bill came to visit me two years later in Tasmania, his right arm was four inches shorter.

BAR TOP

My friend was delighted with the results of that bar top I had made for him. During one visit to my new home he saw the kitchen cupboards I had made myself, also the spiral staircase. Everything in the house was new. Most of the internal woodwork I had done myself. He asked if he could use my house for the location of a new cigarette TV commercial that involved a party scene with lots of extras. In instances like these, extras were usually made up from members of the staff and their families; all the wives were at that party.

Now everyone knew that I was handy, and I was continually being invited to dinner and always ended up fixing something or other from fridges, washing machines and lawn mowers. I discovered that an awful lot of service agents don't really fix things. They just get them going again, consequently to break down almost immediately.

The wives were usually involved in some craft or other. Again I got totally involved in their problems, cutting glass, how to centre a pot, silver soldering, the use of tempera. I now knew that there was almost nothing that I could not do with my hands. I also knew that everyone was probably the same, but it was just that they weren't interested in how things work. The only things that I really failed at were things that I never saw value in, like spelling and grammar (was it Mark Twain who said he had no interest in anyone who could not spell a word at least six different ways before breakfast?). Annes friends, who were involved in every new wave venture sought my company, if only to help with their latest problem, mostly to do with sewing or silk screening. It was amongst all these demands for my talents that I lost sight of who I really was; who was George? There never seemed to be any room for me. Psychologically I was confused with all this crap going on in my head. Somewhere in there was "I." The ego was big enough, but the identity was confused. My income was huge, I owned two cars, two motor bikes, two dogs, I was Irish, the flavour of the month. I could do everything. My marriage was in a mess, sex had been confusing, my wife needed me only for an income! What next?

MY MUM

My mum wanted to come and visit us in our new home. I was now earning stacks. I was 29 years old and earning $30,000 a year, which was an enormous income in those days. So I paid for a return trip for her to Australia.

Mum staying with us exposed Anne and our relationship for what it was. Mum never spoke. She had no opinion of her own about anything. Every opinion was my father's. The happy little woman whom I remember from South Africa was emotionally destroyed, and had long given up thinking for herself. She was but a poor reflection of the little dictator who was my father, and yes, I was concerned about their opinion of me.

Our son Fintan was now about one year old, and Sunita was four. Anne and I had not had sex for over a year. I had not even cracked a fat. I was just not interested in sex.

AMAROO (Aboriginal for a beautiful place.)

I sold that house to a couple that I let move in before the finances were settled. After their deposit cheque bounced and their rent cheque also bounced, I had to have them evicted. The police were present while they watched the tennant throw my keys over the cliff, and the police were there when I took possession. They grinned at me when I looked at the kitchen, which had been burnt out, and the entire house blackened from the smoke. It cost thousands to replace the kitchen, paint and remove the odour of smoke. The police? Well, they just hated anyone with a beard in those days.

This was about the time when I realised there was a pattern evolving in my wife's demeanour. She settled down for six months or so, and I was thinking to myself that maybe I was beginning to get this marriage thing right, when Nimbin loomed on the horizon.

Nimbin was the Nirvana of the New Age and a wonderful, terrible beauty. Drugs, sex and freedom.

YOUNG MAN FROM KIANDRA
Traditional Irish folk song from the town of Kiandra.
Learnt from my mother at her breast, 1941

I am a young man from the town of Kiandra
I married a young girl to welcome me home
But she goes out and she leaves me and truly deceives me
and leaves me with a babie that's none of me own

CHORUS:
Oh the day, rue the day ever I married
How I wish I was single again
for its weeping and wailing and rocking the cradle
And nursing a babie that's none of me own

Well every night she's out on the rantan
On the rantan with some other young man
She goes out and she leaves me and truly deceives me
And leaves me with a babie that's none of me own

Every night it's a ball or a party
Leaving me here with a babie alone
And the poor little laddie, he thinks I'm his daddy
But ne'er will he know that he's none of me own

Now all you young men thats a fancy to marry
Be sure you leave those flash gals alone
By the lords sake tarry, if one you should marry
She 'll leave you with a babie that's none of your own

HORROR

About this time another horror appeared. I started bleeding from the arse; not occasionally, but continually, for about seven days, then it stopped. My relief was immense. About a month later it started again, once more for about seven days, and about a month later it recurred. This had been going on for a while, and I noticed the pattern that had started to emerge. Well, of course it was obvious. What with me not being interested in sex and the periodic bleed it was obvious; I was menstruating! Shit! Panic! Anxiety! Paranoia! The end! Full stop! I was too frightened to talk about it to anyone who would understand.

Eventually I consulted a doctor. The bleeding was nothing more than internal hemorrhoids. And as for the floppy dick, the doctor could do nothing about it, but he did suggest that I see a psychiatrist.

It was about one week before Christmas, and I was at a Christmas party held by one of the outside studios who did my assembly work. A girl whom I had been chatting with invited me to a party to which she had been invited. I had brushed aside the invitation with polite interest, as I had always done. This may seem of little relevance, but it happened that around that I was recovering from the hemorrhoid operation, and I was considering what to do about the psychiatrist. I took the bull by the horns and made an appointment. I spent about three sessions with the psychiatrist. His advice to me was to the effect that my problem was a classic case of mental castration. We discussed the many incidents where I had failed to live up to the expectations that I thought that my father would have had for me. As a punishment, I had denied myself sex, and was punishing myself with abstinence.

I suppose a lot of monks may do this, but I did believe the psychiatrist. I thought, "I'll just see what will happen when I give in to the seductive charms of some lady."

I phoned up the lady who had invited me to the party. Even Billy and George agreed that I should go out with her (I had asked their advice). Well, I did go to the party, and I did go out with her with again and again. I was never the sort to have a casual fling, and I started to get involved deeper and deeper with her.

One Saturday morning after a huge row, my mum had returned to Ireland. For the first time in my life I stormed out of the house and went to meet my lady at the Sydney film festival. Anne followed me, and found us in my Land Rover. Our marriage was over.

I moved into a flat in Northbridge. My lady designed and made jewellery. I used to watch her struggling with copper wire, beads and soft solder making wonderful designs that would fall apart. It took me back to my student days when I was doing lettering with the teacher who also taught jewellery and silversmithing. I knew that there were a lot better ways of doing what she was doing. It wasn't long before I had all the gear necessary to do most silver fabrication, except she always worked in copper, but now because of the silver soldering, her jewellery didn't fall to pieces. I myself started to produce a range of black oxidized copper jewellery that I sold under the label Druid. These I sold at Aladdin Gallery in Kings Cross.

BERSERK

What I learnt from her blew the lid off my chauvinistic, naive, arrogant world and made me an outcast among my cronies. My sexual technique I had learnt from the Irish sex manual; in and out, and repeat if necessary. I had been using this technique with as many variations as possible (none). From my perspective, my partners seemed reasonably satisfied. So I thought that my lady friend, like all the rest, was reasonably satisfied with my performance. This had been going on for some time until one night, while bonking on her mother's bedroom floor whilst her mother was out of the house, she went berserk. All her Christmases seemed to have come at once. She told me later that her head was spinning. She was totally out of control. She was the first asthma sufferer that I had ever met, and I thought at first that perhaps this might be a severe asthma attack; but at no stage did her enthusiasm cease. I was totally confused. Then she started to quiet down. She must have assumed that I knew exactly what had happened, for she politely thanked me for the occasion. What the hell had happened? I was supposed to know exactly what had happened, but I didn't have a clue. "You're welcome," I replied, as if it was a daily occurrence.

Apparently this had only happened to her once before, about two years before meeting me, and she had tried everything to experience the same feeling. Now that she had repeated it, she thought that it was my doing. When you feel a complete idiot, it's better to shut up and say nothing. This way you won't say something stupid and prove to all that you are an idiot. So I shut up and let her chatter on. Of course it transpired that what had happened was the big "O." and went on to tell me about her friends who enjoyed regular orgasms. She said that she thought most of them were lying. She was talking as if all this was old hat to me; after all, I was an old married man. This was her first involvement with a married man, and married men know it all! All the guys that she had known were so selfish and could not be bothered with the woman's needs. She also told me how most men don't know what a woman's needs are. I let her rave on while I thought about how I would cope with all these revelations. We parted company when I discovered she had an obsessive personality. She phoned me about 30 times a day. As a result I am now conditioned like Pavlov's dogs, and go into a state of anxiety when the phone rings.

SNAP!

Some Irish friends had invited me to dinner one evening and after the meal, we were sitting and chatting about nothing in particular when a loud *snap* sounded from somewhere down the hall. "Quick!" shouted our host. "It's my rat trap!"

The girls ran into the kitchen while we followed our host into the bedroom. In the corner lay a rat trap. Next to it lay a huge rat. It was still moving. Our host flung a large book across the rat hole just as the rat became fully conscious. I slammed the bedroom door shut. The rat proceeded to scamper around the room. Running up the tall boy, under the bed, onto the bed and over the mirror. Eventually the host threw a blanket over it and the other trapped it under his foot. "What will I do now?" he asked.

"Squash it!"

"No fucking way!!"

With that I stepped forward and put my foot on top of his and leaned on it with all my weight. I felt nothing, but he felt every bone of the rat being broken and squashed; he fainted!

He was a rather gentle man. From the moment he arrived in Australia his mother, a religious zealot, sent him Bible tracts every week. When she died we heard that, on the day that she was buried back in England, the father took the television set out to the back shed and removed the TV from the cabinet. He then attached two doors that he had bought from the do-it-yourself store and voila! A drinks cabinet! He was reported to have stayed pissed, singing lewd songs for three days.

Back to the rat, and yer man who fainted. He was back on his feet, or rather he was sitting in a chair, and we were discussing both the "Machismo" of the average male and the prowess of the male lover. The host observed that it was all right for a woman to be deprived of the sexual services of her male partner, but a man just had to have sex at any cost. Should a man be away from his wife on business for an extended time, he would seek out a woman or masturbate, whereas a woman's sex urge was a "take it or leave it" attitude. They do it to please the male. It is a woman's duty, conjugal rights, etc. I was familiar with this tedious old tale. Yer man nodded his agreement and the girls, as usual, agreed with a less than enthusiastic, "Umm..!"

This was my opportunity. I was amongst friends, so I stuck my feet straight in. "I reckon you lads are both wrong, have you ever asked the girls about this without intimidating them into agreeing with the answer that you want to hear?"

I occasionally feel guilty for what happened next. Pandora's box was opened.

Apparently there were times in these girls' sex lives with their partners when they had become immensely frustrated. The women had often tried to gently guide their partners without harming their fragile male egos. Worse, of course, was in store. The women told of how they masturbated to get satisfaction, as there was no other way. The formula of "In and out. Repeat as necessary" had nothing to do with satisfactory sex as far as the woman is concerned. All this was a total revelation to these men. They even suggested that this was only part of the psyche of Australian women. They were appalled to think that women should masturbate. Worse was the clear intimation that masturbation was more satisfying than "the old in and out" with their partners; it was intolerable. Over the next couple of months the men's relationships with their wives started to crumble.

I think that it's clear that the wives' sexual problems were caused by the puritanical British/Irish attitude. Certainly I have read that the Irishman's attitude to sex is probably the most naive in the civilised world. This attitude seems to have been taken to Australia when the Irish and English immigrants flooded into the colonies. For over 100 years Ireland's greatest export was its people. These people brought with them their religious bigotry, their racism and their chauvinistic attitudes toward sex.

Now my mates in my workplaces in the advertising industry were mostly Australians, or as Australian as you can get without being an actual aborigine. The entire staff of art directors, senior designers, assembly artists, freelance guys and finish artists, people of distinctly eccentric natures, these folk were the creative heart of the agency. There were usually also about half a dozen others who could be relied upon to take frequent extended lunch breaks. The art directors and writers would also take three or four secretaries and a couple of art buyers to eat and drink at the 729 Club. If all the art directors went, then the creative side of the agency may as well shut down for the remainder of the day. And this often happened. The secretaries and the art buyers usually stayed with us to look after us and made sure that we did eventually return to work some time that afternoon.

During one of our mammoth lunches, in the heat of one of our numerous conversations I threw in my ideas on the needs of women, and how most of the guys had been ignoring these needs. By this time I was not on such shaky ground. I had been reading and reading and reading! I had read every relevant book in the Dee Why Library, the Manly Library and the Mitchell Library on the subject of sex. Well, at least I read all the books that had nice, easy words!

I sort of knew where things were, who was supposed to do what with what and to whom. I also knew about all the various combinations. It was like music. You can do an awful lot with eight notes! I was aware of every sort of deviant sexual practices, and then some. But I was still unable to cope with where I fitted in to all this. These men were so confident. They knew it all, and had satisfied so many women. They were legends in their own lunchtime! At my suggestion, the discussion was thrown open to the ladies. The men took it for granted that the ladies would support them, and support them the ladies did.

This went on all afternoon, and what an idiot I turned out to be! But by the next morning, the two art-buying ladies and the three secretaries came to my studio individually. Without exception, they all apologised for not supporting me at the 729 Club. Not only did they apologise, but admitted that what I had said was all true! Interestingly, some of the men would sneak into my office to discuss their sexual problems. But if anyone was in earshot when they entered my office, they spoke in very loud voices so that everyone around would hear that they were not discussing sex. Eventually I was completely ostracised.

Some of the guys came close to panic if one of the female writers or secretaries entered my studio. They probably thought that they were being talked about. The closest any of the men came to understanding the needs of a woman came from a comment one of them made about how his wife seemed to want to lie around a lot longer than he did after he had ejaculated. Perhaps, after all, she did have an orgasm, and was totally exhausted? I knew this was not the case, as his wife had told me that she considered sex to be dirty and boring!

All this of course was 25 or 30 years ago. Probably everything has changed now. Certainly I ceased to argue the case back then. Magazines such as *Cosmopolitan* and *Cleo* spell it all out for anyone to read. I wonder, however, how many men read women's magazines? Perhaps it doesn't matter. Even some of the men's magazines which once confined themselves to pictures of naked ladies and articles about macho things like cars, war and hunting now include the occasional article on pleasing one's partner. I really don't know for sure, as I only look at those sort of magazines to look at the women's tits! For the moment my temporary final position on this issue is based on a comment made by a lady friend. "George! Most men still think Clitoris is a town in Greece!!"

SAFETY GLASSES

"FUCK THE RAILWAYS!" Mike would declare at the oddest of moments. He was a welder when he worked on the railways. At the end of a particular run of arc welding he neglected to wear his safety glassed to remove the slag from this run. His slag hammer chipped off a piece of red-hot slag into his eye and destroyed it.

By the time he recovered and realised his situation, he was exactly one day too late to make an insurance claim.

I met Mike at our folk club, the Shack, in Narrabeen. He was singing and swearing into the microphone, at the same time playing the classical guitar; a very expensive one, badly! Later he would sing his favourite folk song "Ramble away."

Mike had an engineering workshop on the industrial estate at Warriewood near Narrabeen, where he made dog exercising machines. Regularly through the week I would visit Mike when I was having a slack day at work. I would help him often, and for my troubles he taught me to weld. That is where I built my trailer to take to Tasmania.

Mike was a complex guy, one of those people who should never take drugs or alcohol, and should avoid at all times deep and meaningful questions. No one could handle Mike. He was confusing, manic and brilliant. I, myself, never had a problem with him, and he lived with me in Hamilton, Tasmania for over eighteen months. The rules then were simple; we will discuss as many questions as you want to about "How," but never will I discuss with you the "Why." Why do men of science, when asked the question why, answer the question with how?

Mike learnt from somewhere that the laws governing the land between high tide and low tide were ambiguous, so he harassed the Warringah Council on this issue to the point where they gave up and actually left him alone. I personally think they were letting sleeping dogs lie, especially as Mike discovered that an exceptionally high tide had eroded the sand banks at Narrabeen Lake, and the tide entered the lake, flooding Narrabeen Flats as far as Warriewood way back in the 1930s. Are all those houses on disputed land?

In the early days, Mike was renowned along the northern beaches as the golden wonder boy of the surf. In later days he became known as the nutter who drove and lived in the lorry with a cottage, complete with veranda, on the back tray.

After weekends, Mike would salvage sunken sailing pleasure yachts from the bottom of Narrabeen Lake that the yachties had sunk. He would offer them back to the owner at a suitable price, or sell them on.

As my daily companion in those days, Mike was a gentle soul. Somehow, however, he got lost along the way.

Mike had invented the snowboard years before its time. I went with him myself to the Kosciuszko snowfields to modify it several times.

THE SHACK

Mike James, Ann Hisinck, Rhonda Moore, Graham Lyons, Bernard Bolan, Greg Quill, Danny Spooner, Phil Levy and many, many more were folk musos who had all performed at The Shack in Narrabeen, along the north shore of Sydney. It was the home of folk music, in its heyday, and it opened once a week. In those days everyone knew just what folk music was. Today, no one knows. Those were the early days, and The Shack played a huge part in presenting folk music to Australia. It was a huge beginning in influencing all the folk festivals to come, including the National at Canberra.

I was part of a group called And Others, named because of the list of acts of a particular night always ended with "and others." Occasionally we headed the billing, which commenced on the poster with And Others, blah, blah, blah, "and others." We had done a gig out near Parramatta. Rod and Phil went on to a weekend shack up the Hawkesbury River. Rod went out, maybe for a pee, in the middle of the night, and fell off the cliff's edge into the water and drowned. That was unknown until we had searched in the bush all day for him. Shock went through the folk community, and The Shack was never the same for years.

Phil, the other member of And Others, saved my sanity by taking off to Nimbin with my wife.

NARRABEEN BEACH

I was now living in a very large, modern house in Narrabeen on the beach. When I came home from work early, the house would be full of flower-power hippies, producing leatherwork, sewing dresses, silk-screening material, and making plastic tubular furniture. Ideally this would have been very industrious and wonderfully productive. In reality they were all stoned, the place was a mess and their workmanship was crap. This was all to be sold off at Paddy's Market in Sydney, where they operated completely at a loss, and I was paying for it all.

It was here that Peter Stone and his entire family – three boys and one girl – invited themselves to my house at Narrabeen for Christmas dinner. They arrived in the company of two priests. The three of them had concocted a book called *Traveling to Freedom*.

The surf and being drunk brought out everyones true personalities. Those two priests just couldn't keep their hands off each other…say no more.

Chapter Six

Tasmania

Where I learn how to give up 30,000 dollars (180,000 todays coin), become a TV star, turn down job offers, repel wankers, search for truth and become a real artist, visit James Craig, the lure of the folk singer, about Sweden and more bloody boxing!

SOLICITOR

At last things were starting to make sense. I had been in advertising all my working life and was used to the high-flying, extremely fast-paced lifestyle. The wife had taken off with our children to live the real working life in Nimbin, the Gondwana land of the new age. Now a year later and I'm still earning a huge salary and spending it all on maintenance to a family living in a cowshed in a commune.

I felt that I needed legal advice as to where I stood with regards to guardianship of my children, so I consulted a solicitor. There were several avenues open, He jokingly commented that the only option open was to live below the poverty level, then I couldn't be garnished for maintenance.

At this time I was earning thirty thousand a year and owned my own house outright. I was paying rent on three flats; one in Manly, one in Northbridge and one in Narrabeen. The one in Manly had three garbage bags of mail behind the front door. I burnt the lot without opening one letter. I had three cars; the Land Rover, the Fiat, and a Morris Minor convertible, fully restored. When the solicitor's advice was to sell the lot and live below the poverty level, I took him seriously, considered it, but before I could reply he said, "I'm only joking!"

But it was too late, I had already decided. There was no joy without my children. The only solution was to come from them. Perhaps I should create an environment that would appeal to them.

"You can't be forced to pay maintenance if you are living below the poverty level," was ringing in my brain. I would pack up and move to Tasmania NOW!

I bit the bullet and packed in the cushy job, explaining to, the director, that I was leaving to become a farmer in Tasmania. The boss was totally sympathetic, as he himself had just bought a farm and was what everyone called a hobby farmer.

With the trailer Mike and I had made hitched up to the Land Rover (always down to earth; the workmates in the agency owned Porches, Alpha Romeos and Lotuses!) loaded up, I headed for Tassie.

The advertising agency had sent me down to Tasmania two years before. I fell in love with the soft, green, rolling, pastoral hills, the entire countryside was on a scale I could relate to.

That was when I had bought my second bit of land, five acres of Tasmanian bush. This was purchased in *my* name, and it had been paid for with cash. Plans had been drawn up for a house, submitted to the council, and approved.

The house at Amaroo had been built by professional builders. I had personally inspected the progress at each stage and came to the amazing conclusion that none of the workmanship demanded any more than what was expected of me by my father when working alongside him, building his caravans in Ireland!

Several letters to and from the Kingston Council in Hobart refused me permission to live in a temporary dwelling while I was building my house. A tent, caravan, a garage, a shed; they refused them all. And here I was looking at my five-acre block surrounded by adjoining five-acre blocks, one with a shed, one with a caravan, another with a bus, another with several tents. I went directly to the council and enquired as to why I had been refused permission. Was it because I was Irish?

"No! Mr. Callaghan, you requested official permission, and officially we had to reply no!"

Ah ha! Permission is harder to acquire than forgiveness.

I had made a friend at a caravan park in Narrabeen on Sydney's north shore. The friend now lived in Tasmania, close by in North West Bay in Howden. He was married with two children.

I must explain Julian. Other than Stef, he is my dearest, closest and most annoying friend, ever maddening each other. We met in a caravan park in New South Wales arguing over the ownership of a genuine original copy of Robbie Burns' book, *The Merry Muses*. There were only eighty-odd ever printed, with great disgusting verses. This was a poor abused one, completely worn and indented from continual thumbing through. It had no cover. A bloke called round to visit Julian. He had it, it had been left in his house by an antique dealer who had stolen it from someone who apparently had also stolen it. Julian reckoned he now owned it, as he now had it in his hand. "No you don't, I've got it now," I said, snatching it out of his hand. I owned it for quite some time until it was stolen from me. You can't trust anyone.

Julian moved to Tasmania to play bassoon in the Tasmanian unsympathetic orchestra. He had been to Gordonstoun School in England with his brother, and they attended the same school and were mates of Prince Charles. Julian knew how to fix, mend and destroy everything. He had been brilliantly schooled in everything except how to do it himself. Like everyone he played music with, knew everything about music except music itself. Regularly I would babysit for Julian and Inger. One evening when he came home from a concert, he complained how during the whole evening's performance his toe had driven him mad with the itch! He took off his boot to have a look and out hopped a frog!

HOWDEN COUNTRY HOUR

I was about to learn the most important lesson of my life – ego. While digging the foundations for my house, the radio was my constant companion. A programme of little importance was Country Hour. There was a story of a farmer who was growing strawberries. These strawberries were dipped in chocolate, and then injected with crème de menthe. He was selling them in America. The next week they were talking about someone who was growing aloe vera and how successful that was, and that there was a huge developing market for the plant. Two weeks later there was a debate on the commercial success of a farmer who had started growing kiwi fruit in Tasmania. Then they would be talking to a young lady who worked in the next bay from me in Howden. She was making a fine income from fishing a particular octopus that the Greek restaurants were buying from her.

Several weeks later, and they were interviewing the same farmer with his strawberries. Since his first interview, about dipping and injecting strawberries, everyone was now doing this, and they were all going broke. Likewise with the aloe vera. Kiwi fruit too; they were going broke. The poor girl in the bay next to me with the octopus--every Greek in town had come down that weekend and fished the bay out. If you're onto a good thing, **SHUT UP** about it!

The foundations of the house had been dug, concrete poured, brick work had been laid to floor level, supporting pillars erected and the floor joists were in place. All approved by the building inspector.

During these months I barely spoke to anyone, treating myself like a true Presbyterian, working like hell for existence and hourly asking questions of myself. I was constantly searching for truth and honesty. What were my beliefs? Had I inherited them all? Were they all my parents'? Was I processing all information according to those beliefs? If I saw an iceberg floating in the harbour was that science, or God? Were friends necessary? Was I an island? Was sex necessary? Who was I? Should I try to survive? I never longed for anyone's company. There were too many questions that filled the space of conversation.

SCREWED

The walls of the house were complete, and the iron had arrived for the roof. I needed a hand to lay this iron, as the sheets of iron were 24' long to accommodate the curved roof.

My friend Julian was to help. He arrived with a screwdriver that he swore by, one of those you pulled out revealing a very long spiral. With a downwards push it was supposed to twist the screw into the wood. That was the idea, in principal…in practice, Julian not only pushed the driver bit through the iron, the entire screwdriver followed suit, making a gaping hole. After six such holes, I told him to fuck off!!

AUSTRALIAN BROADCASTING CORPORATION

At Howden I continually kept an eye on the weather, as I needed the water not only for building and daily cooking, but also for my batiks. In the summertime the thunder clouds rolled out of the southwest, but usually exhausted themselves in the Huon Valley; by the time they reached Howden, they were spent. The local radio station was continually referring to the damage done to the apple orchards by the heavy rain and hail. One of my favourite Australian ballads is "Waiting for the Rain." I decided to adapt this to the farmer's plight in the Huon. I was pretty happy with the result, and decided to bite the bullet and wandered off the streets of Hobart into the ABC television studios and asked to see someone from their current affairs programme. I sat on the corner of his desk and strummed my guitar and started singing my song. At first I thought that they hated it, as they stopped me after the first verse. They took me straight down to makeup and recorded me for the programme going to air that weekend. I went to Julian's house to watch the programme on TV. They had done a wondrous job! They had married my song with some superb clips of hail damage to the apple orchards in the Huon.

Over the years I have done some marvellous programmes with the ABC. There were six 5-minute sections on sea shanties. They were filmed on board a cargo vessel. There was a problem with filming. A Goanese steward from the ship who had ambitions of becoming a star took full advantage of the TV crew's presence, and he kept popping up in front of the camera. He at last disappeared, only to reappear with a guitar, which he strummed continually while he stood behind me! The cameramen solved the problem by introducing a second camera, cutting and recording from me to the other camera, and confused the poor bugger completely.

PORT ARTHUR

I was on my way to Port Arthur in Southern Tasmania when it occurred to me that I was so anti- drugs that my opinion was not quite valid, as I had no terms of reference that were my own. I decided that at the next opportunity to experience the stuff, I would give it a try. I was a heavy smoker, already addicted to one drug, so when the next opportunity presented itself, I would give marijuana a go.

Twice I was presented with the opportunity on the way to Port Arthur; nothing! I was now at my destination and had completed several drawings, when a rather lovely guy came over to me and admired my drawings. He rolled a joint and asked if I indulged. "Of course!" I said nonchalantly. Then after several puffs, my mind started doing things that I didn't like. I told him that I had lied, this was my first experience. He stayed with me for three hours, trying to help me enjoy the buzz, but I wasn't having any joy. Three hours later I was trying to draw, but the slight warp in the paper was too confusing. I appeared to be drawing on a flexible tablecloth. I fell asleep in the mud.

ALCOHOLIC ADVICE

Food was the main problem while working on the house at Howden. Before leaving Sydney, I had met an alcoholic photographer who had given me a recipe for a simple subsistence diet:

3 tablespoons dried milk powder
1 teaspoon dried yeast
2 raw eggs
All beaten into a glass of milk.

This was consumed for breakfast. Through the day I soaked dried peas and soup mix (barley and various pulses) and added two stock cubes and simmered for two hours. This soup was my staple diet. Dessert was half a packet of dried apricots, and the other half-packet was munched in the evenings while reading Alistair MacLean novels, the evening's quota of rubbish!

Water was always a problem, but this was solved after I bought a caravan. It was of the ancient type, made at the time when things were overbuilt and made to last. In true ocker fashion, a lean-to roof of corrugated iron was added, and a length of guttering to collect rain water. It was frustrating to see the clouds roll out of the Huon Valley across the bay day after day and rain themselves out before they reached the Northwest Bay.

ANOTHER FALL OF RAIN

Written by John Neilson of Penola, a bush worker, farmer, and balladist, and the father of Australia's greatest lyricist, John Shaw Neilson.

The weather has been sultry for a fortnight now or more
And the shearers have been driving might and main
For some have got the century who ne'er got it before
But now we all are waiting for the rain

Chorus
For the boss is getting rusty and the ringer's caving in
His bandaged wrist is aching with the pain
And the second man I fear will make it hot for him
Unless we have another fall of rain

But the rains did arrive, and there was never a scarcity of water.

The house was built from the three months' earnings squirreled away in Sydney, after my savings from the sale of that house at Elenora disappeared north to Nimbin.

RON BANKS

As I approached the encampment there was something unusual; nothing obvious. Yes, that was it, there was a note pinned to the flap of the tent.

I had just returned from the building supplier's with a load of ship lap planks in my Land Rover.

Who could this be from? Not my friend Julian, I had just chatted to him hours ago at the bottom of his drive. Unfolding the note, it read:

"Could you please contact Ron Banks at the address below?"

What the hell would anyone want with me? Shit, it meant going all that way back into town. "I'll do it tomorrow," I said out loud, making friends with the crows.

Approaching the address written on the note the next day, I realized that Ron Banks was an advertising agency. Without going any further, I knew that there would be an offer of a job, but curiosity got the better of things and I proceeded. As I had expected, I was shown into Mr. Banks' office. He was the owner of the recently opened advertising agency. They were making a pitch for the government's road safety account.

"Thanks, Mr. Banks, but I'm done with advertising., I'm burnt out!"

"But you're only 30 or 35…"

With thanks and apologies, I left. After collecting another load of ship lap planks in the Land Rover I proceeded home, or to what I now called home. What? There was another message, this time written on a piece of floor board leaning against the tent. It read: "Mr. Kay of Jackson and Wain, Tasmania branch, would like to see you ASAP."

"You're going to work for Ron Banks, aren't you?" boomed Don Kay.

"No!"

Don Kay was the director of the Tasmanian branch, and there was no way that he was going to let this art director from the mainland work for their competitors!

"Look, I'm burnt out! I just wanna paint and build my house."

"How about we put you under contract as a consultant. We'll pay you a retainer. You'll probably never hear from us, anyway. That'll keep you away from that Ron Banks bugger!"

"And you'll PAY me to keep away from him? For how long?"

"Two years!"

Without explaining, I told him that, for personal reasons, I couldn't be seen earning any money.

"We'll pay you in cash! Collect it at the front office. We have no need to see you or contact you, just keep away from that Ron Banks!"

The other job that I rejected at this time was head of print department at the newly built University of Tasmania Art College. The position was offered by Udo Sellbach, the newly appointed head of the art college.

Also, I was offered the job as head of the Art Department at Rosny College. Both jobs I turned down, being as I was very aware that "those that can, do, and those that can't, teach."

PRICKS

I attended a few functions run by Art Institutions around the world. Here I met all the people in the "Real Art World." The first thing that amazed me at one of the functions was a poster for a design department at a college. The poster illustrated about eight recent designs of furniture produced by the students at the college that year, six of those designs had actually been created in *my* living room by my wifes hippy friends years before, I listened to some pontificating prick rave on about those innovative designs.

I do recall one art college lecturer saying to me, "You're one of those advertising guys, aren't you; you spend your time lying to the public?!" I asked him if he was a teacher at that art college. When he said yes, I replied that he belonged to a group of people who not only lied to each other and themselves, but actually believed their own lies.

At a another time a fellow artist, on being told that I was an Atheist, passed the comment that, "The trouble with you, George, is that your head is empty!"

I wasn't actually aware that there was any trouble with me at all. Anyway I replied, "Well, there's lots of room for new ideas, not like *your* head that is full of crap and no room for anything new!"

At these functions of the arts and craft societies I kept my cool; after all, I considered myself a well-balanced person. I have a chip on both shoulders! Also I had a life to get on with, and all was going well with my new lady friend. She even invited me home to meet her folks. She had mentioned that her sister and brother-in-law were artists, but I hadn't taken much notice. I was much too busy trying to get into her knickers! She took me home to meet her mum, sisters, brother, and brother-in-law. Where they the very teachers who had been pontificating about the innovative furniture designs at that Art college? War and love make strange bedfellows, and over the following year, in conversation with the arts community, I was assured of any arts grant funding that I applied for. I did apply for a grant to mount the first sterling silver exhibition in the state, but there were wheels to be greased and arses to be licked and forms (what are forms?) to be filled in. By the time a grant has been approved, the idea has long since died in the ass.

I didn't give up the lies of advertising to live with the corruption of this shit. I had to escape this influence. I had to remove myself from these spin doctors and become my own, born-again artist.

GANGSTERS

The following collection of incidents that I have experienced from around the world, illustrate why I deplore arts funding and the corruption of Institutionalised Art establishments

I had once worked indirectly for the Mafia. But I never realized that when I turned down the offer as head of the print department, at a certain art institution, that I narrowly escaped working for the most corrupt society I have ever encountered.

A group of weekend artists used to meet at an older lady's house. They were a harmless group with a common interest; landscape painting. When the owner died, that art institution moved in and gained control of this situation, eventually taking possession of the house, which they then sold. With the money they bought a flat in Paris, which was used exclusively by their staff. The city Art Prize was taken over by the institution and administered by them, assuring that only their staff past and present received their prizes. I personally entered that competition and was late with my entry. Their main hall was laid out as a viewing gallery. I went into the room with my exhibit; the only vacant space was behind the door where I now stood. At that precise moment in walked a member of the staff, ushering God into the room. They walked straight up to a specific painting. God declared, "I can't give it to that! Have they anything else?"

"Yes, there's another hanging in the office; shall I fetch it?" She left and shortly returned.

"Ahhh! That's better!" and the complete entourage left without looking at any other pictures; also without noticing me behind the door.

I never entered another competition after that!

This art institution gave approval to all arts and crafts grants, even to each other. They used the obvious system of approval. All of them had applications before their own board, and they each took turns leaving the room whilst approving that person's applications.

One year, the tutor who was to mark the passing out examinations, became ill. An examiner from the mainland was called in to assess their trainees. Without exception, he rejected the lot!

The grumbling of the trainees was eventually appeased by waiting on the recovery of their tutor, who re-assessed and passed the entire class.

Two of my associates, who were staff members, had to disrupt their summer vacation to return to the institution to assess the new applications. There was a dilemma, as they needed an intake of thirty trainees, and they had only fifteen applicants. I enquired as to why then were they interviewing them.

"They could be socially unacceptable. Last year we had to reject two on these considerations."

Laughable to think that the main quality for election to such a society the staff rejected!

I knew one of those socially unacceptable applicants and yes, he was social unacceptable. He was the son of a friend, and potentially a creative whizz kid. Artists are supposed to be socially unacceptable; that's their job!

Art College lecturers have become a law unto themselves. They are aware of any projects on the horizon, and snap them up before they are presented to the greater public.

THE COWARD

Poor Mr. Johnny Howard, one of our ex-prime ministers, has the unfortunate name that rhymes with coward. It could be claimed that he was many things, but certainly not a coward. When he arrived at the new parliament to take up office, he was confronted with an office full of furniture that was totally unsuited to his persona. He couldn't stand the sight of the stuff, and demanded that it be removed. There was an outcry from the Art College of Tasmania, deploring Mr Howard's attitude. I wrote to the papers defending Mr. Howard's rights to work in an environment where he could perform at his optimum.

The local radio station asked if I could defend my opinion live on air. Of course there was someone to argue the point against Mr. Howard. After a lot of to and fro-ing, I finally declared that the designer who was head of the design department at the college of art who had produced the entire furniture installation had made a huge elementary blunder. He had designed and manufactured the items for THE MAN, not the OFFICE!

At the time of the furniture's creation, the encumbered officer had a totally different persona, an aesthete who most certainly would have loved this contemporary plastic furniture, which was already out of fashion and out of date. The designs should have been timeless, ageless and adaptable to any changing minister.

To those who would have seen *Yes Minister*, the only amendment that the incoming minister is allowed is the choice of his own personal chair. I have seen many, many dead, useless designs produced. There is an island, off an island, off an island that is the resting place for all that crap.

REAL ART

Before leaving Sydney, I had been exploring batik. The principal was similar to lithography, which I'd majored in at art college. Both worked on the same principle; water and wax don't mix. Lithography is printed on paper, while batik is printed or painted on fabric. I was using this process to produce a single image, not for repetitive printing.

In Tasmania there were only two art galleries, and one of those was an Italian restaurant that hung and sold paintings. It was said that you got a free splash of spaghetti on every painting that you bought.

Saddler's Court was the only real art gallery. It was run by Alice Krongard, literally an aging matron; she had been a midwife nurse. Although she was quite happy to show and sell my work, she wasn't overjoyed until she came to the section in the folder that contained the batik. Sure, she had just been to town that morning and bought a book on batik. Could she have an exhibition of these pieces as soon as possible, and more, could she have, at a later date, an exhibition of sterling silver jewellery? I had brought along with me some of the jewellery that I'd been toying with in my spare time.

Everything seemed to be coming together at once. The house was almost complete, the exhibition of batik was working out fine. The lack of copious amounts of water had proved to be a problem with the batik, but my friends Julian and Inger allowed me to use their laundry to boil out the wax from the dyed images.

I was sorting out the problem in my head of what had gone wrong with my marriage, who had gone wrong, and how to avoid repeating the same faults in the future. I had rejected religion many, many years ago, even before I had left Ireland at 21. Life's not a rehearsal. The time spent working on the house was a sort of soul-searching period. There were some really important questions that needed answering. If I spent all day really working hard, sweating my guts out, at the end of the day was I was really dirty? Did I really need to wash? I hadn't once come into contact with any real dirt; what is dirt? I hadn't shaken hands with anyone or had any physical contact with anyone--*that's* how you got really dirty! Fuck! I'd hit my thumb with a hammer, but what is the point hopping around like an idiot? There is no one to see. Why scream? No one will hear!

I had been making regular visits to Saddler's Court Gallery in Richmond, and realized that I enjoyed this village relationship. It had a sense of purpose. Like any real township that was never purpose-built, it just happened. Houses had grown up around the necessities of the community and had been added to, in what might have been thought of as willy-nilly. Things seemed to grow together; the village had a heart.

Not like the sterile thing I had built in Sydney, and now another sterile building on a beautiful hill at Howden. Major decisions were never a problem. Sell up and leave.

CAMBRIDGE HOUSE

Peter Stone reappeared on the Sydney beach of Manly wearing the exact same bathing costume as mine, that we had bought from the same shop in O'Connell Street, Dublin. He reappeared again as the kitsch designer of that copper rose fountain at Roselands Shopping Centre in Sydney. Then he moved into the flat below me in Manly. At last I got away from him when I moved to Tasmania; well, for a while. I came home one day to my caravan at Howden, to find written in lipstick all over it "the Stones have arrived," which was weird, as I didn't think Christina, his wife, wore any makeup. They had bought the most fantastic house in Geeveston, the original Cambridge house, huge, and now a historically preserved wooden house. We found the original bill; it had cost £49 for the material when it was first built.

I was really enjoying folk singing then, and was making a visit to the Stones' almost every two weeks. Peter was a fantastic flautist and a superb jazz pianist; his wife played superb cello. We would spend the evening recording various arrangements for the most recent folk song I was having a love affair with. If I wasn't happy with the arrangement, Peter would produce another in minutes. Now this was totally flabbergasting and amazing, as Peter was completely tone deaf. When I appeared on a Saturday morning with a new song, it would take Peter a whole day to work out the simple melody and write it down. He just couldn't discern the note I was playing. After that, arranging for him was child's play; it's all mathematics.

JAMES CRAIG

On one of my trips to Geeveston, I went a little further down to Recherche Bay. I had my yellow canoe that I had made with me, on the roof of the Land Rover. On the distant shore was a strange structure.

I paddled over to investigate. It was a disbanded steel-hulled ship. I had my pastels and drawing gear with me, so I jammed the bow of the canoe between the hull and rudder of the wreck and concentrated on my drawing. This took an hour. When I had finished I went to move, but the canoe just wouldn't budge, the bow was jammed. Not only was it jammed, but it had risen 12 inches up in the air. Then I realised, no, the water had fallen. The tide had gone out! I looked behind to grab the paddle. The stern was 12 inches under water. I levered and levered with the paddle, and eventually freed the canoe. The canoe shot backwards and almost flooded. I bailed her out and paddled a hasty retreat. That boat is the now completely restored *James Craig* which is anchored in Sydney Harbour. The drawing I have done is the only record of the hole in the *James Craig* and is now owned by my friend Julian – that's the drawing, not the boat!

TRACTION

My daughter Sunita came to live with me for six months, and my friend Julian arrived every morning to collect Sunita to take her to school with his daughter. My driveway was really steep and Julian, who was ever a paragon of logical thinking, stopped at the bottom of the drive. He then loaded his boot with six Besser blocks which had fallen from the delivery truck at the bottom of my drive. Julian drove the car in reverse up the driveway using the added weight of the blocks for traction.

I never did finish that house. I rushed to finish the floor so that Sunita had somewhere to ride her bike that I had bought her for Christmas. At the lock-up stage I had lost interest. Actually, there were much more interesting things happening in my life, and things started to come together in my head. I became aware of that thing between my legs when I met a really interesting girl at a folk club in Hobart where I was performing.

BEETHOVEN

There was only one folk club in Hobart, Beethoven's, and I was singing there in my very posey Russian shirt. I got talking to two very interesting ladies, who invited me to their flat for a late bite to eat after the club. Always suss of drugs, I nipped into Kentucky Fried Chicken for a take away and brought it to their flat. That didn't go down too well, as they were vegetarians (atheist ones). Much later I went in search of these two ladies, but they had moved. My search provided many blanks, as I didn't know the name of the one that I was interested in. Perseverance prevailed, and they were located. Our involvement was intense, as Stef was intent on returning to England to pursue a degree in nursery nursing. Our mutual interest which brought us together was the culinary aspect of food.

How Stef, the everlasting love of my life, ever managed to get through my spot-welded, riveted and bolted filtering system I never knew, but she did. There was a whirlwind encounter, then she buggered off to England to pursue that career in nursery nursing.

WALSTEDTS

The house in Howden sold rather quickly. I flew to England and put my proposal plain and simply to my lady.

"Why study nursery nursing when you could live it first-hand and raise a family of our own with me in Hamilton?"

It worked, the smooth talking bastard. So here I was, an emerging, sucessful artist with enough cash stored away to pay daily expenses.

Stef and I had written to each other for some time, and it seemed a good idea to go to England in person and seduce her to come and return to Oz with me, and become each other's symbiotic concubines. The problem was the sale of my house; it hadn't been finalised, and I needed cash for the trip. I approached Julian for a short-period loan. His reply astounded me. "No problem, if you take my wife, Inger, and the children to Sweden with you and make an in-depth study of dismantling a factory and relocating it here in Tasmania."

Inger was to inherit a cottage weaving factory in Sweden, Walstedts, in Dala-Floda, as the business was being taxed out of existence. That trip was a nightmare. The kids, all three of them, Tussi, Sonja and Tommy, were totally out of control: I had no influence over them whatsoever!

I left Inger and her Katzenjammer Kids in Sweden, and I went on to Bristol, in England, to tempt Stef to join me in Oz. We spent several months of that long, hot summer in every curry house in Bristol while Stef traipsed through the landscape in her Laura Ashley accoutrements. I bought a set of very expensive amber beads to incorporate in a sterling silver exhibition that I had planned in Saddler's Court Gallery in Richmond.

As a result of my smooth talking, Stef agreed to help prove all the pleasures and return to Oz to live with me in Hamilton. But firstly we had to go back to Sweden to make an in-depth study of Inger's factory. Her father, Lasser, was a genius. All his machinery for handling wool he had made himself, from washing the wool, to automatic carding and ways of spinning wool I had never seen before. The systems for weaving were mind-blowing.

Stef and I wove a table runner that we'd had for years. That weaving re-introduced Inger's kids. They were now behaving like the gang at St. Trinian's, climbing over every machine, getting tangled in the spinning threads, wrapped in the carding machine and using the warp at the back of the weaving looms as a trampoline, including the one that Stef and I were weaving on at the time!

A group of Australian spinners were shown around the factory. Stef and I followed them around. Lasser demonstrated every aspect of spinning and weaving in true showman fashion. He asked the Aussies to demonstrate to him how they spun wool back in Oz. The award-winning spinner sat down in front of his spinning wheel and demonstrated her dexterity. Lasser then sat down to the wheel. "I sit at the side of the wheel, and while you use two hands, I use one! I can spin the wool fine enough for embroidery." Producing a fine sewing needle, he proceeded to thread the wool through the eye.

Walstedts used stainless steel vats down in the basement to wash their wool, which the entire family used also for their bath. Stef and

I were in it when it overflowed and saturated all the nearby wool. We were distracted, as Miche was being conceived in that vat!

On returning to Oz, I had a complete feasibility study drawn up on relocating the factory, ready to present to Julian. He wasn't the slightest bit interested, as he had pissed off with some other woman!

VEGETARIAN

Stef was terrified of coming over to Ireland to meet my parents. We'd been living in sin in Bristol for months. Also, in those days, who wouldn't be anxious about going to Belfast? I decided to go on my own a few days ahead of her to sample the atmosphere. Now it was my mum's turn to be terrified. Stef was a vegetarian! Mum wasn't sure if she was a Protestant or a Catholic vegetarian, and we were unmarried to boot. Never mind, she'd make up the box room for Stef to sleep in, and I could bunk down on the sofa.

"No, Mum, we sleep together. We have done so ever since we lived in Australia."

"No, what would Stef's mother say? Not while you're under my roof," declared my father.

"OK then, I'll stay with my sister."

This might have been all right, but mum won out. She wanted her son at home.

The evening before Stef arrived, in what I thought was going to be a heart-felt moment, Dad, out of the blue, commented, "You know, the only thing I've ever regretted was the beating I gave you that night when you were in the billiard hall all those years ago." Ten or twenty minutes later he was still apologising. I tried to ease his mind by saying that at the time I probably deserved it. Forby, I was big enough; I could take the punishment. His fists clenched, and his blood pressure was rising. "What do you mean by that?"

I now said something every angry son wants to say to his dad.

"Well, ever since I was 15 I could wipe the floor with you."

We had sparred together all my training days, and I had been pulling my punches since I was 14. He went into a rage that took three hours to calm him down from. The only way to solve this, as far as he was concerned, was to climb up into the glory hole and retrieve the boxing gloves, and we would solve this there and then in the front parlour. It never was resolved.

All the boxing gear that I had was stored in the glory hole. I learned later that visit that my young nephew, his grandson, had endured the same treatment as I had, and had also been pressured into becoming a boxer, even though he had a hole in his heart when a baby. Luckily, he escaped to England.

Chapter Seven

Hamilton

Where I learn to untangle the tangle, the charm of our stone cottage, living at the poverty level, about simple country folk, the wrath of God, of trouble in paradise and how to harp on!

1846

I was of the opinion that art made us better people, yet the very people who were actually creating works of art were collectively the most unkind people that I'd ever met. I hated the arrogance and the egos and the religious attitude which they applied to their work. I found the average artist very hard to accept; their opinions were clouded by their egos. The art that was being pursued could be produced at the rate of three per hour! The current crop of artists were 5th or 6th generation teachers from the time when it was discovered that art had a therapeutic effect, not only in schools, but in hospitals as well. For this, the institution of art needed teachers; the problem was that there just were not enough artists to teach. So the question was addressed in two simple ways: lower the standard of artists to become teachers, and broaden the terms of the word *Art*. The result and impact of this was that within three generations, teachers were being taught by teachers who had no aptitude for art whatsoever. The definition of what an artist was changed so much that I could no longer see in Contemporary Art what had attracted me to art in the first place. What was I to do with my ability to draw? I was highly skilled in the techniques of art and the entire craft of handling all mediums. I did not consider these skills as absolutes, but what was being done in the contemporary world of art offered me no challenge at all.

Great individuals in the art world rise to the top like cream, in spite of the art institutions, but even they can be trapped by their own success. The collection that I had made of different definitions of art were enough to put me off forever.

Art- "The pursuit of that which is not essential to human existence."

I found this quote in my Encyclopedia Britannica. It upsets most artists who don't give a fuck about the 76 percent who make up the starving masses throughout the world. The yuppie lot who read National Geographic and admire the noble savage in their natural habitat, ignoring their cultural and religious icons and imagining that their art and culture are far more revered than a bowl of food.

Art- "It is what you can't do."

No matter which artist's work you're looking at, be it Arthur Boyd, Leonard French, Michelangelo, Leonardo de Vinci, Van Gogh, etc., etc., you are looking at what they could do. They were certainly not doing what they couldn't do.

Art- "Art must present, not represent."

And yet there are so many artists continually re-inventing the wheel. However, it is by striving to re-invent that the occasional breakthrough is made. It's also like opening oysters in search of the pearl; a lot of oysters die that way.

Art- "All art is quite useless."

If it is useful, it is either a tool or an item for intentional use. A religious item has or had an intentional use, but was never made purely to exist as a useless article out of context.

Art- "Easy to do if you don't know what you are doing."

This level of work is encouraged in Kindergarten and promoted throughout the artist's life. Art is for all people, and all people are artists. The fridge magnet is the totem of this culture; fortunately, there is a finite limit to the amount of children's drawings that the fridge magnet will support. The drawings will eventually fall to the ground to be chewed up by the dog, and eventually disappear. Some will end up in frames; these are usually better than the final year submissions by art students.

Art- "If you know what you are going to do, then go and do something else!"

Did Picasso say this? It's the quote that bugs me most. My favourite artist was a friend of a friend who went to college with me. He knew exactly what he was going to paint, and could vividly describe in detail the way it was going to look; he never did get around to doing the paintings. Usually I know exactly what I want in a painting; achieving that end is the challenge. Once I see the problems being solved, I lose interest in the piece. It is sheer persistence and discipline that completes the work. It is also the dissatisfaction in the finished work that is the springboard for the next work.

CHARM

The exhibition at Saddler's Court proved that I could go it alone. I had lived in the country in Ireland, in Ballinderry, when I was a kid and loved it, so I looked for a house in the country, something with charm, something old and with a bit of history. I had been sketching up in the Derwent Valley when I first came across Hamilton, a sleepy town once planned to be the capital of Tasmania until someone noticed that it was 60 miles from the sea.

Moving to Hamilton was a great idea, mainly because it removed me from all the Art Farty Wankers I'd met in Hobart. None of those guys were living in the real world. The stone cottage that I'd bought appealed to all my romantic notions. It supposedly had a ghost; maybe that was why I had a dog, for by now I certainly did not believe in ghosts, but I was still afraid of them! I had grown out of all that juvenile crap that was fun to scare the girls with, and although I had convinced myself that I had at times seen several ghosts, I now knew that it was all a load of crap! I feel rather sad that there are no such thing as ghosts, as they are a great idea, and if I were a god, I certainly would have taken advantage of the idea.

The title that came with the house said that it was first sold in 1846 and was one of three workman's cottages. It was sandstone with convict brick chimneys (convict tally bricks were used on all the windowsills, a brick with a thumb mark in it for every hundred made). All of the chimneys were not pseudo; they worked.

The north wall needed repairing badly and had no windows. Fun was had with the kitchen lean-to when I first arrived. It had moved away from the main building, and there was enough space to allow a rope to pass through. So I was able to completely surround the badly built, rickety structure, tie it off, attach one end to the Land Rover and drive off! Then set fire to the whole bloody lot, including the skeletal remains of a rat that had been walled up a hundred years ago!

Three stone cottages stood on separate blocks of land which backed down to the river where the pump shed was located. Water was pumped up from the river to a header tank on top of a tower 15 feet high. Numerous lengths of wood leaned against the tower on three sides. (Stef later showered under this tower using a paint tin I'd punched holes in.) Craig, our twelve-year-old neighbour, copped an eye-full once.

There was a confusing shed that leaned against several ash trees. It was collapsing, yet the roof was new (I lifted the entire roof with a block and tackle anchored to the tree above and rebuilt the shed). Against the fence on the south edge was a garage which was ancient; judging from the tools found inside, it went back to the days of horse and buggy! In the floor was a motor car pit which must have previously been a saw pit, as it had layers of sawdust lying in the bottom.

The house had caught fire at some time, almost burnt down, as many of the beams were scorched but not completely burnt. All the roof beams had been replaced, but none of the original shingles remained beneath the corrugated iron, unlike the adjoining two houses.

Along the south fence were plum trees and the outside dunny. In one corner was a peach tree which bore delicious, white-fleshed peaches; beside it was a gooseberry bush.

At the garage door stood another white-fleshed peach tree, and in the middle of the cobbled yard was a horrible-smelling flowering currant. In the north corner grew the most magnificent orange ball buddleia plant.

POVERTY LEVEL

Living just below the poverty level was an art. In reality I was living way above the poverty level, but financially and officially below it, as my banking accounts showed.

At my father's side in Belfast I had learnt many hands-on skills. We had built five caravans, maintained our brick house, repaired the bodywork on my father's cars, and rebuilt all sorts of petrol engines. My father had also taught me how to fight, though he taught me nothing about sex. That was Belfast; there was nothing to teach.

Electricity, as long as it didn't involve resistors and such things, was dead easy. It was just plumbing only more dangerous; never mix the two together!

Australia was used to this attitude; if you could do the job, you did it, simple as that. This gave rise to all sorts dodgy business, but as long as you were working for yourself, who cared? You didn't have to employ anyone to do your work. Any income I had only needed to be spent on materials and food. The only entertainment at this time was canned or homemade, and the library. TV reception was dreadful.

Firewood was free from the surrounding bush. I cut up one large pine tree that had fallen in the church graveyard; what a blunder that was! The bloody thing wouldn't burn, it just sat there in the fire, charred black, and stayed like that! "Struck by lightning, mate!" was the old bushy's verdict!

Because of my bearded and preoccupied appearance, for quite some time I was mistaken for a hippie, and singled out by hippies passing through as one of them. For a while I was inundated by them hoping to freeload off me as a "kindred spirit", which I am not! I'm sure of this, having had first-hand experience of their talents when I visited the self-sufficient commune of Nimbin. Intellectuals, maybe. Pragmatic? No way!

The house was on the road to the dairy which sold the village milk, illegal because it was raw and not pasteurized, but perfect for making cheese, butter and yoghurt.

EXPERIENCE

They were getting closer. What should I do? Experience had told me they would give me a hard time; no one wore a beard these days, especially in a country town like Hamilton.

The beard was a remnant from days in Sydney, my badge of passage. It might have to go.

They were almost upon me, and now I noticed they had guns, rifles or shot guns. Then I saw the several rabbits they were carrying between them. It was said that when you are drowning, your whole life supposedly passes before you. It is thought that your on-board computer is searching for a way out of maybe a similar past situation.

"G'day, guys! What on earth have you got there? Rabbits? They look incredible! Did you shoot them yourself?"

Their chests visibly swelled! I climbed down the ladder and approached the five lads. They were 16-18 years old and dressed in typical Aussie fashion; farming gear, Blundstone boots in varying stages of disrepair, a mixed variety of checkered flannel shirts, and there was just enough material left on their legs to be recognized as trousers!

It was the expression on their faces that made them so enjoyable. Each had an ecstatic expression. The rabbits they had bagged that Sunday morning on the north hills of Hamilton were their passage to heaven. They usually went rabbit shooting every Sunday morning.

"Why don't you come along next Sunday?"

"I'd love to, but I've got this place to fix up. But I wouldn't mind buying one of those!" I pointed to a rabbit which was instantly hung on my outstretched finger.

"Here, you can have that one, mate! Buy us a beer when ya sees us in the pub!"

With that they proudly strolled off past the post and rail fence, down the gravel road.

I shouted after them: "I'm George!"

As I climbed back up the ladder, I was remembering how I had gotten out of a previously tight situation. It had happened down the Freycinet Peninsula at Recherche Bay. I had towed my overweight, dilapidated caravan behind the Land Rover down a very boggy four-wheel-drive track. The place was deserted, and I was in the process of setting up camp when there was an uncomfortable rumble in my stomach. It turned into a sound that got louder and louder…then absolute thunder, as 30 or so motorbikes neared into view!

"Hells Angels! Oh my God! The beard! Should have shaved it off when I left Sydney!" What was I to do?

I stepped out of the caravan.

"Jaysus! I'm glad that you lot showed up!" I said, holding the bottle of butane gas in my hand. "Any of you guys know how to connect one of these bloody things?"

I was nearly killed in the rush as 30 or so Hells Angels descended to assist!

Now I was on top of this roof, trying to nail down the final sheet of corrugated iron on what was going to be the Art Gallery. Just at that moment there was a gust of wind that took the sheet out of my hands and cut the telephone cable that was attached to the telephone pole just behind me on the street!

"That'll make me popular!"

The house had been bought for a pittance; 2,000 Aussie dollars. It was a four-bedroom cottage with one large lean-to, which was divided into three smaller rooms. Behind that there was another lean-to kitchen. Australians do that, they add on a lean-to, onto a lean-to, as many times as they can get away with, until the roof is far too low! You can go on forever if you build on a hill!

The main road went through a narrow, enclosed valley. There were two parallel tracks to this. At one end of the town, where the approaching road turned immediately left, was the local garage. The main road passed stone cottages, joining streets, the vicarage, a school, church, three shops, the post office, the old school, and the library. The village ended with a pub, an old flour mill and a saw mill. In the old days there were sixteen pubs in the town.

The north wall of the cottage was leaning eight inches out of line at the top. This was the result of the usual problem with all stone or brick buildings in Tasmania until the 1820s, when most houses were re-roofed with corrugated iron. Wooden shingles, split wood tiles were used before then. Water was never collected from these roofs, as it was undrinkable. Nearly all the water was collected from the river and transported to wherever it was required. With the advent of corrugated iron, water ran evenly off the roof, collecting in guttering that went all around the building. It was collected in a tank at the corner of the building. When this overflowed, the ground under the building became waterlogged, and the house sank into the marsh. Likewise if there was a leak at any one point in the guttering, the ground got overly soggy and the wall would sink only in that spot. This was exactly what had happened to this wall.

Harry & Jan

"If you need any stone or wood, there's a lot to be found where I'm demolishing an old stone pub." It was Harry from down at the old schoolhouse.

I'd first met Harry and Jan when I arrived in the village. They had bought the old double-storey schoolhouse at the other end of the village for a song. Jan was a weaver, and they had converted one classroom into an art gallery. Jan also made and sold coconut ice. They had sung around the same folk clubs in Sydney as I had. They invited me to Sunday evening dinner to play and sing some folk songs.

Harry had called early on Sunday morning along with a friend named Richard. They were off up to Hamilton Plains above the village to duff a sheep. (This is a sort of Aussie tradition of sheep stealing. Legend has it that it's okay as long as you leave the skin on the fence. It isn't really understood what exactly the purpose of this gesture is!)

Richard, Jan, Harry and I had literally sang for our supper. Over the past year Harry had been demolishing one of the 16 original pubs that had first been built in Hamilton. This one was called the First and Last, as it was next to the original bridge that crossed the river into the village. The bridge had washed away in a flood. Perhaps the village had been first settled because of the coal mines, which were all over the hills. At the First and Last I was able to scrounge enough floor boards for the gallery, and two lintels for the three windows to put in the new wall.

There was also a wooden double-panelled louvered window. It opened and closed with an ingenious comb-type lever. This went into the wall between the kitchen and the living room.

Next door to Harry and Jan there was a public library; lots of people seemed to have the key to the building, which would account for the large number of books that went missing!

The Teacher

Being out and about at the gallery and the side wall of the house, I was continually encountering most of the locals. One of these was the headmaster (the only teacher) of the local school. After a rather long chat, the headmaster offered me a job; a rather odd job, as a remedial teacher, music teacher, and teacher of children with social problems. Strange offer after a fifteen-minute chat!

The qualifications from Belfast did not include a teaching qualification, as I had been advised not to even attempt the exam. I even failed the teacher's interview, as I stuttered terribly. This you know about; my stuttering slowly vanished after learning to play the guitar and sing.

The money offered was just enough to officially keep me below the poverty level, so I accepted the position, more as a social responsibility.

Lola

Lola owned the local garage at one end of the town; she drowned in her own vomit inside her car. She had been to Hobart City, which was sixty miles away, only once in her life. She claimed that she had seen the lights of Melbourne across the waters of the river Derwent. Melbourne was actually 2,000 miles away across the Bass Strait! She "drowned" one week after I moved to Hamilton.

Barney, her husband, fell asleep in the downstairs living room. He had thrown an old tyre onto the fire. The light from the burning tyre could be seen from the other end of the town. Oddly enough, the garage did not burn down!

However, like his wife, Barney also drowned. A year after Lola died, he was out fishing with two friends on the local lake. He was drunk, and tried filling his outboard engine without switching it off. Of course the engine caught fire, the boat caught fire, Barney caught fire. He jumped overboard, not knowing that he couldn't swim!

George

Further down the road lived another George. He was ancient but as fit as a fiddle, and chopped all his own wood. He never spoke except to mutter, "TV won't work," and "Follow me." I would follow and fiddle around with his TV aerial, stopping when the appropriate grunt sounded like "Stop!"

When George died, it was discovered that he was a hit man at the Victoria Markets in Melbourne in his prime.

Sonners

At the far end of the opposite street lived Mr. Sonners. His vegetable garden was as only a non-organic gardener could grow! He was a regular visitor every time he couldn't get his rotavator, lawn mower or chainsaw to work. Check the spark, clean the plug, NO spark! Clean the points, spark? Joy!

This was a good arrangement, as it meant free access to all his tools.

Roy Bailey

Roy Bailey was an oxymoron. He swore like a trooper, and lived directly opposite us. He regularly stood outside his home in the early hours of the morning threatening to castrate his wife if she wouldn't let him in! I often wondered how on earth he could castrate his wife! No one knew if he ever gained admittance, but he always eventually quietened down. He hunted possums for their skins, stretched them out on his shed walls. He would never hurt a fly, and was kind to all his neighbours.

Mrs. Webberly

Mrs. Webberly next door was always cooking up some strange bush tucker, possum stew, Wallaby rissoles; she even cooked Navens! These are a native hen similar in appearance to the Roadrunner of Coyote fame.

The Recipe:

2 river stones
2 plucked Navens
herbs and spices
Water to cover
Boil for several hours. When the stones are tender, remove Navens and eat stones!

Mrs Webberly was always passing her culinary delights to us over the fence.

Garth

The foot valve of the pump was clogged with debris. I was completely submerged under the river trying to remove the accumulated gunk. I had to remove the filter cage. Upon surfacing, I reached behind myself to search for a spanner on the river bank, cursing loudly, "Where's that fucking shifter?"
"Ahem, is *this* what you are looking for, my son?"
"Who are YOU?"
"I'm the new rector!"
Garth had just moved into town. He was living in the rectory, a large, convict-built building, two large rooms on either side of a wide hall. All the rest of the rooms were contained in the usual lean-to.
Most of the buildings in the town were convict-built, either stone or convict brick. Even the architect might have been a convict.
At a later date Garth had been rearranging his furniture to allow for me to use his front two rooms and hallway for a huge showing

of my paintings. The deal was I would have access to a list of all his parishioners in the surrounding areas of Hamilton to invite to the exhibition. In return, the church would receive the thirty-three-and-a-third percent gallery commission.

Now Garth was grumbling about running out of time to write his sermon for that coming Sunday's evening service. "I'll write it for you!" I declared.

That exhibition was opened by the then Premier of Tasmania, Angus Bethune, and was a complete sell-out on the opening day. That Sunday evening, Garth insisted that since he had attended my exhibition, I must now attend his church for evening service. As we were both pissed, I conceded. I attended the church service. Garth was there in all his finery (it is the uniform, it gets to them!). As usual there was no one else at the service, but still Garth proceeded to preach to me and me alone from a sermon that I myself had written! He didn't seem to register the irony.

Of course we fell out. " The abuse of greatness is when it disjoins remorse from power"

Post office

The shop and post office were opposite the rectory. Fred Bradshaw, the owner, was unbelievable, generous to a fault. He allowed everyone to run up a monthly account, and he still managed to keep ahead of the game. He mentioned in passing that he had been a table tennis champion, and talked occasionally of playing the saxophone. Later days found him out; he *was* a champion table tennis player, *and* at the saxophone he wasn't just good, he was brilliant!

The Midget

Diagonally opposite the post office was a white box of a house of no consequence except for the size of the woman, Sally, who lived there. She was huge! One morning neighbours woke to find a sign had been erected in her garden. In dreadful English and in barely legible writing it declared:

"If the person who ran off with my wife ever returns here I will shoot 'em both!"

Apparently she had taken off in the middle of the night with a midget from the circus that had been passing through!

Sam

Sam is my realest, true Aussie mate. He drinks like a fish when there are drunks around, otherwise doesn't touch the stuff, like many other drinkers (that's around me.) He never registered a car in his life, always got his registration window sticker from a window at the wrecker's yard. "Shouldn't have been bloody well-made if you can't fix it with a screwdriver or a hammer." He referred to a shifting spanner as a Holden tool kit. Whatever he was doing he would always pack it in, and go and live in the outback with the Aborigines. After every trip he would give us a call with the most incredible stories, like how when the white man first arrived in Botany Bay, they recorded that the natives could only count to four, using his thumb to point at the other four fingers, not noticing at which joint they were pointing to. They could add, multiply and divide in multiples of four.

Sam told of seeing a VW engine sitting on the back seat of a Holden, held in place by two Aboriginals, the fan belt going through the floor onto the drive shaft. They had travelled 400 miles that way. He told of how the Aboriginals would travel hundreds of miles to see and listen to Slim Dusty of the 'pub with no beer' fame. They would arrive at the concert, which was usually out of doors, with their guitars, and sing and play along with all his songs. They had their own method of learning the guitar. This would make sense to any of you who play guitar. D – two black fellas behind me. A – three black fellas in a row. C – three black fellas climbing the stairs. G – one lonely black fella. They keep it simple.

Sam's father was building a concrete sailing boat way out in the woop woop past the black stump. Sam would pass our house every two weeks or so to get his dad something in Hobart, and he would call in for a chat. Perhaps he'd call in at his friend in Hamilton who owned a junkyard. Sometimes he worked for him. I once bought 20 round poles, 6 feet high, from which I built my chook run. Neville, the owner of the junkyard, called to see me a week later looking for his marquee tent poles that Sam had sold me.

I had been to see Sam's dad's boat. He had taken months to do the concreting. When I had lived at Howden, Julian had a friend next door who had built a concrete boat. We did all the concreting in one hit. There were at least 10 of us working on that at once. Seven hours to get right around, working from stem to stern, both sides at once.

When the time came for Sam's dad's boat to be launched, someone alerted the TV stations. I watched it myself. The boat was lowered into the water with a crane. It floated on the water for quite some time, and then it slowly started to break up and sink. It was rescued and taken to a children's playground. Sam's dad had numerous kids, and he would seek solace out in the backyard for years, working on his boat, so the project had been worthwhile for him.

Judy & Mike

Judy was the grand lady of Hamilton. Mike, her husband, was the original cockie farmer. They owned thousands of acres on the surrounding hills and thousands of sheep. I got my building sand from Mike's property. Judy was a humanist and an aesthete. She organised an art class where I was to teach housewives of all the landed gentry. Here I learnt how to pronounce all my colours in proper 'strine (Australian accent)! Brauwn instead of Belfast bruunn! Certainly NOT brown!

Judy was a dynamo, and when the arse end fell out of the wool industry, she kept their boat afloat by renting out several stone holiday cottages that she owned around Hamilton that she'd bought for a song, including mine that she eventually owned. She also helped to keep me afloat by buying several works from me. She had grace and charm.

TO CHURCH

At the end of the town stood a Catholic church, to which most of the locals belonged. It was a wooden building which did not burn down, as it was not in a vulnerable position for lightning strikes.

Usually churches were built on a hill above a town, not down in the valley where the pub and brothels were. God with his lightning bolts always struck the highest buildings, i.e.. the church! Most early churches were made of timber, and were consequently burnt to the ground, while the dens of iniquity on the lower ground remained intact! Benjamin Franklin with his lightning rod was a hero to most Christians.

On the hill above our village, on the approach side from Hobart, stood the Church of England. It was stone, and probably convict-built. It had a lightning rod! The most notable of the graves was one on the west side. It was inscribed "This young child came to the church to pray." Her dress had caught fire on one of the church heaters and she burnt to death.

Blind Rupert welcomed the congregation, occasionally getting a feel into the bargain as he pawed them in greeting. "Welcome, Mrs Partridge."

MARRIAGE

If Stef wanted to get married, which I had no objection to, I would have to get a divorce. Also, it might help to keep Anne out of my hair anyway. Marriage has no logical foundation, but then neither has divorce; so during an illogical moment, I got a divorce. My friend Julian also got a divorce about the same time. A year later he invited Stef and me to his new wedding. I knew both of the couple well, and I asked jokingly if they could give me 10 good reasons why they were getting married and if they did, I would attend their wedding. As the date approached I reduced the reasons to one. Since Julian could not think of even one good reason, I refused to attend. Stef went. Seven months later they were separated, and divorced six months later.

Stef and I did get married (gypsy style). My daughter Sunita performed the ceremony on the cobblestones outside our back yard in Hamilton, the podium being an old cast-iron broken cooking stove. Sunita had written to Stef and me asking if she could come and live with us. Miche, our first daughter, was one year old. This was beyond all my wishes, as I knew that this was solely her wish, and not the result of my bitterness. Without much ado we secured a cupboard drawer in place with an octopus grip in the back of our Land Rover to put baby Miche in and headed straight up to Nimbin, almost non-stop, stopping only in Sydney to overhaul the gear box at Billy Longridge's garage. There was bugger all wrong with it. Julian had over-adjusted the handbrake on the drive shaft. Before heading out on that trip, Julian assisted me by dismantling 10 different areas of the Land Rover, leaving me to reassemble them – the bastard. There's a great Australian poem – "The Bastard" by Jacko Kevins.

At our appearance in Nimbin, Sunita hesitated in shock for three seconds at our prompt arrival; but her belongings had long been packed, and in four days' time we were back in Tassie.

THE WRATH OF GOD

I am a lover of oil lamps. Hanging above my head were two of the largest and nicest-looking pair I had ever seen. We were in a building in the middle of nowhere at Strickland. The doors were locked, cobwebs and rust indicated that the building hadn't been entered in forty years perhaps. A few planks had rotted out near the water tank. That was where we entered the building. Dilemma!!! Should I souvenir them or not? Eventually conscience got the better of me and we left, leaving those two superb oil lamps behind. We had been in a church forty miles north of Hamilton.

We then travelled westward towards bandit country, where the inbreeds lived. Locals named them after John Wyndham's book. This was an area of saw millers and truckers. We stopped when we saw another derelict corrugated iron church. I can never resist the temptation to enter a derelict building. We waded in four-foot-high grasses. Through a broken window we saw that it had been gutted, except for a superb aisle sea grass runner, ideal for our long hallway at home. There was also a lovely wall bracket lying in one corner. God had deserted this place, and obviously had no further use of these items, so I nicked them!

On the wall bracket at home I mounted a wooden model ship that I had built of HMS *Bounty*. The carpet was laid in the hall.

Stef and I had just woken up the next morning; she was sitting up in bed. "That carpet we laid in the hall is going out the front door! Look!"

It was slowly disappearing underneath the front door. I hopped out of bed, through our open bedroom door and into the hallway and flung the front door open. Before me was the largest pig that I had ever encountered. He had eaten more than half of our carpet!

God moves in mysterious ways!

One evening Stef and I were sitting in our living room by the fire, reading. The children had been put to bed. Suddenly behind us was a mighty crash, as the complete window frame, glass and all, fell shattering onto the floor, followed by a totally confused sheep! An uninvited stranger!

THE CROZIER

Someone of pseudo importance had been very, very impressed with a copper religious processional cross I had made for the Anglican Church in Hobart. Garth, the Hamilton Rector, got to hear about it, and his friend the newly appointed Bishop of Bendigo in New South Wales wanted to meet me; he was from Tasmania. Could I make a silver crozier for him? Of course I could. Also a processional cross and a Bishop's ring? Of course!

"What's a crozier?" I thought. I'd agreed to make one, but what the fuck …? Hold it, he's a Bishop. Luckily he presented me with some photographs of a crozier. Ah, a full-size shepherd's crook.

Oliver was a modern Bishop. He didn't want any of that ornamental lacework or frills like the French. What the French put on, the Swedes take off.

At the time I could only buy silver in a 12-inch-square sheet, and the crozier was 22 inches in circumference, so I chased it into a shape at each end, the join continually fractured until I got it tapered and into shape. Then it was finally hammered into shape, and was reinforced and finally silver-soldered. The seam was on the inside of the curve, which also kept opening, so that's what all that ornamentation was for; to hide the seam (form follows function). But perseverance paid off. The entire crozier disassembled into four pieces. The staff was of Tasmanian Blackwood, terminating in a silver ferrule.

The amethyst Oliver had was an heirloom from his grandmother. Was it glass? I had discovered a bubble in it. Oliver went over to Melbourne and bought another. I was told later it might have been a genuine amethyst with a bubble of Argon or some other gas.

His two sons commissioned a large necklace cross on a silver chain. By his attitude I knew Oliver was delighted with his crozier, but he never said a word until after his inauguration. "George," he said, "While other Bishops were cracking tiles during the procession through the church, my crozier made a gentle whisper." I had put a rubber doorstop on the bottom. Sixty-eight cents' worth of rubber; acknowledgement at last.

This commission led onto a design for a silver and gold chalice to commemorate Field Marshall Montgomery's connection with Tasmania. Then someone noticed people weren't going to church anymore, except for those 12 people who dress up nicely every Sunday morning and are always seen outside their church at the bottom end of Davey Street, Hobart, saying good morning to their minister, who's dressed up like a Christmas cracker.

THE WEED

Harry had restored the old council chambers and discovered not only a cash of old coins and paper money, but also a lot of valuable stamps.

A strange thing was happening to this town. Not only had I moved in, but another artist, a potter and a writer. (He was very interesting; he was trying to graft his hop plant onto a marijuana stem. He was also growing marijuana in his hedge.)

I also had been investigated by the police in case I was growing the stuff too, probably because of the beard!

It had started with someone dobbing in Harry for growing weed in the guttering at the back of his house. The amazing thing about this incident was that the police had searched Davids belongings, a visitor who was staying with them. They emptied the contents of his case onto his bed. They didn't find any marijuana! What they hadn't noticed was his eight passports in different names!

David made his income from traveling the world losing his luggage, which he had insured. He obtained passports by applying in names that he found in the birth notices in the newspaper. A simple phone call claiming to be a friend of the victim, "Remember, we met in London?" If the person replied that they didn't remember him he would hang up.

But if the person claimed, "I have never been out of the country, mate, couldn't be me!" Got ya, that means you have never applied for a passport. A birth certificate and a photo in that person's name using a post office address…another passport and an identity under which he could insure another lot of luggage!

The town had what people were calling an artists' community, and other artists were always looking for empty houses to buy or rent. Hamilton was becoming a refuge for drop-out artists. We now had a weaver, two potters (the craft society of Australia sent me a 25-page survey form to fill in, the result was that the average craftsperson in Australia was a woman, a potter and over 52!), three painters, a sculptor and a few hangers-on.

Whiskers, the general store, was a real emporium, which sold the weirdest things. It was the original Chicken Feed! I recall buying a set of roller skates from there for Sunita one Christmas. These skates only had one set of rollers per skate, they were called "Skeelers." The city shops couldn't sell them, and Whiskers shop had bought a job lot. Twenty years later roller blades hit the market and made someone a millionaire!

THE BOTTOM OF THE GARDEN

The stone cottage I had now restored, and came to the decision that it was a continual, full-time job to maintain it. The dust falling from the walls had to be swept up constantly, floors polished, and there were rats that lived in the inner walls that I somehow could never get rid of, even though I had sat up night after night and shot them with a slug gun! The cottage was cold in winter and hard to heat. The property was a long block; at the bottom of the garden, it looked out over the river. I decided to build a studio that I could later convert to a house.

I had put word out for any old buildings, sheds, etc., that people wanted demolished and removed from their land. This way I was able to accumulate an amazing amount of building materials, and for a while we looked like a builder's salvage yard! But I eventually became selective.

It is a fact that split timber lasts almost forever. Most of the fencing around Tassie is post and rail, sunken six-foot-high posts buried 18 inches into the ground, twelve feet apart, spanned by four runners slotted into drilled slots in the posts. These post and rail are over a hundred years old, and barely a sign of rot as they are all split.

> I'm not a shingle splitter,
> I'm a shingle splitter's son.
> I'm only splitting shingles
> till the shingle splitter comes!
> (Incidentally, a proper yew longbow is split, not sawn.)

Splitting wood instead of sawing it does not expose the capillary tubes for water to enter. Roofing shingles were always split. I have seen shingle splitters working so fast as to have one shingle in the air at all times, i.e. split one, throw it over your shoulder and have another split before it hits the pile behind you! Most of the wood that I had collected was split and weathered to that wonderful Ozzie grey, just like her ever-grey trees.

Eventually I had enough material to build myself a large studio at the bottom of the garden. This was built in a fashion of a Wild West movie set, as each wall was only erected when it was completed windows and all, constructed flat upon the ground. The wall panels around this entire structure and the roof cost me nil, until the internal walls needed lining with plasterboard, which I had to buy new.

Coincidence was kind to me. When asked by the local council who had given me permission to build such a structure, I steered them in the direction of the local building inspector, who had been found dead in his car that very week.

BALLS

Among the oddballs of Hamilton I felt quite at home. Not only was I an oddball myself, but I entered the idiot stakes when I turned my hand to raising calves. I had gone to our local dairy for our usual fresh milk and asked the dairy farmer who had a herd of about eighty Friesian cows what he did with his male calves when they were born. He told me that he knocked them on the head and fed them directly to the dogs. I asked him if he could give me a few.

About a month later I received a message from him saying that he had six male calves for me. I went straight round and brought them home. By this time I was really feeling like a fair-dinkum farmer. I could shear a sheep in the real old way, with hand shears. I knew how to kill sheep, skin them and butcher the meat, and now along with my chickens and ducks, I had cows!

The problems started when the calves got the scours, a form of very debilitating diarrhea that formula-fed calves suffer from. Their shit literally turns to brownish-green water.

The local cockie farmers gave me numerous traditional remedies, and eventually the scours cleared up except for two calves who continually passed water from their rear end. My friend Traps came up to Hamilton to help me de-knacker the calves. The method was to place a rubber ring around the testicles, and this would cut off the blood supply and the testicles would eventually fall off.

During the de-knackering, Traps casually commented that two of the calves were female; gee, did I feel stupid! These were the two calves that I was treating for scours, and all this time they had just been having a piss.

The news soon got around the village of what an idiot I was, not knowing the difference between a male and a female cow…maybe the fool was the dairy farmer who had given away two perfectly good milking cows!

Traps and Sally

Traps got his name from the job that he'd had at the University of Tasmania. It was his job to procure live animals for the staff, who studied these animals. Traps' passion was fishing up in the highlands, in direct competition with the professors he worked with. He always won the bets that he had wagered, and as he didn't like fish, he passed them onto us. Consequently, we always had a constant supply of fish.

He often went hunting and took his wife Sally along. She bought a gun, but always spent the day sitting under a tree reading a book, occasionally firing a shot into the air to keep Traps happy.

Traps once showed me how to fish for trout. He was working at the salmon ponds, a place specifically for breeding salmon and trout. On the bank of the river that passed the property, he spread a sheet. He crawled under and emerged with a couple of insects. "If there's a fish here on this stretch of water, this is what they're living on," he said, holding up the insects, which he put on his hook. "If I don't catch a fish within four seconds, there's nothing here." We caught one.

THE TASMANIAN SYMPHONY ORCHESTRA

Once music has parental involvement, the entire concept changes. Parents see little Johnny or Samantha bowing on stage to an admiring audience. They see the entire concept as safely controlling their child's future. Music is something that you discover for yourself. If you are dropping your kids off for music lessons, then you've got it all wrong, as far as I'm concerned.

Every couple of weeks, Stef and I would venture into the big smoke on a major shopping spree and meet up with our friend Julian for lunch. We would rendezvous in the lunch/tea dressing room of the Tasmanian Symphony Orchestra. In all the years that I have known those musicians, never did I ever see one of them playing their instrument outside that establishment, with the exception of the bass player. During the chats and discussions that I had with them, not one of them ever picked up their instrument to play for enjoyment. The only passion that related to their performance was the union rules, and several times they would get into a fury if the conductor conducted a concert too slowly and they did not get the concert finished in its due time. There was even one occasion of stopping a concert that was running late when management refused to pay overtime rates when the concert went past its time slot. The entire orchestra downed tools and literally left the stage in the middle of a performance!

Of course, when you understand what is expected of a classical musician, what else can you expect? All those hours that you should have been out playing, instead, hour after hour after hour, practice, practice, practice.

Oliver Schroeder, a friend and one of Canada's most experimental and contemporary violinists, recorded all his scales and played them in his bedroom, convincing his parents that he was practicing. In the meantime, he was messing around on his computer.

After a few years of that crap, any moron can pass an exam. What is expected of you is a mindless, accurate response to a conductor's baton and the patience to sit still and do nothing until the conductor tells you it's your turn!

I was at a rehearsal of the TSO when a very famous French horn player made his definitive recordings of Mozart's four horn concertos. It was confusing watching him reading his newspaper while waiting for his cue from the conductor.

He once watched me play the harp at Salamanca and enquired as to who had taught me to play the harp.

"Why?" I enquired.

"It can't be played the way you're doing it!"

"I taught myself."

He replied, "As it should be!"

An artist's sketch book can be a passport to many places, and I could move freely among the musicians during rehearsals. Once I played a vital role in their presentation of Tchaikovsky's 1812 Overture. They needed to know exactly just how loud to play their recordings of the cannon fire. At the time I was middle of the audience seating, drawing.

I was also invited to one of their concerts when they were performing *La Marseille*. My part there was to lead the audience in booing, as the French were conducting nuclear explosions in the Pacific.

I witnessed the odd ins and outs of the preparation of the musicians themselves, how when dressed in evening gear half of it was held together with safety pins, sticky tape or even drawn on bare flesh with eye liner. Julian's underpants had to be regularly blackened with boot polish when his crotch split. Black underwear was very popular because of such wear and tear!

SAUSAGE

I once saw three harps in a shop in Dublin called Walton's. Walton's had a slogan something like: "If you are going to sing a song, make it an Irish one!" I promised myself there and then that when I reached old age, 50 to be exact, I would learn to play the harp. There I was, 37 when my friend Julian had just returned from South America with a harp. I knew that it was a harp because of the triangular shape, but it was nothing like the Celtic harps that I had seen in Ireland. The pillar was straight up until it met a curved neck, at the end of which there was a carving of an Incan Indian chief. The sound box was faceted, and the sound board had a complex frame rather like the bulkheads in a model aircraft. Julian asked me to restore this harp, but the wood was rotten and beyond repair. The idea fired me up, so I decided to make my own harp and copy Julian's, except for the carvings. The South American harp only had a few strings on it, and I had no idea how to string my prototype, so I used guitar strings. The result was not as I expected. It certainly didn't sound like any harp that I had heard before. It certainly was not what I was interested in sound-wise, but the challenge had started!

It was about this time that Derek Bell, the harp player with the Chieftains, was making a name for himself. But there were no plans available for making harps. All I had to go on was a small photograph of his harp on the back of one of his LPs. My only available reference to an actual harp was in the orchestra, which had more scales on it than a fish, and was not my cup of tea! Still I measured the string lengths, and it gave me some idea of the construction. Of course all this information is available on the Net now! Eventually I constructed a harp that met with all my requirements, and it looked and sounded like the one that Derek Bell played. The nylon strings I used from classical guitars, but the longer strings I had to make up from sausage skins. These I soaked in the bath to remove the salt, and then I stretched them across the longest room in the house. Each string consisted of ten or twelve sausage skins twisted together, about the thickness of my little finger at first, but they shrank to the right thickness as they dried. They sounded perfect, but on hot, damp days salt would surface on the strings, as I had not washed them thoroughly enough before twisting and drying!

Living in Hamilton, there was no way of finding anyone that could teach me to play the harp. But I did have an auto harp (like a zither) that worked by a set of dampers which stopped certain strings from sounding when you strummed your fingers across them. I used this principle to play my harp, by using the fingers on my left hand to dampen certain strings that were not necessary for the chord. It sounded really pretty. Eventually I met up with a concert harpist from the orchestra on the mainland who spent an entire day showing me the basic playing techniques. I knew that this would be my only opportunity to learn, a one-day lesson, thank you!

THE BROAD RIVER

A complete fool is what I felt when I was offered the keys to the fenced gate "A Taranaki"* that blocked our entrance to the upper reaches of the Broad River. The gate was secured by a chain that had a group of at least 10 locks along the chain, each lock owned by an individual farmer. My friend who owned land along the Broad River had several copies of his key, and was now offering me one. He held it out to me for my personal use.

"But I need ten keys to get through that gate."

"No, you don't! Open one and you have broken the chain!"

Jaysus! He was right!

I had just been given the keys to the most beautiful river imaginable for our own private swimming holes. Mile after mile of meandering river, through massive rock formations, banked on either side by pasture and bush, no buildings forever!

One New Year's Eve all the family were up there, 60 miles from Hobart, when Stef smashed a lemonade bottle that she was carrying in a plastic bag at her side. It sliced deeply into her leg. We had to beat a hasty retreat to the hospital. She got the strangest of stares from the hospital staff. What sort of celebrations had she been up to? After all, it was New Year's Day…

The Broad River empties into Meadow Bank Dam. On the west bank there is a valley called Traps Valley. We had ventured into it in the Land Rover down an almost impossible track. Garth the Rector, Julian and Stef were beside me as I was driving. While Julian and Garth were working out a way of souveniring a particularly great diesel generator at the abandoned homestead, Stef and I were rummaging through a mound of empty bottles. A particular one caught my eye. It was corked, and half-full. It was ornate, and rather beautiful. I sat down, removed the cork and sniffed. I spoke urgently to Stef,

"If anything happens to me, it was that bottle!"

She hollered for Julian's and Garth's assistance. I was breathing in and breathing in and breathing in; I could not breathe out, nothing was happening! My mouth opened, my chest deflated but nothing came out of my mouth. It seemed to take about an hour before I recovered.

The guys appeared, and Garth recognized not only the bottle but what exactly had happened. CYANIDE! Cyanide had been used by the cockie farmers to eradicate rabbits. That was before Myxomatosis. Years later I read in a first aid book how cyanide destroys the oxygen in your body. (Incidentally, Julian's father had received some British honour for poisoning rabbits in Oz.)

*A wire gate in a wire fence as protection for Aborigines against radioactive fall-out at Maralinga by the Brits.

BACK TO LEO BURNETT

I had provisional tax to pay on that money that vanished before I left Sydney. I had felt confident that I could eventually pay this off, but it was getting out of hand. There was only one alternative; return to advertising in Sydney, and pay the bill off. Mea had just been born, so we loaded the Land Rover and were in Sydney one week later.

During my first week the accounts executive, the copywriter and I were hauled over the coals for not servicing the Sunbeam account properly. Months went by, and we still hadn't done anything. During drinkies with management on the above floor, I was asked how I was settling back in. "Great, but I'm concerned that no one is interested in servicing Sunbeam. We could lose that account."

He looked at me as if I was stupid, then it dawned on him. " Oh, yes! You wouldn't know; we are now owned by Leo Burnett. Leo Burnett are owned by £$%^&*(! who own Oster in America, who own Sunbeam here in Oz! Simple; we can't lose our own account." So indirectly I worked for the £$%^&*)!

AWARD

Advertising agencies handle blokey stuff and girly stuff, and Leo Burnett had several girly accounts, including Helena Rubinstein.

The girly artist in the next office had been having problems with a prestigious design for an award for their silk fashion design. Helena Rubinstein had rejected designs from all around Australia, including England. He was in a flummox. I could hear him having a feminine rage about their latest rejection through the wall partition. "You do know," I said, "I'm a silversmith. Would you like me to have a go at that for you?" He jumped at the chance, and they approved the design. In the world of silversmithing, it's normal for the designer to hand his design over to a craftsman so that they can work from their drawings, but Helena Rubinstein and the agency wouldn't have a bar of it; I had to make it. Primarily there was the quote. How much did I owe the tax man? Eleven thousand dollars. OK, it would cost them $11,000. "There's still the problem of my tools," I said. "They're all in Tasmania."

"Well, we'll equip you to do the job here in Sydney, and in addition, we want a smaller copy for Trent Nathan, the current winner of the award, to keep."

Two months later we were back home in Hamilton. Our house had been rewired. The freezer was buggered, its entire contents had turned to liquid and stank to high heaven all the way down the main street of Hamilton.

HIPPIES

I was totally disillusioned by the "Real Art Scene." I loved painting, and when I didn't come into contact with other artists all was well; but there were so many of them passing through Hamilton, including every alternative hippie. I had a beard, Stef had bare feet, the kids ate wholemeal-bread sandwiches, and as a consequence of this, every passing drop-out was directed to our house. Most times conversation eventually came around to the decadence of modern society and the traps of possessions while they helped themselves to our stove and hearth. Art college teachers came up from town, grumbling and moaning about life at the art college, grumbling about the continual back-stabbing. The conversations were so predictable and boring. I was continually being told how to teach my grandmother how to suck eggs. The only way to be diplomatic was to appear ignorant, and to be told for the hundredth time how to design a chair, how to make a pot or how to re-invent a thing called a wheel! Art was crapping me off, and artists, so I was being drawn more to the self-sufficient idea of farming. I needed to get further away from artists! My friend Julian had 70 acres of land just south of Hobart, but he fancied moving and buying a larger farm. He asked if I was interested in sharing a property of 800 acres on Bruny Island. An island, where? Bruny Island is a half-hour ferry trip from the Tasmanian mainland, $10 fare to get across. That would keep the wankers away!

I would become a real farmer, shearing cows and milking sheep! Now there were about eight artsy types living in Hamilton, and we decided to put our home on the market.

These were the last days of Hamilton, and the beginning of the Bruny Island phase of life. Hamilton had a saw mill which I had painted several times and I knew the owner. He cut all the timber for the new house we were to build on Bruny at the right price for me.

SELLING HAMILTON HOUSE

As Tony Hancock would say, "I'm outta here, mate!" It didn't take long to sell our house. I had just completed the last of 30 paintings for my exhibition. They were all leaning against the wall of our gallery. An American lady, along with her daughter, called at the house. She had seen our for sale sign.

"Are there two houses on the property?"

Well, one was a studio, really.

After the hastiest of viewing, she insisted on buying and paying in cash. She was quite prepared to pay the asking price for the house at 600 percent more than I had paid for it! I recall that she needed to go to the loo, and had hollered for Stef to come and help her with her knickers!

She was curious as to whether I had any paintings on hand for sale.

"Yes! An entire exhibition," I replied, and led the way to the gallery. Honestly, she took the top one without looking at the rest. Her daughter appeared at the door. "I've just bought a picture! Go on, buy one!" she said, pointing to the next painting in the pile! She bought the next one as well!

A right pair of nutters! We were allowed to stay on in the house for two months. Within four months every artist in Hamilton had left the town for different pastures. One year later I could have bought back my house from that Yankee lady for almost the original price I'd paid so many years ago! Hamilton sits in wait for the next bunch of weirdos like us!

MURDER

Julian and I spent the day on Bruny Island checking the boundaries before we decided to make our purchase of the 800 acres. We spent the early part of the evening in the local pub chatting with the resident pyromaniac, who the previous week had set fire to his mate's shed for him to collect on the insurance. The problem was that his mate had not cleared out all his important possessions in time, like his 20-foot aluminium boat, complete with outboard. We left the pub early that night to sleep in the shearing shed on our intended property. Stef and Julian's wife came down to the island early next morning just as Julian and I were waking up. On the radio they had heard that a murder had occurred in the Bruny Island Hotel the previous night.

Chapter Eight

Bruny Island

Where I learn about the dangers of partnerships, how to fall from a great height, about Dutch iris's, drunken Christians, snakes alive and playing possum.

BRUNY HISTORY

The island had been known for its huge stands of timber, most of which had been felled and shipped to England to construct their piers. Almost all of Bristol docks are from Bruny Island timbers. They were so long that the front and back gunwales had to be removed from the ships used to transport them. To be a left-handed tree feller was a valuable asset, locally known as a Molly Duka (Aussie slang).

Bruny is made up of two islands joined by an isthmus two miles long. There is also coal on the south island, near the landing strip where the flying doctor landed. Our farm was at Sheepwash, directly opposite Gordon on the mainland across the D'Entrecasteaux Channel, where the mail was first delivered. Fishing was immediate and in abundance. Half the land had been cleared and left in long windrows, which we finally set fire to. They burnt for weeks, snakes fleeing in all directions. We had three small dams. When it came to the farming, Julian was boss.

Bruny was serviced by two ferries, running every two hours, depending on the weather or how sober the skipper was! But a trip to town usually meant a day off school for the kids. We had our own boat, *Buttercup*, with a Seagull outboard. When we wanted fish, we knew exactly where to anchor within five meters by lining up homesteads on the horizon. Ten minutes' fishing at a fish a minute!

"Do ye ken John Peel" was written on Bruny, and Captain Cook planted apple trees and climbed the lookout on the isthmus. Adventure Bay has a very interesting museum. When I lived there, there were records of the first settlers, and convict records detailing the reasons for transportation. The museum has a wooden replica of the *Bounty* which sailed into Adventure Bay, and Captain Cook hopped ashore and planted his apple trees there. The Bligh Museum was run by a lady who stood for council on the promise that she would have all the lupines (not native flora) eradicated from Bruny if she got elected. She became known as the Lupin Lady, and like everyone who lived on Bruny, was iffy, she became known as the Loopy Lupin Lady! She was my mother-in-law!

SHEEPWASH

Stef and I and our four kids (Fintan was living with us at the time) entrenched ourselves at Sheepwash. Here I learnt how to split fence posts, make droppers and fence. I learnt that a "dead man" is a post buried in the ground horizontal to the main straining post. I learnt how to drive a tractor, how to bog a tractor, shear sheep, clip sheep, throw a fleece, sharpen sorbies, how to de-knacker lambs, de-tail 'em…all the important stuff that God is going to ask me before he'll let me into heaven. I know that if you swing a gate from a young tree the gate will not end up twenty feet in the air!

Julian and his wife Christina, Stef and I, formed a partnership, and we bought a farm at Sheepwash on Bruny Island. We had every known farming animal, including some 800 sheep. The idea was for each couple to build their own house, but after one year, just when I was learning to shear sheep properly, I realised that no way was Julian ever going to build his house. Ours was finished, and we'd been living in it for six months. I had built this entirely with a chainsaw; we had no power. All the doors and kitchen cupboards had been made in Hamilton before our move.

Julian was eating me out of house and home, never making his own sandwiches, and his wife was always in town working. Julian realised this before me – well, he didn't really – and he offered to buy us out. Good riddance to 800 bloody sheep, including the 20 we'd raised from lambs who made it impossible for Julian and me to use the sheepdog. Shepherding works on the theory that sheep run away from you. Hand-reared lambs don't. They grow up and they run towards you. Sheep follow sheep, half-running towards you, and half running away. The blind leading the stupid. Julian, the dog or me?

The farm at Sheepwash had a mile of waterfront facing Gordon across the two-mile stretch of water. In the old days, the postman rowed across here with the post. At one time he swam the distance. There was superb fishing including crawfish and abalone, mussels and oysters. The Aborigines only ate shellfish, not fish with scales. There had been coal mining on this stretch on the peninsula. We also had bee hives, and the cows that we had reared at Hamilton. Arum lilies grew on the edge of one dam. They reminded me of my mum, as she held six of them in her wedding pictures.

A LIFT

As I said, Julian was my closest and most frustrating friend. For our large working farm we erected a row of 18-foot posts. They needed trimming off equally at the top. He lifted me up in the air to their height, me standing in the bucket of the tractor with my chainsaw running. I should have known better, as Julian had repaired the trigger mechanism of the bucket with No. 8 fencing wire. Suddenly the bucket tilted and I fell out. In the 18-foot descent to the ground, luckily I thought of throwing the running chainsaw as far away from me as possible. Julian was of course devastated. For many reasons which I forget, he is still my best friend.

My own chainsaw I had bought second-hand and had impressed him so much that he bought a new version of exactly the same model, a Farm Boss. As a standard precaution, we always cut our firewood together within visual distance of each other. I had occasion to stop my saw while I cleared some light bush that the tree had fallen into. Julian's saw eventually stopped when it ran out of petrol and he came over to me to souvenir one of my sandwiches. I could see by the look on his face he was perturbed about something. Eventually I stopped when my saw ran out of petrol. "What?" I said, as I looked at his confused face.

"Have you only just run out of petrol now?" he said to me. "Yours has been running 10 minutes longer than mine, and mine is brand-new." He was most upset about that issue, and I never let on about turning mine off for that 10 minutes. Serves the bastard right for nicking my sandwiches.

As I write this I remember my friend Terry from Belfast. We were clearing an area of woodland up the old Hollywood Road behind the man's house on the corner, who always let us drink from his well. Terry had been up a tree chopping down the branch he was sitting on. As he fell, he threw the axe into the air. I looked up and the blade of the axe hit me in the eye. Another time he was clearing bush ahead and I followed too closely behind and the large bread knife caught me across the front of my three fingers on my left hand, cutting an artery on my ring finger. Blood spurted all over Terry. I died there as well.

THESE BOOTS

Kemp and Denning were dismantling their warehouse and selling off the buildings. Julian, Chris, another friend, and I bid for their corrugated iron, which we won. As we dismantled and loaded up our truck, I continually passed a pair of superb, expensive boots in the slowly disappearing office shed. I tried one on and it was a perfect fit. "I'll go home in those!" I thought. At the end of the day Julian carried my shoes out to his truck, leaving me to don the amazing boots. What a fool! They were two left feet!

Nils

Julian not often got it wrong, but this time he got it right. His son Nils could and did drive every vehicle on the farm ever since he was ten! How Julian ever taught him anything was a mystery to me. I watched him filing something intently in his Tasmanian convict vice while Nils was kicking the shit out of his ankles trying to get his attention! Nils failed!

However, the point is that on his 16th birthday, not only did Nils pass his driving license test, but also passed his pilot's license!

ABALONE

The Japanese pay a fortune for abalone. We were told to venture into the small bay at Sheepwash at low tide in water up to our waist, wearing heavy-duty gardening gloves, and feel under the rocks for these ashtray-shaped shells clinging to the rocks. These can be removed with the aid of a heavy-duty screwdriver. Inside the shell there is a large round mussel about the size of the palm of your hand. Beforehand you should have prepared an implement that looks like a heavy-duty wire brush but instead of wire, there should be three-inch nails. On the stump of an old tree you proceed to smash the living daylights out of this beast. At the stage when you've beaten it to a pulp, you're halfway there. Keep going. Cut the pulp into small pieces and cook for seconds in a pan. If you choose, as I would, throw them away or feed them to the dogs and never go abaloneing again, or you could end up like those gits who come down to rape and pillage the island.

SIMPSON'S BAY

We re-located directly over the hill from Sheepwash Bay to Simpson's Bay, the most picturesque place we have ever lived. Here we established an almost self-sufficient lifestyle. A brief description would have you believe that life could never be more ideal. The view from the house from left to right looked over the hills and mountains of Woodbridge to Margate, Snug and then onto Kingston, all in the backdrop of Mount

Wellington. There's more; in the foreground was the Isthmus, a narrow strip of beach with the ocean to the east and the shallow, aqua-blue waters of Simpson's Bay. To the right, east, was Adventure Bay, of Captain Cook fame. Years ago, the Aborigines waded into Simpson's Bay and trapped fish which they clubbed to death for fun. The island was populated by nutters even in those days.

Islands are microcosms of society. It's probably truer to claim they are populated by society's rejects, including us. Think on it. Australia is an island off Asia. Tasmania is an island off Australia, and Bruny Island is an island off Tasmania. Does this suggest anything?

In the five years we lived there, I did not do one painting. I did, however, build a lithographic press from the guide posts that I had knocked down with my Land Rover, but only from safe stretches along the road. A boat winch was used to pull the stones through the pressured edge of the press. The stones I used were marble from gravestones which I had cut for me by a grave monument sculptor, and the etching acid was vinegar. I have noticed several of these lithographs on the Web recently.

IRISES AT SIMPSON'S

I had not really listened to the farmer who sold us his property at Simpsons Bay. He had told us of the three orchards on his land, and of the beds of Dutch iris that grew between the rows of fruit trees, 48,000 of them! A purple profusion!

Towards the end of that first summer, Stef pleaded with me that we should try selling these blooms at the Salamanca Market in the capital's state town of Hobart. There was no way that I was going to sit at a market stall and sell bloody flowers! There were thousands and thousands of jonquils, and the same amount of daffy fucking dillies as well!

At this time I had just completed making my first harp. There was no one on the entire map of Australia who could teach me how to play it. No one to help with lessons or advice. So I was having to learn it the hard way, trial and error, and logic. I brought my harp along to Salamanca Market to sit at the end of Stef's flower stall and make some sense of the instrument. I had made a cover for the harp from an old blanket, which now lay beside me on the ground. After two hours of very bad practicing I got up to leave, as Stef had sold out of her flowers. There was more money lying on my harp cover blanket than Stef had made selling her twenty million irises! We repeated exactly the same performance week after week while the irises lasted, with the same results.

I practiced the harp while Stef sold flowers. Soon the season for the irises ended, but I continued playing the harp, only now I was being asked for recordings. This was the time when young folks were buying super-duper recording machines and were trying to set up sound studios. One of these enthusiastic young lads, David Holmes, was prepared to make me a one-hour recording, which I could afford. This I had duplicated in Melbourne by the hundreds, and sold every Saturday morning. Salamanca was now our main source of a weekly income. With the advent of the new one-dollar coin, busking was bringing in at least $100 a week.

I had made a fret saw to cut jigs saws. The designs were of native animals. They were a bore to make, and each piece was hand-painted. We sold about five a week, but the biggest earner was the tangram made in the shape of a bird's egg. From these pieces you could make over 50 different-shaped birds.

SEVEN DAYS APPRENTICES

The man we bought our farm from at Simpson's Bay was a seventh day apprentice. They had weekly meetings in their front parlour. This state of suppression became obvious when I started clearing the rows of blackcurrants on the small fruit orchard at the bottom field across the road from where the house was. It was on the hillside facing north. The road cut the farm in two. The bottom half met the water's edge of Simpson's Bay. At the end of each row of berries when I cleared it, was a weatherproof box. In each box was a stash of some empty, some half-full bottles of liquor, and a collection of great dirty magazines.

I disturbed two snakes. After some pursuit they made for a depression in the middle of the orchard that was overgrown with blackberries. I don't like snakes, especially in Tasmania. There are three kinds; tiger, copperhead and whip snake – all lethal.

As I was using a brush cutter I had petrol close by. This I threw over the bush. I couldn't find my matches. Crossing the road, I dashed up the hill for my matches. I also grabbed more petrol, as what I had thrown on the blackberry bush would now have evaporated. I also brought my 410 ladies shotgun. I threw more petrol onto the bush, lit a match and ran back. *Whoosh!* Up went the fire. About half a second later there was a mighty boom that shook our house behind me, also the entire of Simpson's Bay. When the fire died back I saw the reason for the boom. There was an underground pipe, 18 inches wide, going all the way up to the house. It must have been the fumes that filled it that had exploded. I was pondering this when the two snakes appeared totally unharmed. I shot both. Aborigines declare a snake only to be dead after sundown. I often thought that this might be because the venom might remain active until then. I have since discovered that the venom can crystallise and still be lethal ten years later.

I have encountered many snakes, including a huge one just outside our new house in Sheepwash. I had run into the house and grabbed the rifle but Julian had been using it last, and there was a telescopic lens on it. I climbed onto the bonnet of the Land Rover but I couldn't find the snake in the telescope. Stef drove around and around the windmill washing machine. Eventually I ripped off the scope and shot the snake. There is now $1,000 fine for killing any snake in its natural habitat. A bit of a reversal from the days of Lady Franklin, who in around 1837 put a bounty on snakes. Richard, our neighbour, paid $2 a foot for them; he ate them.

That windmill that Stef drove round and round was made from four half-15-gallon metal drums, made from a design in the Whole Earth catalogue, which was a softback book of half-baked ideas of things that never existed, impossible to buy or simply just didn't work – well, most of them. The drums were welded on a cross-frame, each concave of the drum catching the wind. The entire rotating shaft was oar-shaped, and revolved in a copper drum made from an old hot water cylinder.

It worked superbly as a washing machine until it disappeared on one stormy day, over the horizon, along with all the washing.

THE BOG

The shed where I made my harps looked out over the south end of the island's isthmus. This was an area we referred to as Julian's Bog. It was a strange, flat area. Succulent plants grew in the salt water. The area was subjected daily to tidal flooding. There were draining ditches that had been dug years ago in an attempt to drain the area. At one time there was a mile-long timber bridge which traversed the bog. From my shed I caught a glimpse of movement in my peripheral vision, which is more sensitive to movement than the front part of the eye. I looked straight down to the bog and could just see Julian waving frantically, standing on the top of his tractor, right in the middle of his bog. I ran to tell Stef that I was off across the fields to help Julian, as he seemed to be in trouble. At the time I was working stripped to the waist, as I usually did. Of course I didn't hesitate to stop and put on my T-shirt.

When I got to Julian he had the tractor well and truly bogged, up to the back axel. I could offer no assistance, although we struggled for an hour or so. Eventually, as it was getting dark, we had to abandon our efforts. Without my T-shirt, I was absolutely covered in mosquito bites. When I got home my explicit instructions to Stef were, "Don't touch me anywhere!" I sat still in the chair until bedtime when all the stings had quieted down. There were literally hundreds of them.

One of the usual considerations of living in Europe now, or the UK or France, is that people want to hear about the biting and stinging things that we have in Australia. There is nothing so annoying as the insects I live with each summer here in France. Each sting means a continual week of itching. The fly sprays are totally useless. Eventually I sent to Australia for Aeroguard, the stuff the CSIRO developed in 1960 for the Queen's visit. Odd too, if at any time you are seen stripped to the waist unless you're at the beach, your mode of attire is referred to as "half-naked," or maybe you're a gypsy.

Gerald, one of the farmers-turned-deck-hand on the Bruny Island ferry, told Julian how to un-bog a tractor that was up to the axel in mud, with wheels spinning freely in the mire. It was not dangerous as long as you don't sit on the seat of the tractor.

> Step 1. Bring to the site one or two short, stout, split fence posts, 4 x 4 x 7-feet long and No. 8 thick fencing wire.
> Step 2. Remove mud guards from tractor.
> Step 3. Clear mud away from area between back wheel and engine, all the way through from wheel to wheel.
> Step 4. Pass fence post all the way through from wheel to wheel and attach to each wheel with several turns of No. 8 fencing wire.

Julian and I did as instructed. We then started the tractor after putting it into the lowest gear, letting out the clutch. The tractor gently and slowly lifted out of the bog. The precaution of not sitting on the seat was in case the tractor rushed forward and the attached fence posts caught the operator and terminated him. We turned the engine off, removed the fence posts and drove straight out of the bog.

OSCAR WILDE

The arse end had dropped out of the art scene. Tasmania had more artists than you could point a burnt stick at. The place was a wasteland of useless artists, but then all art is useless (Oscar Wilde). Although we were eating regularly, we were not eating healthily. Stef milked three cows every day and made butter – too bloody much. When I killed a pig--pork, pork, pork. And when I killed ducks-- duck, duck, duck (poor bastard, wait till you get to France!). Food was either a feast or a famine. Trading with locals was impossible; they were also in the same boat. No one could afford petrol or electricity. All the locals had applied for and received National Assistance (the dole). We hit rock-bottom when the Salvation Army came to our rescue with food parcels. We had three children, so like everyone else I applied for National Assistance. I was the only one on the entire island to be rejected. My job as an artist was deemed as professional, and I was deemed self-employed. We were eating well enough, supplementing our farm produce with fishing. Our pizzas were a philosophical disaster – all topping. It was the base we couldn't afford.

I mentioned my dilemma to a member of parliament who had years before bought several paintings from me. Six weeks later there was a call from Social Security for an appointment. Stef and I were shown into a very sour-faced civil servant's office, who sat us down in front of a pile of forms. The bottom one had my signature on it from when I'd first applied for their assistance almost a year ago. "Sign these forms," he demanded. Eleven months' worth of them, and in return I received a cheque for 11 months' dole money. As a result of my case, the law was changed to allow self-employed artists to be eligible for the dole. I was also eligible for the dole until the economy changed three months later, and we were back on our feet at last.

FLYING DOCTOR

The flying doctor came to Bruny Island once a week, and our entire family had visited him for one reason or another.

Mea had her first and only attack of croup in the middle of the night. She was rushed to the north end of the island by the resident nurse to be met by the police launch. We arrived at the rendezvous point to see the police launch illuminated by torchlight, stranded, 200 yards offshore.

It was the first time their brand-new emergency launch had ever been called out and they had run it aground on a rock! Eventually they lifted it off the rocks; luckily the tide was coming in, and the launch had no holes.

The item was on the news the next morning with the usual accuracy: "A girl from Bruny Island had fallen from a cliff and broken her arm! The police launch rushed her successfully to hospital!"

Mea had a further encounter with the flying doctor, many years later. He was at a reunion of his old college associates which was held at Saint Andrews golf course in Scotland. Mea, who is now a chef, was doing the catering. We learnt about this when he telephoned me to see if I had any further information on Lord Franklin,* who sought the Northwest Passage through the pole and disappeared. He had read the song in a book that I had published *Art Works*. His friend was writing a book on the subject.**The husband of the lady who put a bounty on snakes.*

LORD FRANKLIN (TRADITIONAL)

(Recorded and sung by everyone under the sun)

It was homeward bound one night on the deep
Swinging in my hammock I fell asleep
I dreamt a dream and I thought it true
Concerning Franklin and his gallant crew…etc…

I myself had a brief encounter with the Bruny Island nurse at 11.00 one moonless night when my spastic colon was acting up. We arranged a rendezvous at our property entrance gate, and by the lights of her car I dropped my dacks and she gave me a pethidine injection in the arse! I was to drive like a bat out of hell home, the one mile along the shore just in time to make it through the front door where I collapsed in a heap, To Stef's amazement. I know I shouldn't say it, but I love getting Pethidine! I've had it about six times.

PAUL TOLLEY

I had a friend for a very short time on Bruny called Paul Tolley. I thought him the second-biggest liar that I had ever met. I can give his name now as I know that that was not his true name; he had got it from a bottle of brandy that was on the shelf of the local bar when the police cornered him. He told the strangest stories, and I was sure that he was full of bullshit. He was a Maori from New Zealand, a real one. He invited half of Bruny to a Maori Hangi feast which he prepared firstly by digging a huge pit and lighting a large fire, into which he piled rocks. After many hours, when the fire died down, large leaves were spread across the rocks and then a large pig was placed on top, then more leaves, then the whole thing covered in with the soil that came out of the hole. After another endless time, the process was reversed. The pig was then divided among the guests (boiled pig). In true Aussie fashion as on these occasions, every family brings a plate. This means a bloody big plate of the best of the best that you can afford or produce. The spreads on these occasions were to die for. Competition is fierce, as your status on the invitation list to any occasion depends on your plate. As for the pork, it was fucking awful. A soaking wet, jellied, blubbery, boiled excuse of a traditional disaster. Paul was so proud.

    I went possum shooting with him. I only accompanied him, as I had no gun of my own. The trip through the bush started off at 11 o'clock at night, and with the aid of very, very strong torchlights, off we went, scanning the trees. Above, the possums' eyes were illuminated by the torchlight. Paul had to be a very good shot, as the skins were worthless if they had a hole in them. The possums didn't stand a chance. Paul killed about 15 that night, skinning them on the spot, and the next day he would nail them up on the shed wall. A possum is about twice the size of a large cat, with a long tail and pointy ears and lovely, large eyes. They are renowned for having a sound like they are laughing at you, and I have been told that they have been known to pee on you with alarming accuracy.

    During possum hunting season, the sheds in country areas of Tasmania are covered in these skins. They range in colour from black, brown, and golden to albino white. Paul had been hunting out of season, and asked me to store three sacks of possum skins under the house. He claimed the inspectors were snooping around the island.

    One day he called around to the house. He had to flee the island. No, he had to flee Tasmania, maybe Australia. Could I loan him $1,000? I never said it to him face to face, but as I said, this guy was the biggest liar since…the Greeks, when they said, "We've left you a nice little gift of a Dala Floda horse for you outside your city walls."

    As security he would leave all these possum skins with me. I loaned him the money. Eight months later I got a phone call from a man enquiring about the skins. Could I bring them to the car park of the casino in Hobart Town? When I arrived, without much ado, he put them into his car, all three bags, and asked me to join him in his room at the casino. When I got there I was among six other men. The man, who had a New Zealand accent, placed a suitcase on the bed. It was crammed tight with notes. He selected a pile and divided it out among us; $3,000 to me. I never saw nor heard of Paul Tolley ever again.

THE CELLAR

Stef had a romantic notion that no self-sufficient farm would be complete without a proper root cellar. There was a very steep hill on our property, about forty-five degrees, that would be just the spot for it. She drew a rough plan of a room twelve-foot square and six-foot high. It had a zig-zag entrance and a ventilator shaft. All the necessary requirements for a root cellar. Oh yeah! What a load of bullshit; this was a nuclear bomb shelter. She had been nagging me for years to build such an item, but I always thought that it was just a geg!

But like the preverbal rock that wears away the water, she achieved her goal, and I did build the root cellar, complete with bunks and a pedal-operated fresh air supply. As luck would have it, in all that digging I struck an underwater spring, so this root cellar had its own fresh water supply. The entrance and exit were both covered by fly screens. When it was completed, it was fully equipped with root vegetables, all in tin cans. Once finished, Stef never went near the place, as she was terrified of the millions of snakes that she suspected were living in it! It took me six months and a three-stone weight loss to build.

The nutters of Bruny Island, as well as the morons that the island attracts, were getting to me. Really I should have taken the hint. When you look back at it, all the road signs were shot to pieces. It was always open season on some poor animal. In the evenings when one looked out from the front veranda, the isthmus was ablaze with the campfires of the visitors who had arrived on the ferry with their trailers, overloaded with tents, outboard motors, more tents, aluminium boats, cray pots, guns, and fishing gear. Well, everyone's entitled to a feed, and being a meat eater myself, I am of the opinion that if a man is going to eat his meat, then he should be prepared to do his own killing. But no, these killers left Bruny Island at the end of each season, behind them a trail of massacred uneaten mutton birds, scallops, fish, cray fish – shame on you.

All this killing impacted me. I was now killing something almost every week on the farm, so I considered my philosophy and fooled myself with the word *prepared*. So from now on I wouldn't do my own killing, even though I am always *prepared to* do so.

Bruny was a cultural backwater. There was no music whatever, unless you called Julian playing the introduction to "Puppet on a String" on his bassoon music. Over the D'Entrecasteaux Channel, two miles wide and over the first hill, lay the town of Cygnet. In all, 12 miles away. They were going to organise their first Folk Festival. Not only could I perform, but would I help with the festival?

Oscar Wilde said that people in the country get up early as there is so much to do, and go to bed early as there is so little to think about. The work on the farm never stopped. Every fence was broken, and we didn't have enough money to buy new fencing, so the old ones had to be continually mended. There was so much killing to be done, every time we went near an animal it was to torment it in some way with drenching or rubber bands to tighten on testicles, etc., etc. The romance of being a farmer was beginning to wane.

Bruny Island revisited (or why I hate Bruny Island)

Bruny Island encapsulates why most Australians have a love/hate relationship with Australia. By European standards, the soil on Bruny is crap. It's sandy, and the rain that does fall is almost instantly absorbed like a sponge. The native vegetation can handle these conditions, but all attempts to grow anything else will end in frustration. Most houses on Bruny are surrounded by failed attempts to grow European gardens. Even the failed lawns around the house are just cleared scrub to act as a fire break. The European trees look like tortured willows and are contorted in their search for water during the drought seasons. Why do people grow these gardens? Bruny Island is spectacular, the scenery is amazing, and the coastline viewed from a distance is breathtaking. The native bush can even be inviting. But travel further than from your car window, and you will discover that what looked soft from a distance is prickly and hostile. The first thing that the Europeans want to do is to tidy the bush under foot. The bark and the fallen leaves are the homes for many native fauna. These are the first victims of the insistence in making Bruny Island habitable to Europeans.

Everyone on Bruny owns six cars; three are already rusted away besides what remains of Granddad's 1954 Holden. Two cars are continually being cannibalised to keep the other cars on the road, as they are continually being shaken apart and disgorging themselves on the corrugated dirt roads. Beside each home there are twenty-four sheets of corrugated iron and four rusted-out water tanks. Some houses have the most recent eyesore installed, the green plastic tank. Surely these would have been better in grey or a brownie-grey to blend with the natural flora. There are loads of snakes on Bruny. Most people disagree with me, but they are not artists who sit quietly for an hour or two drawing. I always check thoroughly when I finish a drawing before I move off. Once I counted six snakes sunning themselves on the perfectly sheep-tortured lawn of an old disused house that I had been drawing; one was only about twenty feet away.

Imagine a homesick Aussie living in the Glens of County Antrim in Northern Ireland on twenty acres of land. Within a sixty-meter radius of his home he removes all the topsoil and replaces it with barren building sand scattered with gravel, shell grit, sharp stones and random rocks. Add to this a selection of prickly shrubbery interlaced with dead bushes and several ever-grey gum trees, have a home of breeding flies and gnats, add the occasional feature of piles of corrugated iron or the occasional rusted car and presto! An Aussie bush garden revisited. You never see genuine gardens like this in the gardening magazines!

Often I have taken visitors to the top of Mount Wellington, which overlooked my back garden. I am always amazed by their reaction to the view. Looking east over the city of Hobart they are really impressed by the impact that man has made on the environment. It is this view, the view over the city, where they linger. Immediately behind them is the endless view of virgin wilderness to the Southwest. Few people admire this view. I suspect that it is threatening, hostile, and fills the viewer with unwanted humility.

Bruny is an island off an island off an island. So the locals have a definite island mentality, and while I was there I suppose I was a fucking nutter too! Actually I am a sceptic, but when I visit Bruny Island, I believe in God. My car instantly breaks down when I leave the ferry, now this is evil, and evil is the devil's work. He knows that I hate Bruny, and so he and God work hand in hand to prove each other's existence.

Bruny Island is a seasonal island. There is the Mutton Bird season. This is when everyone on the mainland armed with their killer instinct or with a miniscule relationship to the indigenous Aborigines hunt the Shearwater. This means waiting 'til dark, sticking your hand down the bird's burrows, wringing the young birds' necks and voila, the killer instinct satisfied! As the birds taste like cod liver oil, the carcasses mostly end up on the local tip. Scallop season, the same hordes arrive in their boats, dredge the channel dry, and the scallops prove difficult to open. A large quantity are again chucked on the tip.

Summer holidays on Bruny are an Australian's back-to-nature ritual. Hundreds of aluminium dinghies loaded down with fishing gear, Eskys and carton upon carton of beer. Since the clamp down on gun ownership, I don't know what the possum shooters will do. You can always tell the nature of hooning by the amount of shot-up road signs on the island.

SELLING PUZZLES

Salamanca Place still has the original waterfront warehouses in Hobart. It is the waterfront referred to in literature as "A far distant land," full of cutthroats! As the pier front changed the warehouse buildings became empty, and stood that way for decades. In the seventies, the spaces were almost rent-free, and a bohemian arts community evolved. Glass blowers, silversmiths, potters, weavers, woodturners all moved in. I was there at the start of their folk club, at the same time George Prince and a few of his friends started that market out on Salamanca Road that ran along the front of the buildings.

The history-- they started their arts and crafts centre, then coffee shops opened, then an arts supply shop, then an art gallery, then two photographers, then two restaurants, two craft galleries. Then the powers that be and the City Council took control of the Salamanca Arts Centre. It became so top-heavy that there were more in administration than there were arts and crafts people. Artists started moving out; they couldn't afford the rent! Exclusive galleries moved in. More exclusive restaurants moved in. More artists moved out. Now no one can remember why anyone goes to Salamanca! To pursue art while feeding their faces, or the parking meters, I suppose!

In the meantime, that little market George Prince started is now the largest and the most prestigious market in Oz! But it is just one more establishment that I have run away from. I have run away from the music institutions that wanted me to conform to their rules. I am running away from the French, who don't like me doing my own home maintenance. I'm not allowed to farm without a cow-milking diploma, make honey without insurance covering the entire nation against stings, I can't go to Ireland without my fool's pardon, and I hear that there is an institution being created for those Molly Dukas.

SALAMANCA HARP

My harp was an instrument of mass disillusion...one of the first medium-size, 36-string harps ever seen in Oz. For 16 years I never told a sinner that the CDs I sold at Salamanca Market in Hobart brought in more than enough to pay for my entire family's income for the week, and that was made in just two hours each week. (Also, it was enough to eventually take me away from Hobart, when the Oligarchy made it impossible for me to live here in Tasmania.)

The harp also kept us unusually amused, playing in mines miles underground at Zeehan for functions and concerts; to King Island, where they had to use two light aircraft for me and my wife because they couldn't fit the harp on the first one. Additionally there were numerous concerts for the ABC radio and television, an endless number of weddings, TV specials, and music festivals. One Australian award-winning programme was copied scene by scene by a Japanese film crew – I had no idea that they were doing this until they asked for my donkey to come over to me and nudge me as if he was listening to me playing the harp in the garden; this had happened accidentally in the original. We achieved this by placing a piece of apple down the back of my collar. The original TV show had me playing in the Grand Chancellor, where I used to be their resident harper, but I had stopped playing there, so they hired an entire restaurant for the night just to replicate that scene. I played for a gangster and his moll from Chicago while he proposed to her. Once I lost my appointments diary – the dog ate it – and ended up playing for four weddings in the botanical gardens until somebody came over and paid me.

Myself and seven other musicians performed for an incredibly produced religious TV show for the ABC. Six of us were atheists. Atheists grow rather prolifically in Tasmania. The cathedral in Hobart can barely pay its rent. It probably should be shut down, but Tasmania would go into a panic if a state funeral should ever occur. But the country's quota of religious devotees always stays the same, only now it's crystals – it was acupuncture – while yesteryear it was chiropractics. Most people don't know they don't know while you and me know we don't know, or should I tell you, you don't know.

PLASTIC FIDDLER

I have been the feature of at least 30 travelogues and many interstate documentaries, and then it dawned on the Tasmanian Tourist Department that maybe they should feature me in their latest travelogue for Salamanca Market. They made arrangements with me to use my domain at the market, and to be available for filming between nine and noon. I arrived an hour before the appointed time to tune up, dress up and prepare myself. Cameras arrived, set up and then a clown with a fiddle, which he couldn't play, arrived and the producer said, "Oh, we won't need you, Mr Callaghan, we've got this fiddling clown instead."

"Well, that's all right," I said. "You'll get a bill from my solicitor for my loss of income." These guys were from the advertising agency I still sort of worked for, and they knew I knew how they worked. They paid.

Chapter Nine

Cygnet

Where I learn that the hills are alive with music, Stef finds her voice, the healing power of the harp, that bi-polar was the answer, Australia has an outback, where Snow White lived, the dos and don'ts, that my persona has been hijacked and the Keystone Cops are alive and well.

LEGEND

The Cygnet locals, legend had it, were mostly descended from an Irish immigrant ship loaded with convict wenches that had accidentally sailed into the Huon River in the D'Entrecasteaux Channel – sounds iffy. Before hitting hard times, the local school, church and convent dominated the valley. A change in the world market for apples devastated the area of Cygnet, and most of the apple orchards were ploughed in. The Cygnet Council was absorbed by Huonville Council, and the total area went into decline. The orchardists sold up and left. (I wrote a song about this, and ABC produced a TV programme over which I sang and performed the music; it was awesome.)

Someone had to be blamed for the demise of the orchards. There were now so many musicians on the Cygnet landscape, it gave meaning to song "the hills are alive with the sound of music." And each and every one of those musicians was responsible for the world's decline in apple consumption.

We bought into a ten-acre block in a small bay called Helms Bay. It got its name from the people who lived just across from the jetty. Vick Helm was about 85; what he didn't know about marine engines was not worth poking a stick at. Steve and Jane Ray shared the ten acres with us. The land had been surveyed for two 5-acre blocks on which now stood two houses on a west slope. Our house had been superbly built out of celery top pine poles and clad rather like a Swedish log home. It actually had five levels in a part A-frame, with the very top level an entire double bed. Later I closed in the veranda in true Aussie fashion, and added a larger veranda at the side and built a three room studio at the back, which instantly became bedrooms for the two older girls. For the years that we lived in Cygnet we were in constant contact with Steve and Jane. They had two children, Luke and Connor, and our girls became their babysitters. Jane and I sang together at concerts and festivals for years, occasionally being referred to as a husband and wife duo. Steve was into bluegrass mandolin. They now have a regular bush band known as the Cockies, and they have done fantastic work with school kids.

Self-sufficiency and killing behind me, we moved into this well-made, A-frame, timber, log-style house with three levels. I was so glad to get out of that badly built house on Bruny Island. I reckon Julian and my grandfather between them couldn't have done worse. On the property of five acres there was also a huge shed where a chap was building a boat, soon to be gone.

There were more musicians and singers in the hills around Cygnet than I'd had hot dinners. Enough to pack a hall full every first Saturday night of the month. There was always a music session going on at someone's house every second week – blues, country, Irish, Australian bush, jug bland, bluegrass – no jazz – that's city music.

All three of our girls were at school, and another accidentally on the way. I was working three nights at the Grand Chancellor playing the harp.

THE JETTY

The hills around Cygnet reminded me of Ireland except for the buildings. These were very Australian with their high-pitched hip roofs, the usual lean-to back kitchen and lean-to front and side rooms that had started life as a veranda. Whilst living on Bruny, I had promised myself a three-week trip around these hills to do drawings of the rather romantic settler's homes. When I actually got round to making the trip, most of these homes had been replaced by triple brick-front veneer built by the new generation.

Helms Bay was six kilometers outside Cygnet, and the bay itself had a jetty. It was a great place for swimming. There was even a sunken wreck to dive down to and explore. The bay was great for the kids growing up, especially since we had our own boat. A rocky bay like Helms Bay was more interesting to explore than all the long stretches of golden sands one finds all around Tassie.

The best place to build a supermarket is right next door to another supermarket, that prevailed in Cygnet. The town had four drinking holes, three churches, two schools, four supermarkets, three garages and three take-away shops, all surviving. I'm told that Cygnet was only accessible in the old days by sea. This was the heyday of the apple. When the area was first settled there was a shortage of women, but apparently a shipload of female convicts came to the area from Ireland. This explains the high proportion of Catholics in the region. The locals were dominated by the St. James Catholic Church, and all were educated at St. James Catholic School. With good roads and better bus service, the school started to lose pupils. Also contributing to the loss was the fact that the council in Cygnet was to be decommissioned and based in Huonville. The school, in its blinded wisdom, decided that the fall of its pupil numbers was due to the fact that they did not have an art teacher. I was asked to teach there in the hope that this would attract pupils to the school. I declared that I was an atheist, but the powers that be decided that as long as I didn't undermine the teachings of the Catholic faith, this would be okay with them. I needed the money, I was easily bribed. This singular event was the worst experience of my entire life. It was like stepping back into my father's memories. The school did have a craft room, where one of the sewing teachers did teach something. The shelves around the room were stacked with what my mother would call "wee holy things." All these icons were broken, and had been brought to the school for the pupils to fix. This was craft! I was expected to create a different altar piece for the church each month. Every ounce of creativeness had been surgically removed from each student; they could not cope with the concept of free thinking. A young girl who attended the school was tragically knocked down and killed on her way home from school. The next morning the headmaster interrupted my grade eight class to talk about the death. He was there for the entire lesson, and was not prepared to leave until he had all 30 students in tears. He gave each child an individual guide through their own guilt trip, moving on to the next child only after he had reduced the previous pupil to a physical and emotional wreck. I left in disgust. When I passed through the infants' class to get to the store room, the primary teacher, a friend of mine (a folk singer), had a child standing on her desk, smacking her across the legs and saying: "God is love! Repeat after me! God is love!"

Grant Wood

I had been sent a postcard from America of a landscape artist by the name of Grant Wood. There was something very appealing about the style, and also something very familiar. Around this time, I had been asked for an exhibition by Saddler's Court Gallery in Richmond. My friend Alice had sold the gallery and had moved into a cottage across the main street of Richmond. Abstract painting did not appeal to me whatsoever now. There were so many abstract painters, their canvas' sold by the meter, usually pieces of interior design that were out of date before the paint dried or the building was completed. Of course there was the totally undemanding school of water colour artists; that was an option that I pondered on for 20 seconds. It was this work of Grant Wood that seemed to strike a chord. The power of his landscapes had an impact on me. Then I received a letter from a friend in Ireland telling me how the teacher who taught me at college, John Luke, had recently died. He included in his letter a print of the painting that he had done of the Old Callan Bridge in a style that was almost identical to Grant Wood's. It was also similar to the style that I had been painting when I first left college and moved to London. Everything about this painting was demanding, from the composition, preliminary drawings and detailed drawings, the sort of demands that I was comfortable with. This new work that I was planning demanded my all.

FLEMME FATALES

Stef was now a regular member of the theatre group, the Flemme Fatales. She was also the local librarian, and we were getting too comfortable. Also, the girls were about to leave school. They wanted to travel to Ireland and England. They were entitled to British passports, so they applied for them. Passports were only available to them if their parents were married, so we now had a reason to get married. We did get married, and nothing happened. Clouds didn't part, it suddenly didn't stop raining, and no one served us an Indian curry.

I had another sell-out exhibition, and the money was burning a hole in my pocket, so we were planning another a trip away, England via Holland, as I speak both languages, worsely.

THE BIG FIDDLE

The Grand Chancellor; what a laugh. I was resident harper at the most exclusive and expensive restaurant in Hobart, so exclusive I can't even remember the name. It was within the foyer enclosure. Three nights a week, and three meals cooked from the same kitchen where all the swells were eating. These swells who were shown around the hotel were brought before me, where I was always introduced as the "man who played the big fiddle." I'm very, very versatile.

On quiet nights when the restaurant wasn't busy, I sat in the foyer of the hotel and played the grand piano, even played requests, which was totally amazing, as I can't play the piano! It was nothing more than appearing confident and fiddling around. Occasionally the most beautifully grey-haired lady would wander into the foyer, sit down at the piano and play for hours. She had left her shopping trolley outside in the foyer; no one ever objected. She was Hobart's one and only bag lady.

HEALING POWER

A woman approached me as I was playing the harp at Salamanca Market.

"Ah, George! You are here! I have just sold that last CD of yours; I need eight more. I have used them to heal so many people this year." She was some sort of nature-loving healer; they grow under mushrooms. She took and paid for eight, and off she went.

Bob Brown, a very prominent politician, was standing behind me listening to this. Turning to him I commented, "You know, Bob, if there was any truth in what that lady had said about the healing quality of the harp, I would have to be one of the most healthy people alive in Tasmania. And here I am: I've got kidney stones. I've got cataracts. I've just had a heart attack, and I've got screaming in my head."

"George! Think of the mess you would be in if you didn't play the harp!"

Yes! You are a true politician, I thought.

Harpo Marx played the music from the sextet of Lucia de L'Amour (and yes, I can play it!).

I hummed along with it on stage with those divas in Belfast during the opera season that all of us art students participated in. Harpo played it at various speeds, and it was the only tune that he could play for years. At the market I was playing it when I was joined by a couple of opera singers who were touring Tassie. Booming out in full bloom, we continued our extravaganza until I ran out of my repertoire! It was one of THE magic moments at Salamanca.

THE BLACK STUMP

There is such a place as the Black Stump. It was a chosen surveyor's point, way beyond woop woop. A lot of people out there communicate over the radio. A lady located beyond there had been given a small harp that I had made as a gift by her husband. She had tried all avenues to get a lesson on how to play it. I was approached by the Australian Broadcasting Corporation and asked if it would be possible to give her a lesson over the air. How we handled this was for me to teach the interviewer how to play the harp, and for the lady to follow the same instructions. Firstly, the harp had to be tuned. She had the key to the tuning pegs, and I instructed her on how to tighten and slacken the strings according to my instructions. This we did on-air, humming: "Do re mi fa so la te do!"

"Then place the small harp on your knees and hold it in place with the right hand, leaning the harp on the right shoulder."

Now it sounds too complicated if I write it, and this book is not a lesson on playing the harp! But I think you get the picture.

This was enough to get her started. Several months later she had bought a much larger harp and two years later she was a member of a small harp orchestra.

I was once joined by Janet Harbison, the leader of the Belfast Harp Orchestra, for what was one the most enjoyable concerts in the Lake District. We brought the house down! Well, she brought the house down with her dynamic performances.

BI-POLAR

When I'm asked to teach the harp my reply is a defiant, "NO!" I taught a young girl once who did exactly everything I told her to. Within 10 weeks she was better than me. Stef, like most people when they are learning an instrument, picked it up half an hour before her lesson in the hope that this is all she'd have to do; but practice, practice, practice, is the only way to get to Carnegie Hall.

This young girl gave it up a week later to play the flute. She also ran off with a truck driver who lived next door; she was nursing him as he had a broken leg. Her husband was a genius with his hands. They had both met at a Rudolph Steiner school. They had two young children, and now she'd run off. The husband explained that she had run off many times before, almost without really knowing what she was doing; just suddenly there was a complete change of mood, and he found that it was like living with a stranger. Sounded bloody familiar to me. A couple of years later he and I met up again for a discussion about marriage. His new lady wanted children, but he didn't.

"Ever hear from your ex-wife?" I asked.

"No, but I did learn that she was diagnosed with bi-polar."

VOILA

Surveying was done from the air, and buildings before a certain date were deemed to have city council approval. In the huge boat shed that was on the property when I bought it, I built a huge gallery, without building approval, 12 inches smaller than the existing building. I dropped the shed overnight and voila! My gallery!

Before the shed was dropped I was experimenting with harps. I don't think anyone in Australia had ever made a harp at this time, certainly no one in Tasmania. Once I saw a small one in a museum in Port Arthur, which had come out on a convict ship. Julian had brought one back from South America which he had asked me to restore. As it was beyond restoration, I had no option but to make a new one to satisfy my own curiosity. It certainly didn't sound like anything I'd ever heard before, but my interest had been aroused. There was no structural information available, so I opened Pandora's Box. Hope! I made harps in every possible way I could imagine. Out of every possible material. Square sound boxes, round-backed sound boxes, plywood, fibreglass, carbon fibre, brass, aluminium, even horsehide. That particular harp gave the best sound, but it would never stay in tune. All these materials were tried on sound boards as well. After making 15 harps all the same size, 18 strings, and of all these different materials, I invited my musician friends to a demonstration; a double-blind demonstration. One of my students played the instruments. There was no consensus of opinion as to which harp was preferred. Even the harp made out of craft wood (cardboard) gained equal acceptance.

Barney

When I built my art gallery, I had two additional rooms on the back. One was my tool shed. This had one wall open onto the large paddock where our donkey Barney wandered. The adjoining room was my studio. Then, through an open door, around a counter display and into the gallery. One weekend while we were away, Barney the donkey navigated his way through my workshop, through the studio, passed the counter display and became trapped in the gallery for three days. During this time he removed every painting from the wall, trampled the glass and ate all the cardboard that the pictures had been framed with, backing card as well! ALL the paintings. If I had sold all that work it would have totalled $40,000 dollars!

Everyone I tell this story to blames the donkey. Barney, during the years we lived there, also ate an entire fourteen-foot boat!

DORRIGO

My English acquaintance, Peter Stone, had an empty house in Dorrigo, a very beautiful area of New South Wales, high on a plateau above Bellingen. Bellingen was populated by people on the dole. Very suited to alternate living. The soil could grow anything. The weather was always ideal, and if it got too hot, you'd travel up the steep climb to Dorrigo, to rain forest country.

The alternates failed to secure a member to council during the local elections, by just one vote. The current council refused a re-count. OK, next dole cheque, we will all cash our cheques at Coff's Harbour and buy our supplies there. The alternates had their re-count and gained a seat on the council.

Our trip to Dorrigo took us through Sofala, a gold mining town. I had been there before with two friends, Jim and Terry. Terry was one of those people who changed when they are within the vicinity of a gun or anything military. We (Jim, Terry and I) had gone to Sofala primarily to pan for gold, on Terry's suggestion, the real reason was for him to shoot his gun. The three of us had guns. Terry's first instruction when we arrived at our selected campsite was to give a demonstration of our fire power. "What the hell's that?" Jim and I enquired. "Well, we'll shoot our guns into the air all at once." To shut him up, we fired our guns across the river. One of us hit a passing bird, which fell into the water. It took all our ammunition to put the poor thing out of its misery.

Stef, Miche, Mea, baby Lena and I were in our Nissan E20 van fitted out for camping and laden with art materials, jig saw for puzzles, and my harp. We were hopefully going to stay away for 6 to 9 months, just for a change, and show the girls outback Australia. Our first day was spent panning for gold in the Turon River at Sofala and we found a few specks, enough to excite the girls. The area had been panned out by the Chinese years before. The Chinese went through the workings again, and recovered the spilt mercury that was lost during the battering process. We had some experiences there in the outback. There were goats on the surrounding hills. And once during the night we were alarmed and frightened by the harmless arrival of 15 or 20 motorcyclists, which has become the butt of a standing family joke: "I hope they're not going to the Broad River."

BOX TAPE

Never look a gift horse in the mouth, ran through my mind as I wandered about that house in Dorrigo. Everything was broken and put back together with box tape. Every little thing fell to pieces as you approached it. Mea went to turn on the TV. Not only did the knobs fall off, but the wobbly wicker table collapsed, and the TV nearly fell on her. We enrolled the girls in school and settled in to linger and enjoyed the area, which was fantastic.

The fence posts in the area were made from mahogany rose, a blood-red wood that weathered to the usual Australian grey. It was a useless wood of its time, as it could not be glued because of the oil it contained. But nowadays it can be treated with lime and glued with epoxy.

On the property I discovered a 14-inch square gate straining post made of this wood, which I souvenired. It was buried 30 inches in the ground and barely any sign of rot. I replaced it with a gum tree post.

When we left I took it with me, and made several mahogany rose harps. I played at a very rewarding concert in Bellingen, supporting Paul Adolphus, a Japanese Kyoto player, who also played several other instruments. He suggested we play a duet at the closing of the concert. "I couldn't do that!" I exclaimed. "I know nothing about Asian music."

"It's simple," he answered. "Play any notes on your four octaves – do, re, mi, fa, so, la, te, do. Just don't play fa or te. Or to make it simple, so as you can't make a mistake, change all your scales; do do, re, mi, mi, so, la, do, do. A five-note scale. All your ancient Celtic music was played like that, for example, 'Auld Lang Syne' and the 'Rocks of Bawn.' Gershwin only used the five-note scale." We played to a full house at Bellingen, and our duet brought the house down.

In Bellingen I was able to get guavas, which I grew up on in Cape Town. When we first arrived there kiwi fruit were 50 cents each; a month later they were 50 cents a bucket. The area had a problem in so much that the growing season was just too good, and everything ripened at once.

Strange things happened around the Stones'. I entered Peter's life again when I moved from Belfast to Dublin, or maybe he entered my life again. He was a well-turned-out cliché of an Englishman, who was out of place, living in Dublin, very guilt-ridden for all the sins the Black and Tans had perpetrated there. His next-door neighbour had arrived one evening to babysit the next-door's children, but the parents never returned home, and she had been receiving a cheque for expenses and a weekly income; that was two years ago. She seemed very happy with the arrangement, and she never heard from the parents ever again.

Peter faded off the radar until I phoned him and asked him if we could use his house in Dorrigo. He and Christina called in to see us when we arrived in Dorrigo. As luck would have it, our car had started acting up on that last thousand miles of the trip. I dismantled the carburettor. Then the same mishap occurred every 200 miles. When we reached our final destination of Dorrigo, the local garage man declared, "The condenser, mate. In the distributor. Six dollars for a new one, or leave it alone and let it cool down every two hours."

Peter and Christina blamed all breakages on bad karma. People actually broke things themselves with their own negative attitude, which said a lot for their own possessions--every one of them was broken.

NO ONE THERE

Every time we encountered a collection of motorcyclists Stef declares: "I hope they are not going to the Broad River." I am a motorcyclist myself, always have been. The strangest encounter I had with a motorbike was after I had advertised for a bike with a sidecar in Hobart. I only ever received one reply.

When we arrived at the address given on the phone, the bike was parked in the driveway. It was just what I fancied; lovely condition, black, 350 Honda. I was with a muso mate of mine. We knocked on the front door and looked ahead. When the door opened, there was no one to be seen. Pete and I looked at each other and then back to the door, which had been barely ajar, and now was fully opened. Below us stood one of the most beautifully faced men I have ever seen. A midget. John was his name, and we eventually became quite good friends. Stef agreed with me that he was extremely good-looking. He was also very interested in art. He owned the bike, and was going to have it altered so that he could operate it via a set of levers, which he could reach near his shoulders, as he had no arms, only fingers which emerged from his shoulders. He certainly had a "never say die" cavalier attitude; by his age I suspected thalidomide, a drug taken by pregnant women in the 1950s that had been presumed safe until their babies started dying.

I bought the bike, and Pete drove it home for me. I tried my very best to enjoy the sidecar, but to no avail. So I took the sidecar off, fired the bike up and headed down the highway. I came to a halt at the first intersection. The bike fell to the ground, as my legs weren't long enough to reach the ground, or the bike was too high; either way, I never bothered finding out. I put the sidecar back on and sold the whole disappointing assembly.

SCEPTICS

When living in Cygnet, I was an active member of the Australian Sceptics. In name, this sounds fun. We would look at any ridiculous claim – ghosts, ley lines, dousing, acupuncture, and we'd subject it to the most rigorous questioning possible. We once invited ten of the most highly acclaimed world dowsers to a public challenge. On stage were 12 firemen's hoses. Only one contained a flow of water. Also on stage were 20 empty milk cartons, one of which contained a bar of gold. We had a hidden agenda for publication. Each expert was allowed three go's. Thirty attempts; all failed. Likewise, they failed to locate which milk carton contained the bar of gold. Oh yes, the hidden agenda. What were the excuses why they all failed to discover the bar of gold or the hose with the flowing water? "No dousing ever works in the presence of sceptics," to, "Oh, I was having an off day." It was truly interesting, investigating such quackery as homeopathy, spoon bending (I've learnt that trick myself), reflexology – what a giggle that is. Truly the sceptics do nothing more than create philosophical debate. I left the sceptics, as they were a load of cruel killjoys with no room in their lives for that crap that we all enjoy so much.

PRINTS

We were now selling prints which I had made from three of my works; two typical landscapes, and a fantasy of the waterfront at Salamanca in Hobart. It was titled "The Night of the Tall Ships." I sent a set of these to my friend Billy in Belfast as a wedding present. This was his second marriage. I have never approved of getting married for a second time without a damn good reason, and I am very fussy as to what I will accept as a damn good reason. Getting married for the second time is for really bad learners. People who are easily intimidated, people who have no courage of their convictions, people who just don't have any balls. Stef and I were married for a jolly good reason, and it did not happen until the girls were 18 or 20 and were coming to England with us. They couldn't go on the dole without being British citizens, and for them to get British citizenship Stef and I had to be married. Now that's what I call a good reason for getting married. Lena, our youngest daughter, was witness on the register. Later that day Stef and I stood on either side of the river while Lena divorced us Gypsy-style after the incantation: "I divorce thee, I divorce thee."

KING ISLAND

"How much would you charge to fly to King Island* for the weekend to play your harp at my daughter's wedding?"

"Call back in half an hour and I'll let you know!"

I was used to strange requests at the market, mostly relating to weddings in unusual places or tourism, where to eat, where to visit, which pubs were the best. I should have charged them all commission.

The lady called back. "Well? How much?"

"Nothing," I replied, as I had always wanted to visit King Island. "But it will cost you a flight there, accommodation, and the use of a car for me, my wife and my ten-year-old daughter."

"Done!" she exclaimed.

Two weeks later she sent me a piece of sheet music that she wanted played for the congregational hymn. I don't read music, but Stef can bash out a tune on the recorder, and she can also read music. Of course I knew the tune, "Oh Lord of all Faithfulness," an old Irish air. Or to the Americans, "When First unto this Country."

When we boarded the plane to King Island there was no room for my harp, so another flight had to be arranged just to accommodate my harp. When I got to play that tune at the wedding no one knew it, so we had to teach the entire congregation how to sing it! It really was a super wedding; the food was great! And it was the first wedding ever to be performed in that that corrugated iron church.

The car we had the use of was a complete rust-bucket, as there are few cars on the island, and any that are there have to be maintained against the elements of continual salt in the air. Ninety percent of the year it is impossible to land a boat there. The landscape is totally flat, but on an elevated plateau, and is inundated with wild-tame turkeys. The trees grow at a sixty-degree angle.

The cream from the cows is the best in the world. Also, the cheese is the best of its type, so popular that it is usually sold out. But never mind, they import the milk now from the mainland, rather like those Aran sweaters that you get from Galway, Ireland! The label is stitched and made in Ireland, but the sweater is made in Japan.

* King Island is a flat island located off the northwest coast of Tasmania in the Roaring Forties of Bass Strait, surrounded by the wrecks of sailing ships, of which most are ancient.

Anderson's Coast

With kind permission, words and music by John Warner © 8/5/93

Now Bass Strait roars, like a great mill race,
And where are you, me Annie?
And the same moon shines, on this lonely place,
As shone one night, on me Annie's face.

Chorus:
But Annie dear, don't wait for me,
I fear I shall not return to thee;
There's naught to do, but endure my fate,
And watch the moon, the lonely moon,
Light the breakers, on wild Bass Strait.

We stole a vessel and all her gear,
And where are you, me Annie?
And from Van Diemen's we north did steer,
'Till Bass Strait's wild waves, wrecked us here.

(Chorus)

We fled the lash and the chafing chain.
And where are you, me Annie?
We fled hard labour and brutal pain,
And here we are, and here remain.

(Chorus)

We hail no ship though the time it drags,
And where are you, me Annie?
Our chain gang walk and government rags
All mark us down as Van Diemen's lags.

(Chorus)

And somewhere west Port Melbourne lies,
And where are you, me Annie?
Through swamps infested with snakes and flies,
The fool who walks there, he surely dies.
(Chorus)

SEXLESS MUSIC

Irish music. It's a love/hate relationship. Irish music is absolutely horrid, but only if it's played well. The squeaky, squawking, sexless rhythms, the absence of the middle register, being devoid of bass accompaniment, is lost on me. The continual, frantic rhythm transports one into a frame of mind that is mindless, I've been told. But I'm afraid I've got a life to be getting on with, and sex to do. I do love a good melody though, of which there seems to be an abundance in Northern Ireland. Such a tiz, when all that music is begged, borrowed or stolen. Some of the best Northern Irish melodies – the "Bard of Armagh," "Rout of the Blues," "The Street of Laredo" – all the same tune. Why didn't they stop inventing musical instruments when they discovered the harp? Accompaniment, middle range, melody top end, all in the one instrument; and rhythm, and that's not mentioning what the Paraguayans have done for the instrument. They can make it sound like a complete railway station. As for playing behind the beat, or that sacrilegious use of rubato or vibrato; Jesus wept—that's against the Ten Commandments. I was very flattered once when I was introduced as "The man who put sex back into playing the harp."

DIDDLY'S

I was now playing copious and repetitive amounts of Irish music, and was trying to work my way through the politically correct codes of ethics that seem to occur at the production of the Irish session. What follows is the list of some questions that perhaps some Irish session guru might be able to answer, or perhaps you might just like to add to the list of questions. Or maybe you just divide the list into diddly-dos and diddly-don'ts!

* Is the inner sanctum of the session made up by better musicians?
* Is there a second level made up of less competent musicians, and is this lot allowed to initiate tunes?
* Is the third layer of observers made up of pseudo homesick, crying-in-your-Guinness Irish ex-patriots?
* Are all young musicians to be put down at all costs when they want to get cocky and want to play in everything?
* Is the aim of each member of the inner sanctum to instantly strike up another tune at the end of the last one, giving no time or opportunity for a singer to burst into song?
* If the singer does edge his way in, is this the correct moment for all the musicians to put down their tools and head for the bar?
* Do the remaining musicians now scowl and get depressed until the singer has finished?
* Must the singer perform in the key of D or G, or if they are Scottish, are they allowed to sing in the key of A?
* Is the singer allowed to sing any song as long as it has been recorded by the Furey Brothers?
* Is the aim of the remaining musicians to all join in with the singer and drown him out?
* Are minor keys preferred, or is this because mistakes are easier to hide?
* Is the box player allowed to drown out other musicians?
* Is the rhythm section supposed to outnumber the melody section?
* How many bodhráns are allowed in one session?

- Must harmony and counter-melody be totally avoided?
- Is any attempt at arrangement to be abandoned?
- If a player is playing badly and louder than anyone else, is it correct etiquette to tell him to fuck off?
- Does a session always improve as the musicians get drunker?
- Is it really essential to tune up?
- How many paedophiles are allowed in a session?
- How loud does a banjo really get?
- Is the publican doing the musicians a favour by allowing the musicians to play in his pub, or are the musicians doing the publican a favour?
- Are all the musicians entitled to free Guinness even if there is no one listening?
- Is it taboo to play an electric bass even if it is solar powered?
- Does being Irish improve your chances of making any sense of the above?

SOME OF THE ANSWERS

If you wander into a pub where there is an Irish session in progress, beware; it is not as it may seem. How romantic and how quaint, you may think, and you are probably right; but I doubt it. Let us reflect for a moment, for there are several different kinds of sessions.

Session number one.

This is a group of very serious musicians of a very high standard and steeped in the Irish tradition. They would prefer to play somewhere that is private, away from the public eye, to enjoy their own music. The home kitchen is their preferred venue, or a quiet pub on a quiet night. If you are lucky enough to have wandered into such a session, keep yourself to yourself, and enjoy the music, and keep your conversation low. If you are a fellow musician, do NOT join in this session unless you are of an equal standard. If you are not, then philosophically your balls will be roasted; even if you do not have any.

Even if you are of an equal standard and insist on joining in, they will resent you like hell. Whatever you do, observe the Comhaltas (the mafia of Irish music) rules.

Session number two.

This is held in a pub where there are perhaps two or even three key musicians (perhaps they are even paid by the publican to be there) which are referred to as the inner circle. These guys are there to fire up the session and to encourage other musicians of an equal standard to join the inner circle. There is a middle-outer circle. These are the enthusiastic learners. You will usually find singers among this group. Should a singer strike up with a song, this is taken as a cue by the inner circle to down tools and head for the bar, returning the instant the singer has stopped. Usually the inner circle never pauses between tunes, as this is regarded as an invitation for a singer to burst into song. The outer-outer circle of this session are usually enthusiastic listeners.

Session number three.

If you are an observer, this session is the most enjoyable, and is definitely not as it would seem. There is an inner sanctum of very independent musicians. Several of the melody players--whistle, fiddle and banjo--actually know the tune, and heaven forbid that someone might wander off the melody and play harmony. So American! The middle circle has far too many guitar players playing rhythm, usually drowning out the melody. One guitar might even be playing the melody, which is a complete waste of time, as no one can hear what he is playing!

The middle circle is the domain of the bodhrán. Every newcomer to Irish music plays the bodhrán (supporters of the Republic of Ireland at the world cup football all play bodhráns!).

There are now six of these playing in the session; one bodhrán under these conditions is one too many.

Any dead animal whose skin has been stretched over a round box is going to be extremely noisy, especially one with strings attached, like the banjo. One banjo only in a session, please!

This session has an outer circle consisting entirely of singers. Their duty is to talk throughout the session when it is not their turn to sing. They also know the entire social structure of this session, and are prepared to enlighten the casual observer about all the in-fighting and all the shenanigans that go on in the session.

And you thought that they were all just having a good time!

HEAVY

A heart attack prompted me to locate closer to Salamanca Market, meaning that I would not have to travel so far with my heavy harp and boxes of CDs. The studio we rented was huge, and would allow us to monthly convert into a folk club which we called The Attic. The Attic ran for two years. We invited any folk singers that were on tour visiting the mainland to perform, along with a supporting act that was local, usually nothing to do whatsoever with folk music. My girls are all brilliant cooks and bakers, so at interval we sold and served a huge variety of cakes. Our audience were solicited from clients that had purchased paintings from us. We served wine, but no beer. I personally welcomed everyone through the door. I think the formula must have been just quite right, as we performed to full houses at every event, and usually sold out weeks before a performance. I only performed there once myself, when I presented a concert on the Lagan Canal in Belfast. Incidentally, on the nautical engineering charts of the period for the Lagan Canal, the Irish mile is different from the English mile.

THE TASMANIAN DEVELOPMENT AUTHORITY
(A now non existant department)

We returned from a 3-week trip to Holland to hear people talking about me appearing in full-colour magazine advertisements promoting sport, the arts and the Symphony Orchestra of Tasmania.

To have a full-page ad promoting myself would have given me a great buzz, but the ad promoted aspects of my persona that were totally wrong! There was a link from the advertisement to boxing in my past, which I was totally against. The symphony orchestra was certainly not my choice of music, and I was opposed to and in constant conflict with the established art scene.

They had used a fantastic photo of me which came from a photographer who had created a photographic library of prominent Tasmanian artists.

I immediately enquired who had given them permission to use my persona and this photograph in their advertisement.

"Why, you did!"

"No! I DID NOT!"

I asked the department to write to me as to when and where I had given my permission to use my image and my persona.

Now the solicitor general was brought into the fiasco, giving me dates and the location of my consent. On those dates I wasn't even in the country; I was in Holland, sitting beside a canal.

The solicitor general replied that we didn't actually have a meeting; my consent was given over the phone, along with my approval to use the photograph. I enquired how could I have approved a photograph over the phone?

The reply to that one, still from the solicitor general, was that I knew what they were doing.

On advice from solicitors, I continued writing for an answer. The only possible answer was that they had used two other artists, who had received huge arts grants from the Tasmanian Development Authority, and as part of their acceptance of the grants, their persona could be used by the TDA for promotion; but I had never received such a grant.

The advertising agency who handled the TDA's account had made a HUGE blue! They assumed that my success as an artist and musician was the result of a huge grant from the TDA. My last communication to the department was to reiterate that I was a self-made man, I'd never had a grant from them.

With solicitor's fees, and after flogging a dead horse, I ran out of money and steam. The solicitor general's steamrolling squashed the guts out of me, and I lost interest in Tasmania.

People would enquire of me, "I thought that you hated boxing?"

"What about classical music? I thought that stuff bored you to death? And you told me that institutionalized artists were a bunch of wankers?"

Now it's embarrassing to go back to Tasmania for a holiday, but I still love the place. I presented the case to the ombudsman, whose written reply confirmed that I had a solid case for complaint, even though the ombudsman's letter was also steamrolled by the solicitor general.

Whenever I get homesick for Tasmania, I just think on this issue and the feeling vanishes, and I cry.

STOUT IRISH MEN

Although I'm not a drinker, I do have my own local. It's the New Sydney Hotel in Hobart. Gary, the publican, was a publican after my own heart, and didn't allow drunks into his pub. This became our family watering hole, and was a safe haven for all our girls under the watchful eye of Gary. The entire walls were full of my larger paintings, and for quite some time acted as a permanent display of my work. Several paintings he actually owned. One in particular was a pattern of cloth-capped men, all drinking Guinness. Its title was "Stout Irish Men."

I received an email from a gentleman from London who had called into the bar. His question was simple, "What do I have to do to own a similar painting?"

My reply was, "What do you have to offer?"

His reply came back, "A house in Spain and the use of my car."

"Done! Three weeks, and I'll do the painting over there." Two weeks later, we were in Spain.

I had read that Spain has the highest number of female millionaires in Europe because the girls in the family had always inherited the useless sandy soil on the seafront, which was unusable for farming. Now they'd sold it all off to the English millionaires seeking water frontage.

That was a whirlwind of a trip, and an introduction to the Continent. It started by drinking our host's supply of liquors. I can't stand alcohol, but in liquor you can't taste it, and I do love the feeling of being drunk. When we had sobered up in the morning, we drove away up into the mountains and travelled for hours through spaghetti western countryside. It was dark when we arrived at Ronda, where we booked into a hotel and went for an evening stroll. We were walking down the main road, which was fully illuminated by the Christmas lights. Suddenly the illumination came to an abrupt end, and our way was barred by a high cast-iron fence; ahead of us, only blackness. The experience was mind-blowing, and to be cherished. In the distance we saw specks of light, but the perspective was all wrong. Then I looked down and my legs turned to jelly, and my testicles started to creep. We were standing on the edge of a 20-mile-high cliff, and below were the tiny lights of farms. I have always avoided reading travel books, and don't like to know anything about a place that I should visit; now I was being punished for being ignorant.

We did enjoy some wonderful music in Spain, and bought a tape recording from a group of 12 folk musos, which I have played over and over until it stretched. Tape recordings had long ceased to exist, but these guys were years behind the times. I learnt some fabulous harp tunes from that tape.

All the food we experienced was poor. It has been reinvented by the Spanish now living in Oz. I did bring back with me a bandora, a 10-string musical instrument rather like a large mandolin, which I passed on to the leader of Arauco Libre, our local South American group. I had designed an album cover for them using a painting that I had done of their group. It is still their best seller.

KEYSTONE COPS

My daughter Miche and I had just come out of the bank on the corner of Elizabeth Street and Liverpool Street. Across the road against the wall was a rough-looking lad dressed in agro gear. A policeman had him in one of those throat holds. By one arm he was calling on his mobile phone for help from the station that was 200 meters down the road. "We'll stop and watch this," I said to Miche.

We were on a one-way road. Soon a Black Maria arrived, coming to a halt on our side, the wrong side of the road. The two police officers got out of the van and rushed across the road to assist their comrade. Whoops! They hadn't put the handbrake on in the van, and it slowly started rolling backwards towards their police station. Back ran one of the officers, rescuing the van just in time before it crashed into another car. While he came back up towards the traffic lights, the two other officers dragged the poor confused lad to the back of the Black Maria, wrenched the doors open and literally threw him into the back of the van, slamming the door violently behind him.

The car took off at a great rate of knots, turning sharply up Elizabeth Street up the hill. The back doors of the van both swung open and the young lad was thrown violently up Liverpool Street, the van long gone. Much later I phoned up the police to enquire about the welfare of that young man. Was he hurt or not? They denied that the incident ever happened.

"OK," I said. "This incident was witnessed by at least 100 people, and if I am not assured that that young man is unhurt, my next phone call will be to the *Mercury* newspaper."

"Er, give me a minute, sir," the policeman replied. He came back to the phone minutes later, very sheepishly, and apologised. "You were right, I knew nothing about that." I hope my phone call stopped the police from giving the poor lad too hard a time.

Chapter Ten

The Barge

Where I learn to become a bold sea captain, of a murder of parsons, to have sell-out exhibitions, knowledge of Ireland, about South African junk, and about being blind.

BARGING AWAY!

The Peter Pan syndrome had kicked in; you know, that feeling that you never should have grown up. Actually, I often wondered when I could refer to myself as grown-up. The closest that I have ever come to this is when my mum died. You don't really understand until your parents die just how much you relied on the idea of them solving your problems, even though you might never have presented your problems to them. While they were alive there was always the possibility they would comfort you and dissolve all your hurts. When they are dead, the buck stops with you. You never really get any more grown-up than this.

Among my Peter Pan ideas was being the captain of a barge. This really appealed. I have never fancied life on the open sea, but I did like boats. The idea of living on a boat and never being more than ten feet from the shore, in water no deeper than thirty inches really appealed. Stef also fancied this idea, and as someone once said to me, Stef would follow me to live in a hollow log! Actually, I would follow her to live in a log! Ever in search of new adventures, we decided to sell our house in Cygnet. The house sold rather fast, quicker than we were prepared to go to England. Lena was at primary school, Miche and Mea had not quite finished college, and Sunita was now married and living with her marine engineer. We had to rent a house for a few months. This was my second involvement with a property previously owned by a religious nutter. The house we rented was furnished, and what did I find behind the piano? The inevitable collection of dirty books!

Stef, Lena and I flew to England ahead of Miche and Mea. We had studied all the magazines and books on the inland waterways of England. The canals in Ireland were nothing of note; the locks there were inoperable, and the canals themselves were silted up with supermarket trolleys and bicycles. The canals around Dublin were dangerous because of the hooligan kids who threw stones at the barges as they passed under bridges.

I had lived in England before. Once as a small boy my grandmother had taken me and my sister with her to stay with my Auntie Dora. I have always enjoyed England. It has the lush, sensual landscape of Ireland, really feminine stuff. The English not only tolerated but treasured their eccentrics; was I not an eccentric? What's more, an Australian/Irish eccentric. Ireland brags about her writers and artists, but I recollect that they all fled to England and France. My childhood heroes were all Brits; King Arthur, Robin Hood. But my current and greatest heroes have lived in England; Isambard Kingdom Brunel and Thomas Telford, the great engineers that built England's historic steel ships, bridges and canals.

We had chosen a marina just north of London to start looking at barges. As we passed over our first two canal bridges that approached the marina, I enquired from Stef what she thought of the canal. "What canal?" Stef was like that; she hadn't noticed the two hump-back bridges that we had passed over, and she certainly she had missed the canal! "Is that all the size the canals are?" she enquired, as we passed over the next hump-back bridge. "Surely 20 feet is bigger than that!" she exclaimed. While we were in Australia, the size of the canals had grown out of all proportion.

The cliché that a picture is worth a thousand words is a myth. A picture misses out on one essential element; no matter how beautiful or romantic the inside of an English or Irish pub may appear, the atmosphere is saturated with the centuries of smells coming from the toilets and the presence of smoke that has seeped into the beams from the days of Sir Walter Raleigh. As we looked around the barges it was depressing, because of the smell of tobacco and food-saturated furnishings. We have since discovered that the English/Irish deplore ventilation! We had forgotten just how people in Australia had ceased to smoke in restaurants, and how people were now not smoking in their homes.

There were lots of factors in choosing a barge (of course, they were really not barges but narrow boats; but I shall continue to call them barges, as I refuse to be the captain of a narrow boat. I was the captain of a barge!). Yes, the factors; was it an all-steel boat, or a steel hull with wooden cabin? Was the floor wood, or was it of the older iron riveted boats? Then there were the variety of engines; diesel or petrol? And was the cooking by gas? Gas is always a danger in boats. The shorter the boat, the harder it was to handle. Too long, and it was limited to a specific canal, as some locks did not take boats over 65 feet long. The draft was limited on some canals to 28 inches. Was there a certificate of compliance? This meant that the boat had been inspected and approved of by the proper authorities for gas, 240-volt and 12-volt DC. The whole system was administered by British Waterways, and these guys were the canal mafia! We went from marina to marina looking at all sorts of fit-outs, but most of them were really badly fitted out, or a confirmation of the British concept of design, such as cover every flat surface with floral Formica or wallpaper. We had been avoiding private advertisement in *Waterways* magazine as they were dotted all over the countryside, but now we were so disillusioned with what the marinas had to offer that we decided to re-think the private advertisements. The first one we responded to was close by, so we decided to give it a go. We called the owner. Right away I was put off by the thought of managing the Lister HP3 antique engine. But the guy sounded so jolly, and he was prepared to drive out and meet us and take us to see his boat. When we arrived at the mooring we walked past about 12 boats, none of which we particularly liked. Eventually we approached a superb boat and our luck was in; this was it! She was the classic barge (narrow boat); black hull, green and red cabin with yellow trim, shiny brass air vents on the roof and yes, the traditional barge pole with neatly rolled ropes on the roof of the cabin. The tiller was brass and recently polished. As we stepped down into the cabin, both Stef and I gave a knowing look at each other, this was it; there was nothing pseudo about this boat. The Baltic pine lining inside was real. There was nothing plastic, and all the fittings were genuine. It was 70' long with a long corridor that led to three bedroom cabins, a toilet room with a porta potty and a bathroom with a full-size bath that had to be manually pumped out, as it was below water level. The engine at the back was a magnificent-looking item, shiny new paintwork and all the brass work neatly polished. It was a genuine Lister HP3 with triple nipples! And the barge had two inches of insulation throughout. So why was it being sold so much cheaper than all the rest? We never really did find out why, although there was a minor problem with the engine, as she leaked oil from one of the back bearings. But it never really gave us any trouble except when I came to sell the barge. I had to remove a lot of oil from the bilges.

We finalised the deal within a week. When we had withdrawn our money from the bank that we had transferred our money to electronically from Australia, we were driving around with about 60,000 dollars hard cash in our hands.

PETHIDINE

Two miles down the road from the bank, while I was driving the car, I got an excruciating pain in my back at waist level to the right hand side. We got directions to the nearest hospital. I was in dreadful pain, but I knew what it was. It had happened before. A fucking kidney stone was passing down the urethra (apparently this is the maximum pain that the male can stand before passing out). The doc knocked me out with pethidine while Stef went to the car park to cry, clutching the sixty thousand dollars in her hand! We were in a hire car, and she wasn't game to drive it in England. A very helpful taxi driver took her and Lena to a cheap nearby pub for the night. Next morning when I awoke in hospital, none of the nurses would tell me a thing except to say that I was to have an X-ray that morning. I had to plead with the radiologist to tell me if the kidney stone had left the urethra. She wouldn't open her mouth, but she did nod. I was shown back to the ward, where I put on my clothes and left the hospital, followed by a nurse telling me that I couldn't just walk out of the hospital without seeing the doctor. I did! I sat in the car and waited for Stef to arrive. About three days after we had taken possession of the barge, I pissed out the stone. Marvellous things to look at under a microscope; razor-sharp, full of hooks and barbs!

After some preliminary lessons on how to handle the barge, and with our food and blankets stored, we headed off down the canal. We knew that our first lock was not too far ahead. This was a dramatic moment, a fall in the level of the canal of six inches. This particular lock must have been the smallest fall in any canal in the world. It was the end of summer, and we were mooring for a day or two at a town called Brewood, which I remember well for a shop there that sold the best cheese that I'd ever tasted. It was transported from a small island off the north coast of Scotland. I have never come across it again.

I walked around the village and went into the local church and got chatting with the vicar. He showed me a secret room from Oliver Cromwell's time. This room housed a family when they went to church, and there was a tunnel in the wall from which the family could view the priest in possession of the host.

The main reason for stopping in Brewood was to have a cratch cover made for the front of the barge (a canvas, tent-like structure that prevents water splashing from the lock gates into the front entrance of the boat). Also, to prolong the event that lay ahead. It was a T junction, and I wasn't really sure how to make a left-hand turn. From what side of the canal should I make the turn? It ended up that I did it all wrong, and fucked it up completely, and ran aground on the far bank! After much panic, we were off again. Our moods were not elated, as earlier on in the day, an English prat with a double chin at the back of his neck commented from the stern of his Tupperware (fibreglass) boat that our handling of the barge as we had pulled away from our mooring at

Brewood had been the worst he had ever seen in his life! Luckily Stef had been steering at this point!

We were on the Shropshire Union Canal that travels in a circle around the five counties. This circle was used by a lot of bargees who were on the dole. This enabled them to put in their dole form in from a different office each week, making it almost impossible for officials to check on them. Also, you were never too far from moonlight employment while you were collecting the dole. A lot of bargees on this canal also owned cars. We had only been on the canal for about a week when we discovered that it was almost impossible to travel while the wind was blowing. The front of the barge had to be steered towards one bank, while the stern dragged along the other. The canals were not generally in a good state of repair, and only the middle was deep enough to navigate. This meant continually running aground, as the bends were too tight; but soon we had the knack of things.

Every stop that we made was usually punctuated by something interesting. The canal is the back road through England. At one stop we moored our boat and walked down an overgrown country lane. We were approached by four vicars who looked as if they had stepped out of a Bronte novel; black clobber, wide-brim hats and tight leggings. "G'day," I addressed them in my Aussie accent. "There must be a collective noun for you guys; what is it? A murder of parsons?" There was no reply. So much for the English humour, I thought. (I have told this story to several Australian parsons, vicars, whatever, and none of them found it particularly amusing.)

We were not aimlessly navigating the canal, we did actually have a destination in mind. This was the Llangollen Canal in Wales, where we were going to be joined by our other daughter, Miche. Mea had already joined us at Stone, where we'd stopped for quite some time while we waited for the arrival of our luggage; two trunks, one of which contained my harp. Stone, I had been under the illusion, was where Stone's Green Ginger Wine originated from. The second lock out of Stone was coincidently called the Mea-ford lock.

We settled down to routine barge life. We would travel about six or seven hours, and then moor up for the rest of the day, catching a bus into the nearest village or city, and returning to the barge late evening.

Sometimes we would travel the canal for days only to find that we were eight bus stops closer to the same town that we had visited the day before. The canal followed the level contours of the land, having to take the longest route from A to B. By now we were beginning to look like regular bargees; ingrained coal dust from stoking the fire for heat, chapped hands from untangling crap and plastic bags from around the propeller, never having enough water to keep yourself clean, and a permanent smell of diesel. As a consequence, fellow bargees were able to recognise each other at the pubs that we would stop at along the way. Conversation was easily made. We were now experts at handling the locks, and had acquired the dexterous agility of avoiding the dog crap along the tow path. The tow path was the last refuge for the dog owner; every man and his dog in England, literally, walked the canals. We would refer to a walk along the tow path as the "dog poo shuffle." Stef wasn't really comfortable steering the barge, so she would hop ashore to operate the locks, sometimes opening twenty locks a day! There were endless skills that we acquired (never to be used again). The history and the endless tales and songs of the canals would fill volumes of books; we and our children have endless tales to tell.

Autumn was approaching, and we were headed for Ellesmere, where there was a basin, somewhere we could moor for a long stay. We had made friends with the owners of several barges, all heading finally for the Llangollen Canal where we were all to spend the winter, as British Waterways closed all the canals in winter to work on the locks.

LENA

Lena, our youngest, had made friends with a family who had a daughter the same age. They were both doing distance education. Lena's work was sent back to Australia for marking. A wonderful couple, hippies, travelled in a really good riveted iron boat that they had salvaged from the deep side of a canal. The boat had been abandoned. They had a baby son, who later fell into the canal and was tragically drowned.

It was at Ellesmere where a lady's second-youngest child fell into the canal. The mother was unable to jump in after him as she had another baby strapped on her back. Stef jumped into the freezing water and saved the child. She lost her new glasses! Everyone dried off over the fire in the barge. The lady, I remember, was not particularly grateful; she was rather stony-faced, and she certainly was not in shock. For quite some time I was worried about Stef, as the canal in certain areas contains the bacteria from the urine of rats that causes Weil's disease.

Mea was now with us. She had flown in from Melbourne, and we had all travelled down to London to meet her. Mea was a natural on the barge but I had expected this, as she has very innate capabilities. Within hours she knew the exact feel on the tiller, and understood the exact order in which to start the complex Lister engine; pump diesel into header tank, check cooling water, check oil level in gravity-fed sump, grease and tighten all nipples, press starter button, release when the massive flywheel was in full motion. And the locks were a breeze for her. I now had relief from those endless hours alone at the tiller.

Couples who hire canal boats usually end up fighting in the first few hours for the simplest of reasons. The person at the tiller at the stern has an engine thumping away in their ears, usually the husband (the captain!). The low-life, second mate (the wife!) is up front of the boat, usually 70 feet away, where all is serenely quiet. She is talking pleasantly to him, and he can't hear a fucking word she says. She accuses him of ignoring her, etc., etc., etc.!! You know the rest.

Of course I was painting on the barge. Our bedroom doubled as a studio through the day. The work that I was doing was posted back to the gallery that I was using in Hobart. The last two exhibitions that I'd had with this gallery were a complete sell-out. It was the monies from these two exhibitions that were funding our trip, although we had paid for the barge with the sale of our house. We had by now travelled through many towns and cities, and at times actually went through factories. We were very versed in all the canal lingo. We even knew what a *gongoozler* was; that's some bastard that stands watching you operate the locks, never offering to help, and with an air of total disapproval. We were well on our way to Llangollen. We were moored for quite some time in a basin just before the Pontcysyllte Aqueduct. This is the major aqueduct built by Thomas Telford; seven feet wide, a three-foot-deep water trough, suspended miles in the air, a sheer drop on one side and a three-foot-wide tow path on the other.

By now Miche, our older daughter, had arrived from Melbourne. She had joined us at Chirk, the first village along the canal as you enter Wales. We had been moored just at the Chirk side of the tunnel, again built by Telford. Here there was another aqueduct and another magnificent bridge all spanning the river Dee, all built by Telford.

Mea had been working in Oswestry, a fifteen-minute bus ride away. She was sewing crotches in jeans. Winter had set in. She was 17 now, and an Aussie. She was leaving for work in the dark, and when the poor girl got home it was dark. Like all people in those latitudes, they rarely see the sun in winter until the weekends! We had bought a dog for Lena. The kennel I made sat on the tow path beside the canal.

NEVER LEARN

To escape the barge that was now locked in ice at Chirk Bank near the Welsh border, we bought a camper van to tour Ireland. But first we were taking the barge to Llangollen over the feared Pontcysyllte Aqueduct. I was terrified of this aqueduct. Built by Thomas Telford (the bastard), it was an iron trough, eight feet wide, filled with water, hundreds of miles in the air! I am terrified of heights! Stef never quite believed me until we first crossed over it on foot, wheeling our waste crap behind to the disposal depot on the other side of the aqueduct. Halfway across my legs turned to jelly. I had to lie flat on the ground and crawl back to the barge. When the time came to eventually take the barge across this aqueduct, our daughters Miche and Mea stood on the rear platform, steering, dancing, and laughing their heads off. To the right, a thirty-inch-wide tow path; to the left, 6 inches of water, and 4 inches of iron rail. Below, a hundred-and-fifty-foot drop! Inside the barge, me! A quivering mess!

SALAMANCA COLLECTION

The gallery that I had been using in Tasmania were amazed by my two exhibitions. They had been complete sell-outs, with 30 paintings in each exhibition. I was now working on the barge for my third exhibition with this same gallery. I had by now sent 25 paintings to the framer that I was using. It was at this time that I received a letter from the gallery about the depressed state of the art-buying market in Tasmania, and the gallery owner was insisting that I lower my prices by at least 15 percent. I had been exhibiting long enough now to know that this was the usual panic mode that some galleries go into when they don't think they are going to make as much out of you as they did from your previous exhibition. I wrote to the gallery, trying to put them at their ease on this point, but they were insistent on the 15 percent reduction. I have always been of the mind-set that I never reduced the prices of my work, and while I could afford it, it was better to withhold the work and exhibit at a more favourable time. So I ignored the fear tactic from the gallery, and asked my framer to hold my work until my return to Oz. There were other strings to my bow, or should I say, my harp. I knew that I was able to support the family when things were lean on the art scene. I continued to work in the confined space of our barge. We were now moored at Llangollen in Wales, and were starting to suffer from cabin fever. Miche and Mea had their own agenda and had moved on to Belfast, where they were to meet up with a friend of theirs to explore their Irish roots (which I do believe they did quite a bit of!).

CAMPER VAN ONE

Living daily in two feet of water has a strange effect on you. Imagine you are sitting having dinner at your table with your family, engaged deeply in conversation over a beautiful spread of dinner, when through the window, which is at waist level, out of nowhere the enormous head and neck of a swan makes a snatch at the grandest portion of food on the table. That sort of thing can frighten the shit out of you!

Obviously we had learnt nothing about cabin fever, as we purchased a camper van, cabin fever on wheels. But this was a great vehicle, and gave us liberty from the canal. The car allowed us the freedom to visit more folk clubs and dances, and we had been bitten by the bug of pub quizzes. It was while driving home from one of these folk club nights that I noticed that the headlights of oncoming cars were very flared in my left eye, which started to get worse over the coming months.

I had brought some of my paintings with me to Ireland, and I was in search of a decent gallery to show my work. On the way out of Belfast in the Mourne Mountains around Newcastle, I was sketching when a helicopter appeared over my shoulder behind me. They were close enough to see my drawings with the naked eye. They hovered for quite some time. I held up my drawings, which they inspected with their field glasses, maybe even took a picture. I flicked through the pages. One of them gave me the thumbs up, and they moved off!

Later that day we crossed into the south of Ireland. When we got to Dundalk, we were pulled over by the garda, where a very rude policeman and policewoman abused us for not having our daughter at school.

"Want to test her on her knowledge of Ireland?" They declined.

Now, what is a decent gallery? Some galleries show only contemporary work, and some galleries only show exhibitions. Some galleries must turn out a new exhibition every three to four weeks, some galleries are linked with framers. The would-be exhibitor is usually guaranteed to sell five works; one to his mummy, and one to Granny! Out of 25 works there is bound to be one gem. He is bound to sell that. There is always the idiot who will buy anything, and Auntie Gladys is bound to buy another. The gallery owner is always in front, even if the exhibition is a flop. But the poor artist is left with his framing bill (gallery possibly linked with the framers), 50 percent of the postage, invitations and wine and cheese, then the gallery's 40 percent. Unless you have sold more than 50 percent of your work, the gallery never wants to see you again! These galleries rarely sell ongoing work, they are specializing in exhibitions. This is not what I call a good gallery. I need a gallery that will continually sell my work, i.e. a gallery that has space for exhibitions, and also space for their in-house artists. I had heard that such a gallery existed in Galway, Kenny's Gallery, so it was to Galway that we headed. I wanted to get the painting that I had with me framed as soon as possible. Being used to traveling long distances in Australia, Galway appeared sooner on the horizon than I had expected. I had been promising myself to stop for a piss for the last half-hour, but now here we were, in the middle of Galway. I parked the car at Eyrie Square and Stef, Lena and I looked for the toilets. Percy had been pointed at the porcelain, and I was back outside waiting for Stef and Lena.

I stopped a passerby to ask if there was a music shop nearby. He gave directions and headed off down the road. He hesitated, and then spun around on one foot. He spoke just as Stef and Lena joined me. "Is that a New Zealander's bush hat that you're wearing?"

"No, it's Australian," I replied.

"You wouldn't be George Callaghan?" he asked. I replied in the affirmative as he rocked back on his heels and put both hands in his pockets, fiddled with his keys and change with one hand, and his balls with the other!

"Brian Merry!" I exclaimed.

He was a bloke that I had worked with when I'd first lived in Dublin in the advertising game. Twenty-five years away from Ireland, and the first guy I spoke to, I knew! I had promised to visit him in Dublin as I left for home, but we had run out of time. We had been walking to our car that was parked at Stephen's Green to catch the ferry back then, and he had stepped out of a bus queue that we were passing, exclaiming, "You were to come and visit me, you fecker!"

Brian had now given us directions to Kenny's. In fact, he had just come from there, as he had delivered some paintings for his wife, who was an artist. I was very apprehensive as I approached the building; in fact, I was downright disappointed. Kenny's turned out to be a book shop. Now, I don't really do words, especially if there are lots of them in a book. I've got to have lots of pictures. Everything that I have learnt has come from comics or folk songs, and most recently from videos and TV. Kenny's Gallery? A book shop? Soldiering on, we wandered through the continual display of books. Stef was in heaven; she's a librarian (swat!). I caught a glimpse of a painting through a door. I ventured through into what was a marvellous gallery. We had entered the building through the book shop door; the other street was the access to the art gallery. When Stef joined me, we strolled through the floors of paintings. The bottom floor was used for current exhibitions, while the floors above were displays of ongoing work. This was exactly what I was looking for, the Holy Grail of galleries. On the ground floor gallery there was a classic, jovial Irishman talking on the phone. He was shifting his weight from one foot to the other in a continual rocking motion. You could cut his Galway accent with a knife it was so thick, and he gave a gentle cough at the end of each sentence. When he hung up the phone I introduced myself, and asked if he had time to look at my work. Tom Kenny is one of Ireland's gentle men, with the gift of the gab twice blessed by kissing the Blarney stone. He was bowled over by my work; or was that the blarney? He was delighted to have my work, and he put me in touch with his framer. He asked me to do a drawing in his visitor's book, a properly bound sketch book. He opened it at a special blank page. On the opposite page was a drawing done by Brian Mooney, the very Brian Mooney who busks with his guitar in the mall in Launceston, Tassie. I had met Brian twice before. He had sung around the traps in Sydney, when I was singing with the Leprechauns, and we had also met on the ferry that crosses from Melbourne to Tasmania when I first came to live in the Island State. Since then we had sung together at many sessions. Brian has the clever trick of not tuning his guitar in concert pitch. This means that no other musician can play along with him.

It was in Galway that I became aware of something unusual. I was in the gallery on the day that we left. My paintings were now hanging on the wall, and I was examining the workmanship on the frames. Tom Kenny was talking to a lady from Switzerland in the background. He was telling her how he would introduce her to some Irish painter. There was an awkward silence, then Tom spoke louder: "Sure, George, I'm talking about yourself!" I had been ignoring him as he was talking about an Irish painter. It was strange to realize that yes, I was an Irish painter! I had always thought of myself as a Tasmanian or an Australian painter.

The trip to Galway had been a complete success. I had made contact with what I had considered to be a real gallery. We were now heading to Belfast via the coast around the north shore and down the east coast to Belfast, where I was sketching at every stop.

This was really my first trip around Ireland, and I needed drawings to work from for work that I was planning to send back to Kenny's. Of course we were cooking and sleeping in our mobile home, which was parked in the middle of the road where we had abandoned it because of the snow. That night Lena was introduced to the malady of the Tourette's Syndrome. It was a drunk on his way back home. We could hear him approach the van, getting louder as he passed, and finally fading off into the distance. The conversation he was having with himself had every obscenity punctuated with a double fuck!

Billy Longridge

On arrival in Belfast, I looked up Billy, one of the singing Leprechauns from the old days in Oz. He had long since moved back to Belfast to take up the religion of psychotherapy (question, can you be a Catholic physiotherapist or a Protestant psycho therapist?) which he had studied for five years getting a degree in thinkology. I mentioned the dilemma that I was having with my eyes, and that I would be returning sooner than expected to Oz.

My next stop was to my sister's whom I loved dearly especially since she was the reason that I was never bullied at school as she'd bash any bastard that threatened me. However she couldn't cope with the situation that I was having with my eyes. This manifested itself when Billy called around to my sister's house while we were there. He had good news; a surgeon friend of his would operate on my eye in three weeks' time, and the whole procedure would only take two weeks. My sister saw red. "Your father had to have that operation and he had to wait in the queue for two years! We don't do that sort of thing over here. We don't jump the queue. And if you're going to do that sort of thing, you can go back to your bloody Australia now! And you can keep your money; we don't want any of your money!" Money? What the fuck was she talking about?

Joan, my sister, lived in a brick house where all the windows were brand-new, plastic and double-glazed. They had just been replaced free by the council. Her bathroom was being completely refitted because the council had found a hairline crack in the sink, and next year the kitchen would have a complete new fit-out. And I knew for a fact that the electric meter had been short-circuited. All this lifestyle! Money? We didn't even have a flush loo at home!

My sister calmed down, but my father's Napoleon attitude had left his mark on her. In many ways my sister had actually become just like my father. One of my nieces' children had gone on a school exchange to Canada, and my sister had kept her in her place by continual putting her down on every exciting episode that she recalled about her trip. "We will have none of those new-fangled ideas in this house!" she would growl.

My father's house now stood empty, as he was in a retirement home. None of the family would go near the house, not even to clean it up for sale. It had become a shrine and a place of gloom. Stef and I had a spare day so we volunteered not only to clean the house, but to remove what was supposedly in the attic. The house really wasn't a problem, it only needed superficial cleaning, but the attic? How did this 70-year-old guy manage to get such a clinking clanking collection of collagenous junk through a two-foot hole in the ceiling? Actually, none of it was junk. Most of it was the tools that he had brought from South Africa; a pillar drill, a bench saw, a bench planer. These were all American tools, Delta, superior in quality than I have ever seen in Ireland or Australia. There was also a six-foot screw cutting lathe mounted on the wall of the chimney, and of course his hand tools. It took the entire day and into the night to dismantle all this gear and lower it all onto the landing at the top of the stairs. It was my intention, if no one needed them, to ship them all back to Australia. Sentimentally I slipped a micrometre into my pocket.

ORMEAU ROAD

We then returned to our tour down the Ards Peninsula, where I continued sketching. We crossed Strangford Lough on the ferry and returned to Belfast, and spent some time with Miche and Mea, who were now living in a house with their Aussie friend, Jo, just behind the Ormeau bakery. The bakery made just the greatest bread that you would ever eat, especially their potato farls. I have tried making potato farls but they are always as tough as native hens' drumsticks! The girls had now a few fellows in tow, hard men they were. Naive Aussie chicks blown away by a Belfast accent, "Ousaboutyusthen?" I think that it's Mr. Paisley's accent that gets him his followers!

We made our farewells to the girls. There was a stop-off at Fusco's, or was it Desano's, for an ice cream. We called in to see my sister to say goodbye to my nieces and nephews, and also to advise my sister that I would be making arrangements to ship my father's tools back to Oz. She had sold the whole fucking lot to a junk man for 150 pounds! There was five thousand pounds' worth of irreplaceable gear there! I had no right to enforce my values on these people, so with controlled calmness we made our goodbyes, and made our way back to Dun Laoghaire to catch the ten pound return ferry to England and our barge. As bold as brass I showed my ticket at the counter.

"This ticket was only valid for a special one-weekend offer over a month ago," said the official.

"Yes, I know. This entire venture has cost me a fortune. First I get on a ferry that can't sail in rough weather (was this one made in Tasmania?). I'm left stranded in Ireland because again the ferry can't make the return trip because of the rough weather. We all had to fly home, leaving our car behind, and now we had to fly back to pick up our bloody van!" I replied in my strongest Aussie accent. As sweet as Chinese gooseberries he replied, "Drive aboard, sir!" This was better than the 10-pound fare to Australia I had paid 25 years ago. Mind you, the bastards didn't give me a return fare then!

During this trip we got snowed in, in Leenane, a seaside-lakeside village on the west coast of Ireland, surrounded by steep hills. This is where the movie *The Field* was filmed.

We were sitting around in the pub, chatting to the locals. In the corner was a group of four or five young people sitting on their own. After quite some time I detected their accents; they were Aussies. Of course I went over and after the usual introductory chat, I asked how they were enjoying Ireland.

"They're not very friendly!" they answered, almost in one accord. I was taken aback. I have the most confused accent that you have ever heard, and although people in Ireland can't understand a bloody word that I say, most times it works to my advantage. Irish people, like most people around the world, are genuinely pleasant to strangers.

The penny dropped! "You guys are traveling in a group! You don't need company! Divide yourselves up into two's or one's when you arrive somewhere different. A bunch of Aussies together; you don't need to make friends! Come over and meet these two guys that we have just met. They're from Trinity University, up here measuring the rainfall. Seems like they have to re-apply for their own jobs on a weekly basis." The way of the world?

CATARACTS

I was carrying with me a letter regarding cataracts in my eyes that might give me trouble in about two years' time. The letter was from my optician, Paul McCartney in Hobart, to an associate of his in England, should I have any trouble sooner. Eight months down the track and it was almost impossible to drive at night. A month later, and it was as if I was looking through six layers of polythene.

We sold the barge and headed back to Oz. We had barely used 44 gallons of diesel in our Lister HP3 engine in one year. The engine was a real Technicolor collector's item, and since the barge was a Hancock and Lane, we'd actually made money on the sale. We are now both competent bargees and have the ingrained coal dust hands to prove it! And I can sing my way through, without any prompting, "The Cruise of the Calabar."

THE CRUISE OF THE CALABAR

(traditional Northern Irish Lagan canal song, collected by George Callaghan at Ashfield School 1953)

Come all ye dry-land sail-y-ors and listen to me song,
Tis only forty verses so I won't detain yes long.
It's all about the advent-y-ures of this old Lisburn barge

Who sailed as a man before the mast on the good ship Calabar.

Now the Calabar was a strengthened craft, she was rigged fore and aft,
Her helm it stuck out way behind, and her wheel had a great big shaft,
Witha good strong gale behind her she'd do one knot per hour,
She's the fastest craft on the Lagan canal, and she's only one horse-power.

Now the skipper he was a strapping lad, he stood just four feet two,
His eyes were red, his nose was green, and his cheeks were a Prussian blue,
He wore a leather medal he'd won at the Crimea war,
And the captain's wife was passenger and cook on the good ship Calabar.

Now the skipper says to me, "Me lad, look here me lad," says he
"Would yous like to be a sail-y-or and sail the raging sea?
Would yous like to be a sail-y-or in foreign seas to roll
For we're on the way to Portadown with half a ton of coal."

Twas early next morning we set sail, the weather it being sublime,
While passing under the auld Queen's bridge we heard the "Albert" chime.
Was along by the Gasworks Straight, a very dangerous part,
We ran aground of a a lump of coal that wasn't marked on the chart.

Then all became confusion and the stormy winds did blow,
The bosun slipped on an orange peel, fell into the hold below,
"Put on more speed," the captain cried, "for we are sorely pressed,"
But the engineer replied from the bank, "The horse is doing his best."

We all fell into the waterside and we all let out a roar
There was a farmer standing there and he threw us the end of his galluses
and he pulled us all ashore.
No more I'll be a sail-y-or and sail the raging main,
And the next time I go to Portadown, I'll go by the bloody train.

Chapter Eleven

409

Where I learn that things can become crystal-clear, that I am Irish, that I am Mea Callaghan's father, to become a concert promoter, that animation is a thief of time and memory, about the G bloody S bloody T, that it is time to leave and go back to Belfast, about my second love, archery, that it is time for something different and screaming, fucking, tinnitus!

HOUSE BOAT

Julian's brother had a large sailing boat moored at Kettering, just where you get the ferry to Bruny Island. A moored boat suited my sea legs, so we were able to live aboard while we searched for a house in Hobart. After traveling through the cities of England and Ireland, Hobart seemed no more than a country village, with ugly, giant Lego blocks left in the town square that were an excuse for a city. I love Hobart; the immediate countryside around the town and the city's location is superb. The nooks and crannies are its jewels, you have just got to know where to look. Luckily we have exalted Australians like Leo Schofield telling people what a dull provincial hole it is, just the sort of thing that I love to hear; it keeps all the mainland wankers away. We'd had enough of isolated country life, and really Hobart is like living in the country, if you can excuse the child-minded architects and town planners for leaving their giant building blocks lying around.

We were looking for a home that could double as a gallery, something on the main road, with parking and with good light. We settled for a place in North Hobart. It had belonged to two nice theatrical chappies, so it was rather well-restored inside and on two levels. The top two rooms we converted to a gallery. Of course, I had all the paintings that I had planned for my exhibition here in Hobart, and they had all been framed. Within weeks we were open for business. I was now about to start work for Kenny's in Galway. Well, that was the plan, except that my left eye was like looking through ten sheets of polythene, while my right eye was starting to cloud over. I couldn't drive at night, and was positively dangerous through the day. I had been to see my eye specialist, Paul McCartney, and appointments were made for the operation on my left eye. I would be on the operating table for half an hour, recover in the waiting room for an hour, and home. Or I had the optional choice of going under general anaesthetic, which would take slightly longer. I chose the short method, which meant a local anaesthetic. Now this was an experience. Being the pragmatic moron that I am, I admired the entire procedure right from the first moment. It was explained to me that I would be holding the nurse's hand (I would have preferred to be holding something more interesting than her hand) throughout the entire op. If I wanted to move or cough I was to squeeze her hand. The doctor would then immediately stop whatever he was doing.

The doctor didn't give me a second chance to think. "Look up," he said, and instantly I felt a slight needle prick in my eye. "Look down," and again the needle went instantly into my eye. I felt another needle go into my skull just left of my eye; this one hurt. Strangely enough, that was the only spot that hurt for months. Now everything looked white. This was the effect of the anaesthetic. I could feel, or should I say hear, a dull scraping at my eye. I don't recall squeezing the nurse's hand at any time. I was left in the room next door to recover, and then Stef took me home in a taxi. The next morning I returned to the doc's to make an appointment for my other eye, and also to have the bandages removed. Paul explained that in a way this procedure had been done for centuries; there were pictures on Egyptian tombs of a surgeon poking long, thin needles into people's eyes, apparently to force the lens in the eye from its location. The lens then fell into the eyeball, allowing the person who was blinded by cataracts to see again, although all images would be out of focus. It is also thought that perhaps Christ possibly knew this when he cured the blind man. When a person is old, the muscles that surround the lens get tired and brittle. By squeezing the eye from the front, this can cause the muscle to fracture, allowing the lens to drop into the ball of the eye. The person can see, but out of focus. Perhaps they might even see in focus in poor light, rather like the old Eskimo who makes a small hole by squeezing the thumb and forefinger together. Do this with both hands, bringing the two sets of thumbs/fingers together and squeezing these together, making a small aperture. If you are short-sighted, your vision is improved by looking through the small hole. Paul now showed me out of his subtly lit office into the brightly lit waiting room. This was a large clinic, and there were about 20 patients sitting around the room. "FFFUUUCCCKKK!!!" I exclaimed, much too loudly. I couldn't contain myself; the colours, the clarity, and 20 patients all staring at me. They must have thought that I was as high as a kite! Stef was Cheshire-grinning all over the place as she gave me such a hug. Was my swearing like that really all that amusing? Well, I suppose it was, but what was really more amusing was the look on Paul McCartney's face. I don't think that he had ever had quite that reaction to one of his operations. When I inquired about his fee, after my second operation was done, Paul asked if we could make a deal. Would I paint a picture that represented the operation in exchange for his fee? I was the first artist that he had performed the operation on. He has since become one of my regular patrons.

There was now a huge dilemma; what was all this colour about? If I am correct, even before the cataracts started to encroach on my vision, there had been a natural browning occurring in my lenses. It was the browning that naturally occurs with age, but now I was looking through crystal-clear lenses, and colours now were really over the top.

COLOUR

I started painting furiously to try to get the colours under control, the entire subject being flowers. I exhibited these at Saddler's Court Gallery in Richmond, but I had done so many paintings that I was able to have another exhibition at the same time in one of my favourite Tasmanian galleries run by one of my favourite gallery owners in Tassie, Jane Maxwell, of Bowerbank Mill in Deloraine. This gallery was originally started and owned by a friend called Gary Greenwood, who sang around the same folk clubs in Sydney. He is one of Australia's leading leather craftsmen. When Gary took over the Mill, the enormous chimney needed repair. He tells the story of having the steeplejack to execute the repairs. He talked Gary into climbing up to the top with him, where he proceeded to set the chimney into a swaying motion. Gary said that it swayed about eight feet! If it didn't have enough flexibility to sway, the steeplejack claimed that the chimney would blow over. Gary showed me photographs of the steeplejack in his birthday suit giving a brown eye to passersby. He claimed that this was the traditional thing to do on completion of his work! The photograph that Gary showed me has this guy actually dancing around the wall of the chimney on tippy toes (my balls are starting to cringe).

The exhibition that I had prepared in England now looked extremely bright, and was all hanging in my own gallery. Lena was back at primary school, her first town school, and she loved it. What a contrast to the one day that she'd spent in school in Llangollen where she came home in tears!

North Hobart is a rather upwardly mobile, double-income community. The main street is adorned with numerous ethnic restaurants. It was great to be back in Tassie, just for the food alone! They still hadn't learnt to make a decent cup of coffee in Ireland or England, and although the ingredients are superb, veggies are overcooked, usually in bicarbonate of soda to retain the colour, killing all know vitamins.

The curries in the British Isles have been adulterated and homogenized, blended, and the shit bashed out of it to suit the plebs. Mind you, these curries have now appeared in Hobart. Indian restaurants had been coming and going in Hobart. My favourite was the Taj, although two more had arrived and closed down due to a lack of patronage. Now there is a plague of Indian restaurants serving the English homogenized brand of curry. The era of the Turkish Kebab is with us at present. Hobart is small enough to observe the limitations of a commercial market of restaurants. There is a finite number of restaurants and pubs that the place can support. The secret is to continually change your modus operandi in food, although if the food is really good, it will keep on keeping on. In Hobart it is possible to eat different ethnic food for 20 days without repeating yourself: Italian, Turkish, Chinese, Mexican, Indian, African, French, Spanish, Vietnamese, Asian, Japanese, American steak houses, Macca's and of course, Kentuck Fried Chuck. With such varied and good food, it's not surprising that we eat out most nights. Modern homes and units these days on mainland Australia rarely have kitchens, although they are creeping back into vogue for their ornamental value.

Mairtin

I bumped into an old musical friend, Tom Dunlop, who had just moved into the city from Cygnet. Tom invited me out one night to a so-called Irish pub down in Hobart town called the New Sydney. I have always felt a great empathy for Tom because we both went to the same primary school in Belfast, Carr's Glen in County Antrim.

The New Sydney was not an Irish theme pub, it has just sort of grown that way, with a bent to the Irish thing which had been the flavour of the month for several years. It featured an Irish band every Wednesday night called Rakish Paddy. They had been playing there for three years, and I knew all the members of the band. I had played with every one of them. Dec on the banjo and I had been a duo, and had sung at many gigs and festivals. It was a grand evening's gas. I invited Tom home for dinner the next week to play a bit of music and to have a chat about stringed instruments. Tom was a very skilled Luthier. (That is nothing to do with Martin Luther. I don't know whether Tom is a Protestant luthier or a Catholic luthier; it doesn't matter in Hobart!) Tom arrived with apologies that he had bought along a friend, Mairtin McNahuana. This guy was James Dean/Bruce Willis/Marlon Brando with attitude. He is a brilliant whistle player and an Irishman spelt with a capital, Doric "I." We three played some great music that night; guitar, whistle and harp. Mairtin declared that he had often seen me playing the harp at Salamanca Place Market, saying to himself, "Just who does that wee fucker think he is, playing the Irish harp when he's not even Irish. He's a proper wanker!" He was probably right, except for the fact that I *am* Irish. Tom and Mairtin insisted that I join the Irish session that occurred in the New Sydney every Saturday afternoon, where about twenty musos got together to play Irish music. This has become a regular occasion that I have been attending for the past eight years. At first it was really serious Irish stuff, jigs and reels and sean-nos style singing. I would play accompanying style harp. Mairtin was a man with a mission; he wanted to start an Irish Association. Now up to this point in my life I never really knew that I was Irish, other than the fact that I was born in Ireland. Being brought up in South Africa had deprived me of all that baggage. But Mairtin was a charismatic character, and he managed to drum up enough enthusiasm and followers to attend a feasibility meeting. This meeting was held in the New Sydney Hotel, where everyone with an opinion on the subject would be given the opportunity to speak. The meeting was well attended, and everyone was in favour of an Irish Association, except me.

My reasoning was very simple. In Tasmania we lived in a multicultural society. In previous decades, the island was not only populated by, but almost totally controlled by the Irish or the British. Look around – the suburb names, the street names, the telephone directory – the result of the Irish or British. You've had your chance to intimidate Australia. The Greeks have had their turn, and so have the Italians. Now it's the chance of the Asians; and what about the poor Aborigines? They've never had their turn. There, I'd said my piece. I moved away to the bar in the other room.

About an hour later, Mairtin came round to me at the bar. "Well, we've formed an Irish Association," he said, "but we've struck a problem. We've voted that all the office bearers must be born in Ireland, and we're one short of a quorum. We need you to stand as an office bearer." So in true Irish logic I became a member of the Irish Association. I publicly declared my goal was to destroy this association from within.

A month later, the Irish Association had their first formal meeting. On the agenda, item number one was to stop Ireland being the butt end of the Irish joke (a joke in itself). I tabled a letter at that meeting, pointing to what this harmless platitude could be changed to, and quoted the following examples: How the blacks trembled in fear at the sound of the policeman with an Irish accent in the Bronx in America. How the Irish played their part in the attempted genocide when a tribe of Aboriginals were driven over the cliffs at Dorrigo, New South Wales. How the sound of the Irish accent among the American Cavalry had terrorised and slaughtered the Indian encampment of only women and children and will echo through the centuries, or Ned Kelly and his brothers when they ranged through Victoria, or the drunken wife basher I'd experienced on the streets of Belfast, or to be just like my dad and bash the shit out of anyone who called him Paddy. *The only one to tell the King the truth and get away with it was the fool.*

FORD FALCONS

While living in north Hobart, we had three brand-new Ford Falcons dismantled outside our back door. The third time the police came to make a report they advised me to move, as I was living not only in an iffy area, but also next door to a woman's shelter, and, "Oh yes, Mr Callaghan, are you the father of Mea Callaghan?"

"Yes," I said.

"Well, we have a fine for her for riding her skateboard on the main road at one o'clock at night."

Mea was always doing strange and unusual things. She and Miche were now working and living in their own flat. Homeless youth was on everyone's lips. We even had two government agencies to look after them. Now we had a soup kitchen serving sandwiches, drinks and meals, but the problem was, we had no homeless youths. There was even a TV programme showing homeless children being fed. On the night we watched the show, Stef and I recognised both our daughters in the late-night soup kitchen. Who said, "There's no such thing as a free meal."?

THE COASTER

Our bus was a Toyota Coaster. It had been used as a school bus at South Arm, west of Hobart. Except for the floor, I gutted the inside and re-lined it with fibre board and insulation, which was later completely eaten out by mice during one winter when it was parked up.

People are always curious about my studio. My studio is wherever I am at the moment. What do I work on? Whatever I've got at the moment. What medium do I use? Whatever I've just bought, I don't really care. Anything to make a mark on anything.

On *Desert Island Discs* I was asked about which book I would like to bring along to my island. "Any book, as long as it was blank," I said.

I will use any equipment as long as it is the best. Three brushes for paints, Jo Sonja's paints, bank layout pad, a good sketch book – except for the current canvas – all will fit into a shoulder bag.

The bus was very bright and modern inside, as this was also to be our mobile studio. The kitchen was the highlight, as Stef is one hell of a cook. It had all mod cons. I eventually replaced the original engine with a Holden engine. It was one superb vehicle, and was used over the years by all my family. Health-wise it cost me two frozen shoulders, which every pseudo quack promised to cure. Again my doctor told the truth. One year to get really bad, one year to heal. Two years later he was right.

While working underneath the bus, I witnessed my first optic vision. Nothing like Saul on the road to Damascus. I panicked and phoned Bob, my doctor. "That's an ocular migraine; be prepared for one mighty headache," he told me. But that never happened. I've had many such ocular migraines since and still, no headache.

My son Fintan used the bus, mostly touring around the entire coast of Australia. He left behind a map of every free camping spot on his trip. He is a keen surfer and a superb guitarist, fantastic with his hands, but inhibited by his peripheral vision. He walked through a glass door and sliced his right arm. A blood clot caused a mini stroke. He's always at home in Byron Bay, literally.

When I went to collect the bus for our next trip, I rolled back the carpet in front of the sink while he watched, amazed. My nest egg of 4,000 Australian dollars cash was still there.

SOUTH HOBART

We had a studio in South Hobart where Stef and I could paint and display our work. Originally it was a butcher shop, then a launderette, and we converted it to a gallery. I now basically sell prints of my work; all originals go to Ireland. This has been truly successful through a strange quirk of fate. Come Saturday, come Sunday, Mr. White collar worker gets the guilts about not doing a real job. They need to do something beefy or manly, and there is nothing more manly than getting yourself dirty, taking all the rubbish that has been annoying the wife to the tip. All these fine, jolly fellows pass my studio on the way to the tip. Luckily, they call in on us on their return home. Coincidentally, the first tune I ever wrote on the harp was called a "Trip to the Tip." I called it that as I wasn't very confident about it. Perhaps it was like this book; a load of rubbish!

ANIMATION

I still had my shed set up for the short film that I was working on. The opening scene with Tim Finnegan swinging around the gas lamp staggering down Walken Street and into the pub was absolutely superb. The building site scene with the skyline of Belfast turned out to be all I desired and wanted. I would need to reshoot the parlour scene, which was just so complicated, but I was losing interest in the entire project, as it was much too much work for one person, and my memory was failing me all the time. Manipulate the figure, pan the camera, operate the zoom, move the lights; had I taken a new light reading? Expose the film, had I moved the figure? Did I write it down when I moved the zoom? Actually it wasn't that I was losing interest, it was the fact that the whole process was fucking, fucking boring! Wallace and Grommet, get a life! I convinced myself that I needed the space in my shed to build a double string harp and I packed all the filming gear away. In order not to be tempted to cross this bridge again, I sold off the camera. There are numerous areas of filming that I would like to experiment with, but for this I will use video.

The GST (goods and service tax) had just been introduced to Australia (exactly the same as VAT). This was a nightmare for me. There are two switches in my wiring diagram that don't work; bookkeeping, and the electrics of a car. (I once had three cars on Bruny Island; all of them failed to work because of some electrical fault or other.)

BLOODY GST

I just couldn't settle down to living back in Oz. The nasty taste in my mouth left by the Tasmanian Development Authority was impacting my work. How could I look forward to my next exhibition and confront people? Everyone seemed to know about that issue. I should explore potential alternatives.

I had sent off a couple of prints as a wedding present to a friend who lived in Belfast. Brian Eakin, of Eakin Galleries saw these prints, and offered me an exhibition in my own home town. Apparently I had a reputation in Belfast, gained from the Web, regarding my profile in Australia. Exceptional was the fact that I was one of theirs from the Belfast College of Art. On the strength of this, Stef and I transferred our interests and headed home (?) to Belfast. There was only Stef and me now; Lena had moved into our house in South Hobart.

Brian Eakin of The Eakin Gallery in Belfast asked me for a one-man show. This was to be the first major show in my home town. It took me two years to prepare for this. The opening for me was the highlight. Originally I was going to play my harp at the opening, but the logistics of bringing my harp over from Australia was impossible. Billy and Brian felt it essential that the harp thing should happen, so Billy put out feelers for someone to loan me a harp. In true Billy fashion, he started at the top, jumping in at the deep end by contacting the Belfast Harp Orchestra, going straight to the leading lady herself, Janet Harbison. I knew this lady's work; didn't I have all her recordings at home? Not only with her own orchestra, but also playing with the Chieftains. Not only did Janet agree to loan me a harp, but she insisted on playing at the opening with me. To me this was like Jussi Björling singing a duet with Bugs Bunny, me being Bugs Bunny (I have written into my will somewhere requesting a recording of Jussi Björling singing "I dream of Jeannie with the light brown hair" at my funeral. Although it is still my favourite piece of music, I hope the assembled few will get a giggle from Bugs Bunny's version of this song, 'I dream of Jeannie, she's a light brown hare"!)

GIANTS RING

While waiting for the exhibition to open we drove around Belfast and saw a sign "Giants Ring." You have got to have a look at anything with a name like that! After the first directional sign there were plenty more, but they were half-obscured either with paint or mud. There were several cars parked in the car park when we arrived at the final sign. There was a high, grassy embankment ahead of us which we climbed. From the top we could see a massive, mounded circle. In the centre was a dolmen, made up of huge rocks, with a capping stone.

Coming towards us was a young man with a silly grin on his face. He was now heading straight for us. Eventually he came close enough to identify us. He took a good look at Stef, looked her up and down! His grin turned to horror and he dashed off.

In the background and coming closer was an older man, exercising his dog. "What is this place all about?" we enquired.

"Not much is really known about it," he replied. "Queens University are doing some work on it soon. You've got a weird accent! Where are you from?"

"Oz!"

He went on to explain that we were standing in the very centre of the Poofter quarter of Northern Ireland!

"But we don't have Poofters in Northern Ireland!" I exclaimed "They're all in Oz!"

"Wait around and you'll see when school gets out!"

"Ah ha! So that's why the young man looked so disappointed when he saw that Stef was a woman. The jeans that she was wearing had confused him!"

He went on to explain that if we went back to the car in the car park, what at first seemed to be empty cars actually had drivers. There was some sort of code as to who and what was available according to which direction the car was parked, tail out or tail in! I still think that Giants Ring is a stupid name! I have just checked my facts on the computer, reads really boring. This story is much better!

I arrived in Belfast two days before the opening of my first exhibition to find that the entire exhibition had sold out, over 50 works. I was to do a TV programme the day before the opening at ten o'clock in the morning, but I received a phone call to the effect that a bomb had been discovered on the back steps of the gallery, and the entire block had been evacuated and was surrounded by the Royal Ulster Constabulary. "Don't come near the place," I was advised, which meant that I headed straight for the place. I wanted to be close, but not too close by, when 50 of my paintings were blown to smithereens! All the tenants were lingering about inside and outside the restaurant at the end of the block. Brian, who had originally seen the offending item resting on his back doorstep, described it as being a box about the size of two bricks. It had brass fittings from which came wires that went over the roof of his building. Eventually the bomb squad department of the army arrived. They surrounded it with sandbags and made a controlled explosion. After analysing the remains, the experts declared that it had been the critical data from a weather balloon that had fallen from deep space, landing on the very back door of where I was to have my exhibition. After this type of exhibition, things were a bit tame in Hobart.

By now Stef and I were almost enthusiastic about living in Ireland for a couple of years. We had even come to the conclusion that it might be of great benefit to have Lena brought up there. It was in this frame of mind that we went to visit my father, who was in a retirement home somewhere in the Hollywood hills, just outside Belfast. The retirement home was part of a huge estate. It was while wandering around this huge estate, looking for the exact building that my father was in, that we ended up at the rear of what appeared to be a deserted building, which turned out to be on the adjoining estate. We had wandered too far off course. As we rounded the side of the building, we came face to face with a huge bay window. With our faces almost touching the glass we beheld the scene that lay before us. In the room there were endless rows of chairs on which sat men dressed in dark suits and immaculate white shirts. On their knees were white gloves and a bowler hat. Draped around their necks and over their suits was an orange scarf. They were all listening to someone out of site speaking in a very Hitler-like fashion; the entire scene was very Ku Klux Klan! No! No! I was definitely not going to bring up my Lena amongst this crap!

Eventually we found my dad, and from the time that I stood before him there were faint glimpses of recognition in his eyes. He knew who I was, but I could see no resentment in those eyes. For the short time that Stef and I spent with him I was only able to see and feel the good times that we had spent together, and reflected on all that I had learnt from him. I kissed him goodbye and walked out of his life, but he has never walked out of mine.

That exhibition in Belfast was a total sell-out. We would settle for a while in Belfast. I had many friends from my student days, not only my own year at art college, but the years behind and those in front. I looked them all up and with each one we were welcomed as cousins from the Antipodes. All went well until I enquired about everyone else. "Oh, I never see them." "No, lost contact with those people." "No, never hit it off there."

"This is odd," I thought. "I could have sworn all those guys and dolls got along so well." Then I realised much later that I had missed out on the all-important issue of the Belfast psyche, which I had always thought existed only at street level. I was reared on racism myself, but hopefully had laid that ghost to rest. My friends saddened me to the point that I decided not to live in Belfast but close by, somewhere with easy access to Northern Ireland. Penrith in England is about as far away as Cork as the crow flies. That crow gets around; so does our kookaburra.

I have never had a head for figures, and even now I get physically ill if I have to fill in a form. I was told by some smart arse that there was no GST on exports from Oz to Belfast, where I had studied at the Belfast College of Art. This was to be my passport initially to the art scene of Ireland, but then on to Great Britain. Within months I had a bigger following in Ireland than I'd had in Australia. I had achieved all I had set out to achieve in Australia. It was time to move on. My family were now living all over the world. I decided to live near my market but not in Ireland, where the politics would drive me insane.

Currently I'm living in France, but everywhere has its pros and cons. Oz has more pros than cons but it's so, so far away. I am now able to post my work off to galleries all around the world, and never actually come in contact with any of them.

SETH DAVEY

My son Fintan and his wife had worked the coffee strip in Byron Bay on the northeast coast of New South Wales, and knew exactly how each coffee shop expected all their staff to make their coffee, having worked for each one of almost 24 coffee shops. A triple latte with double cream multiplied by … or cappuccino divided by … a blended mocha shaken and stirred by a chromium plated spoon … to go! Shaken but not stirred.

The coffee at that time in Belfast was crap. The Indian curries weren't bad. A steak, impossible. Sunday roast – fantastic. Fish and chips – superb. Ice cream at Archie's – wow. Chinese – reasonable. Ulster fry – mmm, where does all that dripping go? We'd have to miss out on the culinary delights to live in racial harmony.

We decided to live in the Lake District of England in a town called Skirwith. Skirwith (with a silent 'w') is a typical English rural village, with a beck (Cumbrian name for a stream), several churches, numerous bridges and a road junction that headed off in five different directions. Skirwith is hemmed in by the Lake District and the Pennines Mountain Range and has a lovely feeling of isolation. Stuart, our landlord, made wonderful decoy ducks, but occasionally does the most magnificent sculptural pieces. We had a joint exhibition in the Lake District. I spent many days walking and sketching in this area. But most of the time I spent sitting on the village wall with Lena, whittling a Seth Davey doll for her (this is a leather-jointed puppet doll, with a stick coming out of its back. He dances on the end of a plank that the operator sits on, bouncing the plank with their hand. This causes the puppet to become quite animated). This doll we made with only one tool, a Swiss army knife, and a sheet of sandpaper. The locals of Skirwith must have thought me quite the eccentric.

That trip was in the heat of summer, and from our cottage window it was lovely to hear the children of the village playing in the beck, not the sort of thing that could happen in Oz because of the fear of snakes in the long grass. Of course we had taken the obligatory trips through the Lake District and were suitably impressed, but we couldn't cope with the hordes of tourists.

It would seem that tripping back and forth to Europe was going to be the norm, as I was starting to sell more work in Ireland and England than I was selling in Oz, mostly because I was now involved with Irish subjects. The new studio that we had left behind was up and running, and Mea was in complete control. She was continually framing and selling my work while we were traipsing around the country soaking up the atmosphere.

ARCHERY

Faced with the enjoyment of living in Penrith in the Lake District, the challenge arose of what to do next. The most important thing to pursue, of course, was archery. This was my buzz of self-indulgence. At all sport I was crap. Field archery was my choice of archery disciplines, as it doesn't involve just standing in a field firing arrow after arrow at the same distance year after year. When I first started archery, the club I joined was along the Wakehurst Parkway outside Sydney, Oz, just past the blinking light, laid out like a golf course through the bush. We shot three arrows from different positions, 18 targets. Here in Langwathby it was exactly the same, but with the added advantage of an indoor range through the week. My scores tell me I am very good, but not brilliant. There are no sights or markings on our bows, we are instinctive archers.

LAKE DISTRICT CONCERTS

The English countryside is dotted with town halls, most of which have been recently revamped. I planned a series of concerts at these halls, similar to the workshops that we had presented in Tasmania at the University of the Third Age. I used a slide presentation of my paintings, and two other musicians – a bass guitarist, a guitar player and a singer – made up the three members of the group. I think we called ourselves Yesterday's Men.

A couple of weeks before the event we plastered the village with posters. Sometimes we performed to full halls. Once there were only two people at the venue. We had noticed a large queue outside the door and were very excited at the potential audience; but when we opened the doors we realised the people had only queued up outside because there was a bus stop just outside the hall.

TINNITUS

Just before we left Oz I became aware of the occasional light-headed, dizzy feeling accompanied by what I described to the doctor as minor electric shocks travelling through my brain. It was dismissed as nerves. It was when we were in Skirwith that I woke up with a sizzling in my head (not ringing in the ears). It lasted all day, but by the next morning it had gone. A week later the noise returned with the light head and the electric shocks; this lasted for three days, disappeared again and then returned forever! It was louder than the volume of a jet engine. I was now terribly stressed, as the noise would not stop. I had been to the local doctor, who managed to get me to see a brain specialist in Carlisle in two weeks' time. By the time that I got to see this specialist I was in a mess, and my family were completely distraught. The specialist would be able to send me for a brain scan in four weeks' time. This was the same old story that I'd had with the cataracts in my eyes.

With brilliant decisiveness, Stef managed to get us all back to Australia immediately. Hobart is the capital of the state of Tasmania, and when it comes to amenities, if the other states have got one, then we have got to have one. As a consequence we are amazingly over-serviced compared to the population. We have a population of close to 50,000 people. Within hours of arriving back in Hobart I was having my brain scanned…all clear…brainwaves checked with an MRI scan…all clear. But with this fucking screaming in my head I was going insane. I became totally suicidal. If it was not for Stef continually by my side, I would be dead.

I admitted myself into hospital, as I was a danger to myself, and was interviewed by two psychiatrists who retrospectively were a complete pair of wankers who continually tried to intimidate me into describing the sounds in my head as voices. They sedated me and put me on a course of powerful tranquillisers, which I became completely addicted to after four weeks. I had now seen the last of the specialists, an ear specialist, after a thorough examination diagnosed tinnitus…noise in the head, not life threatening, no cure, Mr. Callaghan, go away and live with it, the best advice I had received so far. However, I was now behaving like one of Pavlov's dogs. The fear element had kicked in, and I was completely conditioned, and I was dependant on these dreadful tranquillisers. Now I was completely vulnerable. There had to be something that I could do. I was advised of the Tinnitus Support Group in Hobart, but those poor people were so ill-informed. Stef had been searching the Internet for answers and had found a marvellous online site, so we were very up to date with current management treatments. Psychotherapy had been recommended, so I consulted with three different therapists who had been exclusively recommended for their knowledge of tinnitus. I explained my particular dilemma, which must have been a nightmare for the poor buggers. They could not use imagery (me being an artist) or music (me being a musician) as I had a thorough working knowledge of how music and art affects the psyche. It is very hard to pull the wool over your own eyes when you are not just a casual observer of art and music. All three therapists recommended that I meditate with calming music (harp perhaps?) and imagine that I was resting in a beautiful, peaceful landscape (like one of my pictures perhaps?). I consulted naturopaths on the insistence of my friends, but this treatment doesn't work on sceptics, even vulnerable ones! Neither did the three chiropractors have anything to offer, although they all promised a cure. The two acupuncturists were so nice about their treatment that for their sake I had to pretend that I was getting better! They were all very happy to take my money and leave me with the sizzling sound of a steak cooking in my head. Through the Internet I located a professor in Melbourne who had chronic tinnitus but who was able to manage his condition. He was the only real help that I had, and sadly, I can't even remember his name. He reinforced what Stef had been continually talking to me about, RE-FOCUSING, learn to live with it. Tinnitus is like one candle burning in a dark room; switch on the lights, and you won't see the candle burning at all. Don't shut yourself down, open yourself up!

I was beginning to manage myself rather well except for the bad moments when I lost focus. I would end up in tears. But even this assisted the management, as the crying seemed to release some sort of sedative, calming effect. There is one other incident that helped me cope. This was when I got a phone call from a friend's ex-wife in a suicidal state. Chronic tinnitus had just kicked in with her. We had long, long chats on the phone, and I know that what that professor was able to do for me, I was able to do for her. The site on the Web informed me that it would take about two years to become used to this screaming. It is now almost four years since Tinnitus kicked in. The screaming is still there, but the fear has receded. There is a pattern. Sometimes there are quieter spells. But I refuse to monitor those, preferring not to give the cycle any power and rule my life. Remembering how I got myself off the Panadeine, I set about with a withdrawal program, moving firstly to a less addictive drug, and then to decreasing the medication. Within six months I was completely off the drugs. Good-meaning people are always asking me about the ringing in my head, usually saying, oh yes, I get ringing in the ears. It is very hard to explain that this screeching is located in the middle of my head, and that I, like them, also get ringing in the ears, which usually lasts only for a minute or two. Some well-meaning people usually have a solution for Tinnitus like aromatherapy, prayer, or one person claimed to be able to cure Tinnitus by singing special harmonies into both ears. Didn't I expose myself to all sorts of different harmonies on a daily basis? Find yourself a good, logical GP who will work with you in your MANAGEMENT of Tinnitus, and help you eliminate your fears through investigation, as my GP did.

Fred Thornett

I was still looking for something more stimulating to do, as the Tinnitus was still impacting. Stef discovered the answer; an arguing class run by Adult Education. This was not really an arguing class, but a discussion group run by a guy who has not only become my mentor, but a friend as well, Fred Thornett. This was a group of ten completely diverse people. Not one of them was religious, so the first topic on the agenda, religion, was obsolete from the word go, which meant that we could become involved in more stimulating and philosophical subjects, although religion always seemed to raise its ugly head. These classes were the highlights of the weeks ahead. What was so interesting was that although I referred to it as my arguing class, I do not actually recall any arguing at all, except for one guy who only attended two classes. He of course broke the rules of discussion and began arguing.

Fred was the secretary of the Tasmanian Sceptics. He is my mentor, as I still have one foot in the gullible camp, and every time that I get carried away on the false hopes of the salvation of mankind, Fred brings me back down to earth with sheer logic, which I am in continual awe of.

THE FOLK SCENE

The music scene in Hobart was becoming rather political, and the infighting was unbearable. For the last couple of years I had been singing in a trio that consisted of myself and two girls. Rose, who is an absolutely gorgeous singer and I got together, me thinking that she would be much better organised than myself. I was also relying on her memory being much better than mine, but her memory was absolutely dreadful. We called ourselves Rose 'n' Me, a pun on the word Rosemarie, but no one ever got the pun, and we were forever being billed as Rose and George. When Miche, my second oldest daughter joined us to make up the trio, we first sang at the Fleadh Cheoil (festival of Irish music) under the name of O'Shadonfreude, which sent all the Gaelic speakers running for their Irish-speaking dictionaries, only to discover that this was a German word used to express the habit of cutting down tall poppies.

We then changed our name to Merosenda, which rolled of Miche's tongue when she explained to someone who was in the group, she had said, "It's me, Rose and Da!" We sang at quite a few venues and at the Cygnet Folk Festival under this name.

Miche took off to pursue her own star, in the wilds of Canada, leaving me with the inability to sing Jesse Winchesters " Sad old Wintery feeling".

As well as a solo performer, I played with several groups. *Reels on Wheels* had six of us doing the usual Irish thing, everyone in on the count of one, two three! No arrangement, parallel melodies all the way, all hoping that we all finish together. As Frank said, "Sure we've got all these instruments, we may as well use them right from the word go!"

It was about this time that I first started playing the harp, and I became part of a fantastic duo with Declan Pickering, who not only sang but played mandolin, mandocello and banjo. We stayed together for about three years, and it was with Declan that I first started playing at the market. At that time there were numerous Irish musicians at the market and we were making a small fortune just busking. I recall Declan saying, "Ders no focking way I am moving away from dis harp!"

Occasionally I did concerts with another harpist. This was part of a tour around country villages. At our national folk festival held each year in Canberra, usually one state is featured. The year that Tasmania was featured I took my harp, but as luck would have it, just as I started to play in the concert I struck one chord and I broke a string. This might sound insignificant, but on a harp the strings beside the broken one instantly compensate for the break in tension, so these neighbouring strings were now out of tune. Then the next neighbouring two were out, etc. etc. This is a harpists dilemma. It's almost as bad as playing on stage and some lighting demon puts a red light on you. This turns ALL the strings red, and you have lost your benchmarks of only the "C" strings being red. Still, my performance was not over, as I was to do some singing with a young man by the name of Martin Spurway Smith, who after the string-breaking performance labelled me as "Captain Ping." We did a bracket of songs, ending the bracket by singing "Peggy Gordon," a folk song which had been flogged to death. I sang this with a very serious approach, while Martin danced around me pinning wooden clothes pegs throughout my hair and beard. By the time I had finished the song po faced I was completely covered in pegs, and I doubt that anyone who was there would dare to sing that song again! Sometimes I played and sang in a duo called Georgian. Ian, the guy that I performed with, sings and plays guitar. We were free thinkers, which is another way of saying that we were not religiously linked to any style of music. Musical whores and will play anything; blues, rock, soul, country, folk…but no fecking rap!

CONCERTS

The concerts that we were having in our studio were a huge success, and to date the Salamanca Arts Centre were extremely happy with our successes. Then there was a change in management. No one came near us from the administration offices, and we were treated with blunt refusal for any assistance, and a hostile approach to the advertising of our venue. This hostility we couldn't understand, primarily because we did not involve ourselves in the politics of the arts centre. Eventually the whisper started to reach our ears; our success with The Attic was not reflecting on the arts centre, it was entirely due to the ability of Stef and myself and needed no input from the arts centre. The centre could in no way bask in this glory, and for this we were being sent to Coventry. Strangely enough, we had been to an art centre in England that reflected an episode of *Yes Minister* where the art centre had managed to get rid of all their artists. They were much too unruly and unpredictable to the smooth administration of an art centre.

The concerts in our studio came to an end when we realised that the folk musicians we were enjoying were OK on stage. Socially, while we were billeting them they were as dull as dishwater, always putting their social energy into their computer, which they consulted every half-hour. I only ever enjoyed one performer at home. He had emerged from his bedroom on Saturday morning after a very good performance, and I was sorting a massive box of broken pastels. Being chalk, the pastels had all taken on the darkest colour in the collection. Picking up one and trying it on a spare piece of paper was the only way to find out the colour, and then place it in the appropriate pile. "Ah, could I do that?" he asked, and without any further chat he sat down. Three hours later he was still at it.

Chapter Twelve

Lherm

Where I learn that France is for the French, all markets are cons, that French food is not food, what really happened in 1066, what is really awesome, how to develop bad taste, what happened to French art and why the French archers lost at Agincourt!

MAISON BLEU

Temporary living in England was getting too expensive. On an exploration trip to France we found it much, much cheaper to rent there. Also, la-de-da Stef could speak the language. We had no intention of purchasing a house, but an opportunity presented itself that we couldn't refuse. We were in the right place at the right time, so we bought a tiny house, much, much too small for our children to linger too long when they visited us.

Stef also owns (not me, that's to stop Napoleon turning in his grave) twenty-five acres of woodland, all regrown over stone walls and garriottes since the days when the grapes got the phylloxera virus.

COMMUNICATION

So why would any fool want to live in France? What makes the French tick? What makes the country chime? For a start, the English can't stand the French; they can't stand each other. The food is supposed to be superb, and then there's the language. Perhaps that's what attracted me most. I have no French whatsoever, and no intention of learning it! Someone once said to me that if you really want to enjoy a country, don't learn the language. They were right. At first I thought I was using this sentiment as a copout or a cheat. No, if you want to communicate or need to, there are so many better ways than language. Use only language and you meet the most narrow-minded gits in the community. Touch, expression, action, demonstration, smell, anger, fear and on it goes. If you're worth knowing, or someone else is worth knowing, you'll get by. Unfortunately you'll have picked up a few foreign words along the way.

Of course, the French got the crap shot out of them by the English archers of Agincourt. The English archer practices hard every day to the point that they are all crippled. The French have better things to do, like having meals with their families, and having sex in daylight.

Food is a comparative thing. If you come from Ireland or England, then perhaps French food might be considered OK; but not if you come from Australia. Honestly, the food is crap. I thought I had found the solution a while back by only eating expensively. NO, it's just as bad!

MARKETS

French markets are no different from markets anywhere else in the world. As usual, more expensive than your local supermarket. The supermarket has the advantage that you are allowed to touch the fruit and vegetables. The French don't make bread for sandwiches; even the supermarket's square bread is far too sweet for a savoury sandwich. Most of it is used as a tool for pushing the fork against and mopping up gravy. It only has to last the duration of the meal. I make my own scones but I have to go without fresh cream, you just can't get it here. Crème Anglaise is the closest you can get, or crème fraiche, which is just sour cream. Potatoes are always a problem in any warmer climate, and I never know what sort locally that I like. If I can't get an Ardglass herring I can't be bothered with fish, and when I do have it, I don't like it messed about with. I'd rather be home in Belfast at any decent chipper with a whack of haddock in batter. Haddock is comparable, but not really as nice as a piece of Tasmanian trevalla, but not trevally (*beware the "Y"*).

The formula for restaurants is constant. Duck, duck, duck. Maybe vegetables – all tasting the same, all cooked in a pressure cooker. Potatoes (they used to be banned), usually of the waxy variety. Dessert – crème brûlée, crème brûlée, or crème brûlée. Within any given 15-mile radius there are at least 12 restaurants all serving the exact same menu. Judgments are made on the price on the noticeboard outside, which is fair enough if you eat to live, but I live to eat. The French go into shock at the idea of spices. You can get excited about the new Chinese about to open, but it will be closed down within a month.

The magic thing about France is not what they have, it's actually what they don't have. They have no household flags, no painted roadside curbing, no religious tracks hammered onto trees, no orange or green marches, and no nasty political murals (*part of our heritage*). You're not intimidated by whatever church you belong to, and no sectarian music.

What the people in Northern Ireland spend on flags, painted curb sides and marches, what the Australians spend on Tinnies, the French spend on their village floral arrangements. The attention to public planters and temporary sculptures is admirable if you like that sort of thing. My wife does!

The rubbish on the streets is blatantly obvious by its absence. As a kid, my father's logic astounded me when I put a sweetie paper in my pocket. "Throw that in the gutter, you're doing a man out of a job!" Further up the road we passed a street sweeper, a man with a job!

The lack of fences in the countryside is confusing, as is the lack of animal stock. And yet on our land there are ancient walls all over the place. I can't walk fifty meters in any direction without having to scamper over one. On the land around me there are maybe twenty small buildings. The information on these conflict; are they shepherd's huts, or for storage? On one of my hills are six of these small shelters. I am terrified of going into them; families of wild boar could be in there. Have you ever seen those guys? Built like brick shit houses!

Once I came to a halt in the car to look at one running along beside me. It was as well that I did, as twelve ran straight in front of Stef and me up the hill to our left, literally brushing the car.

I was about to write that hunters travel all over our land, but they don't; hunters travel over no one's land. Their dogs do all the traveling! The hunters wait, smoking, chatting and talking on cell phones at the end of country tracks, often in the warmth of their heated, luxurious four-wheel-drives! Each one has his own tackle, horns, whistles, elephant guns, machine guns, rifles, hand grenades, and bazookas. If a sanglier appears, twenty or so hunters will blow it to bits!

Napoleonic laws are the order of the day. So trespassing…I don't think exists. We had to take Napoleon Bonaparte into account when we bought our land. I don't own it, Stef does! If I own it, the property by-passes Stef and goes directly to any male descendant. She owns the house in the village and the non-constructible land. Also a ruined building which we aren't allowed to touch (if it falls on me, is that touching it?). Five acres that was at one time cleared for tobacco is now used for hay. We have a tool shed. As the land is non-constructible, we were confused with the French/Irish law of logic. For this building of a tool shed we had to apply for permission to erect a building that you don't need to apply for permission to construct…well, you work that one out!

France has been handy, as it's in the middle of everywhere else that you shouldn't want to go to, that's if you want to go anywhere else; the French certainly don't! I only met and knew one French couple in my life in Australia; he taught me philosophy. His first class was to ask us to make a list of our ten beliefs and present it at next week's class. We were then to strike and remove any beliefs that we had inherited. Without exception, the entire class had inherited ALL their beliefs…time to think for myself! He also pointed out that we process information according to those beliefs. As I said, the French don't travel. These two French people we bumped into in Cahors in the Lot two years before on the very day that they had arrived back in France. His comment then was: "Beware the French! They talk too much, and too fast, about absolutely nothing." So do the Irish!

THE CHURCH IN OUR SQUARE

While Harold was busy getting his arrow in his eye in 1066, the lads in our square had been a long time working on the church that stands opposite our house. It stood deserted for many years when the village was abandoned. When people started coming back to live in Lherm, the wolves had moved into the church. No one knows the order in which things happened around the church, and no one but myself seems to have noticed that it is crooked. All the carvings have been smashed off. These might have been profiles of nobles removed because of the French Revolution. At the rear of the church, up the hill, are the ruins of many buildings. Further up past the graveyards are the foundations of yet another hamlet. The Germans took a lady from one of these farms who was operating a radio during WWII. They shot her in the town square.

At the same time, the nuns from the convent next door removed the silver from the church and hid it up the track that goes through our land on the next hill.

Of course there were many people then in the local resistance, hopefully not stupid enough to sit around in groups with their guns having their photographs taken. There are lots of these photographs of resistance fighters all with their guns in our local resistance museum. Not a good move, fellas! Stupid ego!

The church, like all churches, is important to all communities. Where else can you learn such bad taste?

ARTS & CRAFTS IN RURAL FRANCE

I have no artistic profile in France where I now live, and do not come in contact with other artists. This suits what I have become. I enjoy all of the arts that I am involved with, actually creating and doing the work, but not the company of fellow artists. In this area I find that art and artists promise so much and deliver so little.

Australia was fantastic while it happened, but it was becoming like Great Britain and Europe. In Oz I worked as an artist, silversmith, folk singer, guitarist, harpist, sculptor, luthier, leatherworker, printmaker, builder, and sculptor, but this attitude in Australia is all coming to an end. In France it is OK for me to be a painter, as I had studied at the Belfast College of Art, but it is too much to be proficient on the harp, too much to be proficient at anything else. I am now 72 and about to reawaken my silversmithing skills. I know that this will go down like a lead balloon here in France! Actually, I have changed my mind. I am repairing and building concertinas instead, no I'm not I'm making Northumbrian small bag pipes ...well maybe.

Luckily I was not wanting to establish myself as an artist in France, the land of the Impressionists, or any of the seven arts. France has no more interest in the arts than any other country. It's every middle-class British woman's dream to retire to France and become an artist. The place is crawling with them. Each hamlet has its own public gallery and it's booked out through the summer months, cluttering up the environment. I'm afraid I just add to that clutter.

Never was music for me a total non-event in the same way it is in France. At its heyday in Australia, perhaps I'd sell 25 CDs in two hours at our local market in Salamanca. Here in France at our local market in summer, I sold two in a period of five weeks. Ne'er a coin was thrown my way, so I stopped trying. The harp totally confused the French. I can only imagine their reason. Perhaps I should have been performing in a church. Is this sort of music not acceptable at street level? What qualifications had I? No one even stopped, even out of curiosity. Music is performed in churches regularly, almost exclusively classical or opera, by arrangement with the priest, and the patrons are appropriately attired. Any other sort of music comes under the heading "jazz."

During our honeymoon period in France, I attended several jazz concerts. On each occasion it was anything but jazz, more blues, rock, country, or reggae. French folk music has a lot in common with Irish session music – a repetitive refrain based in rhythm, not melody, suited to the hurdy gurdy or any instrument that is a squeaking, squawking, squelching squalor of tortured arpeggios.

FIRKIN

Luckily we were much too early for our flight at Bergerac Airport. We had time to wander into an antique shop in town. I couldn't believe my eyes! On the wall at the back of the shop was a painting hanging. It was by "Georges (P)?" It was THE very painting that hung in my grandmother's home behind the front door in the hall. A seascape, a stormy heavy sky, six characters in a boat in the foreground, another four in a smaller boat to the right. In the centre of the picture, with a French flag, there is a large boat. In the background, a steamship. One of the last two boats is in trouble; which one?

On a large wave in the very foreground is a firkin. I stood amazed, flabbergasted! Then I recalled that there was small angled cut in the foreground wave. Had it been repaired? Could I have a look at the canvas from the back, please? I held my breath; after all, this was it! It was £11,000.

It was not it. Later I discovered that it was quite common for an artist of that period to paint several copies of a painting that he was pleased with to advertise his wares. I bought the painting, and it's still my granny's painting.

Advice! If you are ever engaged in an art heist, don't roll the canvas with the image on the inside. Image on the outside, please! Paintings have millions of cracks. Rolling the painting paint-side-in squashes the sharp edges of each individual facet together, damaging the crisp edges. When the canvas is unrolled back to its original plane, not only is that damage revealed, but the cracks are now enlarged as the canvas has stretched.

ZEBRAS

A confusing disrespect for the law is magnified by any encounter with a zebra crossing. What's it for? Is it an area for people to congregate and chat? Is it a designated location for cars to speed up? Is it official, or just stripes painted on the road by the café owner for his additional outdoor seating? After all, there's nothing arresting about it, no flashing lights. Both pedestrian and motorist are equally confused.

DETAIL

I take a French magazine here which uses old historical photographs. As I can't read French, I feel and enjoy each photograph, hopefully to its full potential, as I explore every detail to gain information. My wife speaks fluent French. She's not the most observant person in the world. We passed over the crossroads just outside our village, surrounded by buildings, and a truck driver had stopped there. He waved us down. Stef crossed and went over to him. She spoke to the driver and turned around to me, confused.

"Look, what's on the back of his truck?" I shouted.

"Well, a funny crane thing," she replied.

"He's looking for that bloke we passed back there next to all those freshly felled trees." You don't need French language to understand that lot.

ARCHERY

Eventually I located an Archery Club...I wrote about the occasion in a chapter from my novella,

VILLEFRANCE:

Brenda realised as she plodded her weary, way home that she had started making enemies from the moment she had arrived in France twelve years ago. She had vowed not to fall into the trap and become what Bluey the Aussie would call, "Another bloody whinging Pom!" But, no sooner had she committed to this idea, than she had put her foot in it, in one of the worst ways possible.

Her husband, Brian, was a keen archer, and he had won numerous medals in competitions held throughout the UK. Nothing grand like a position of first, second, or third in the national championships, and not even in the top ten. Brenda kidded him that most of his medals were awarded just for showing up, as there seemed to be medals awarded for everything, even for wearing the most successful camouflage gear of the shoot. If only they could find someone to award it to!

During their first months in France, Brian had located the local field archery club in their department. As luck would have it, the club was holding their national championships, and Brian was encouraged to compete, as he had all his documentation from the NFS in England, which proved that he was aware of all the safety rules of the sport (not that safety was an issue with the French archers).

Brian accompanied himself during rounds of archery with his beautiful tenor singing voice, which he claimed he had inherited from Allan-a-Dale. His broad shoulders came from Little John, his firm, deep chest belonged to Much-The-Miller and his dress sense he definitely inherited from Will Scarlet. All in all, he wouldn't blame anyone for mistaking him for Robin Hood! In reality, he looked like Woody Allen in drag.

Brenda was always there to support Brian in these events, and it was promising to be a good day. Brian seemed to be holding his own among his fellow competitors. He even managed a round of applause when he got a hit on the target of the Duke of Wellington!

They had completed the morning round of the course when lunch break was announced. Brenda retired to their vehicle to collect the packed lunch of ham and pickle and a flask of good old Rosie Lee.

When she returned to the meeting place, it was deserted except for Brian, whose French at this time was almost nil. He explained that he thought they were to follow down a particular track and join the others at a picnic area. They travelled down the track some fifty meters, until they reached a clearing in the woods with a huge ramshackle shed. Inside, it was lined with trestle tables and benches. Smoke was billowing from an open spit, and the smell of gold was on the air. A roast pig was rotating on a spit with one of those wind-up things that you buy at Vide-Greniers throughout France, and there was a line of archers waiting for their portion of pork.

"*Rejoindre la file d'attente!*" was the command from Jacques the club secretary, gesturing towards a disorderly queue.

"But, but, we brought our own sandwiches." But an explanation was wasted among the merry men and women.

There followed two hours of French hospitality—foie gras for starters, pork, pommes frites, string beans, carrots, then the cheeses of which there were Heinz 57 varieties, followed by crème brûlée. All the food was washed down by copious amounts of red wine. The two-hour luncheon was rounded off with a special 500-proof cider, specially brewed for the occasion!

Now, for the second round of archery.

At the day's end, the usual medals were awarded for all the different sections: bare bow, compound bow, long bow, women's section, etc. Then came the coup de grâce! The highest score of the day—Brenda's Brian!

What had started as an orderly game of archery before lunch had ended as a drunken traipsing around the countryside, in the words of Fred Wedlock's song, "firing arrows here and there" at anything that resembled a target. There was a stage where arrows were fired willy-nilly above the horizon. Brenda and Brian almost headed for home, when someone started firing arrows directly into the air overhead. Of course, Brian won this award for the highest score! He wasn't drunk! He didn't drink!

During the coming week, Brenda retold the story to anyone who would listen. Looking back now, she reflected that she should have not concluded her story with, "No wonder the French lost at Agincourt!" She thought at the time that she meant this as a compliment; the French had much better things to do than fight a war! Like food, drink, and sex, in that order. But now she knew to never mention Agincourt! (*Based on a true incident...my own.*)

Champion of the World

As he walked to work that morning, his mind drifted to sometime in the future when he would perhaps be champion of Ireland, bantam weight division. This was the weight where the fastest and most scientific of boxers could be found. He wasn't one for the heavyweight bash 'em as hard as you could; 'The harder they fall', scenario. No, he was into the proper way of doing things. He reflected how this attitude had gained him the admiration of his associates in the body building club. Yes, he and his friend James would go this coming week to Helens Bay, where the rest of the club met to sunbathe and tan their immaculate bodies.

He was still trying to make his mind up. Should he become a concert pianist, as his teacher and mother wanted? Or follow his own star with his dance band? He cut a fine figure wherever he went, even in the dance hall where he met James' sister, Sadie. *He had better quicken his pace or he'd be late for work, he thought.* The white satin scarf he'd bought at the weekend would certainly set off his Anthony Eden hat and his pinstripe suit - which was the pride of the Castlereagh Road. His mother had paid for that, but then he was the apple of her eye. Some said he was a mummy's boy, but that was forgivable. Who wouldn't be after the death of his brother two years ago? And his sister during the war?

He wasn't walking any faster. No, he was getting slower. Perhaps he was getting the flu. By the time he came to stamp his card at the shipyard gate, he was five minutes late. They would dock his wages; he wouldn't be able to afford those new brogues this weekend. All thoughts of the new clothes he would buy that coming weekend were starting to vanish. He'd be off work for days at this rate. Normally you would work the odd cold or flu off, but this was a bad one. Should he take the day off now, go home and sweat it out? He kept on at his work bench until the end of his shift and barely stayed on his feet till he got on the tram that took him home up the Castlereagh Road. He stumbled off the tram and just made it to the footpath - where he collapsed. He crawled on his hands and knees the last 100 yards home. His mum put him straight to bed, and there he stayed for two years; polio.

Eventually he recovered, but a shadow of his glorious self, ambitions of Jim, the champion of the world, dashed forever.

This was the state of my father when he met my mother - totally convinced that by being hyper fit he had saved his own life. But had he not been so fit perhaps he would have been aware of the early warning signs of polio much sooner. I have always known this about Dad, but have been in denial, refusing to give him an excuse for his awful behaviour. Perhaps, as the years went by, he became bitter. He must have been terribly disappointed by my diminutive size, but convinced that in order to shine I would have to be 100 per cent fit too, or perhaps he thought he'd try to find a way of having a second chance at becoming the champion of the world through me. He was not often right. And this time he was wrong. Or maybe he was not often wrong, but this time he was right.

Granny and Grandad Mclurg.

The painting I bought in France that hung behind
Granny Callaghan's front door.

Mum when she was sixteen taken in a real photographers studio, all the clothes and jewelry were used in all sixteen photographs of her and her sisters, she also had two brothers.

CA 54919 on the road to Kometchie

John Graham Primary School Circa 1952
Eddie Hybner   Raymond The Knitter   David the top smasher   I'm sorry?
Joseph Borrington   Awlyn D'Arger   I'm sorry?   Peter Catto   C'est moi
I'm sorry?   Christie Hoffman Robert   McAlpine

Strandfontein beach with Lula (with floppy ear)

Ashfield school circa1955 6 smallest in the class
but not the only one in short trousers.

Belfast Education Authority

Telephone No. 56812

A.C. Stanley, B.A.
Headmaster.

Ashfield Boys' Secondary School,
Ashmount Park,
Belfast.

14th June, 1957.

TO WHOM IT MAY CONCERN:

George Callaghan came to this School in November, 1954, from a South African Primary School. We found him to be a boy of good paractical intelligence whose achievement in English was understandably not that of a boy of similar ability educated in this country.

During his two and a half years here he had made steady progress in all subjects, but his work in Art and Craft has been really outstanding. In successive examinations he has been placed first in Art, Woodwork, Metalwork and Mechanical Drawing and his work has figured prominently in a number of exhibitions.

During the past two years he has been taking a course leading to the Junior Technical Certificate, the examination for which is held during the present month.

Callaghan is a pleasant, sensible boy whom we have pleasure in recommending.

A.C.Stanley
Headmaster

The chord of 'D'! With Davey Patterson. Our first skiffle group.

Grandad with full head of hair and my protector Joan
His hand holds me, but his hand flops over Joan

Kennys Studio Dublin with new corduroy coat, tailor made.

Sketch of our stone cottage, Hamilton.

Our mobile studio, a visiting Kookaburra and Stef, the reason to believe.

We used large hand planes made of wood when I got to Ireland.

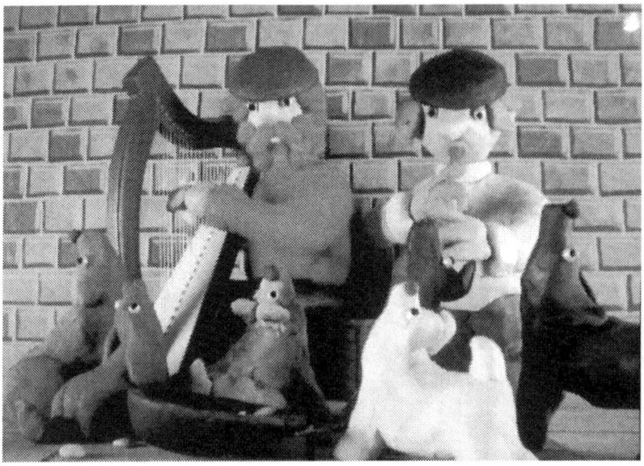

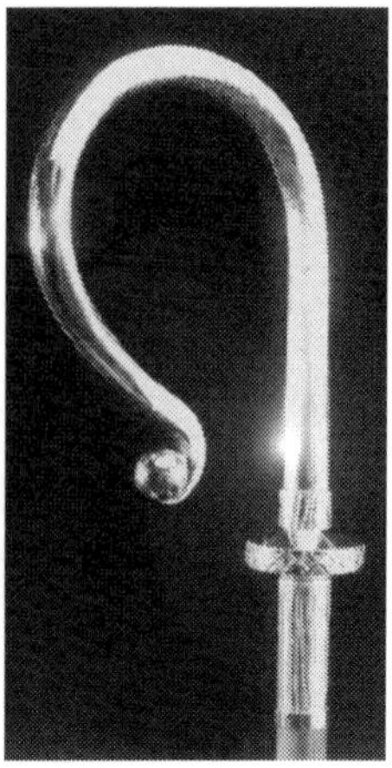

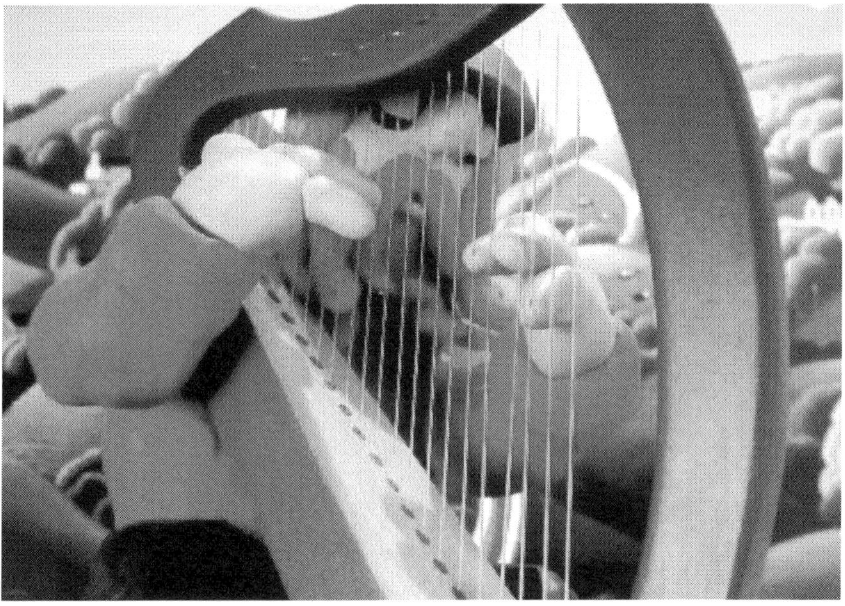

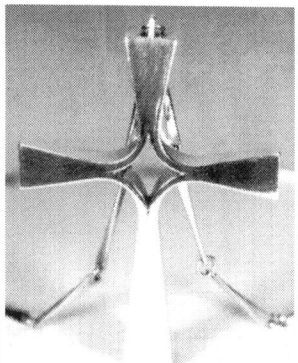

CROZIER & CROSS
for Bishop of Bendigo

Stills from Animation
PADDYWACK, HARPSONG,
PEACE TALKS, COLOURS OF ADAM

Phillips Terrace 2002 Cape Town, where I left the pliers in 1950!

MAITLAND AMATEUR BOXING CLUB TOURNAMENT.

8 p.m. on 15th October, 1953

50 lbs.	D. Dell	(Maitland)	vs.	G. Williams	(Youth League)
60 "	S. Saul	"	vs.	G. Gallagham	(Wynberg)
70 "	D. Mills	"	vs.	G. Kruger	"
85/90 lbs.	W. Prinsloo	"	vs.	J. Jenkins	"
100 lbs.	R. Peyters	"	vs.	J. Wellstedt	(Youth League)
110 lbs.	L. Saul	"	vs.	W. Baker	"
130 lbs.	K. Louw	"	vs.	P. Rheeder	"

Flyweight	R. Reich	(Maitland)	vs.	I. Wassung	(Youth League)
Lt. Welter	J. van Wyk	"	vs.	G. Fisher	"
Welter	C. Simpson	"	vs.	L. Kessel	"
Lightweight	R. Swarts	(Epping)	vs.	A.N. Other	
Feather	G. Vorster	(Lies.Park)	vs.		"
Lt. Welter	R. Reich	(Maitland)	vs.	A. O'Connor	(Wynberg)
Lt. Heavy	P. Murphy	"	vs.	C. Huntley	(Liesbeek Park)

Chapter Thirteen

Age of Enlightenment or things to ponder

Institutions

One of man's most creative areas are intellectual institutions; he will institutionalise everything - then proceed to set up boundaries and rules with which to protect it.

When I first started making harps, I met up with other musical instrument makers - they call themselves luthiers. It was suggested that we all meet up in a pub in Hobart. The chat was fun, we talked of timbers, glues and traditions, and before we knew where we were we had formed an association and we were holding an exhibition of musical instruments. The absolutes that came out of that were laughable! The poor chap that made the sound board from King Billy and not Spruce was crucified! The flute maker who used horizontal scrub and not Ebony or Rosewood was hung, drawn and quartered! The guitar maker was assassinated for not using rabbit glue! And I was transported back to Ireland for making a harp with a squared back! But I never learn, I went on to make them out of aluminum and carbon fibre! These luthiers were all criticised by their own rules. In reality there are no luthier absolutes, as historically they used whatever was available at the time.

Now I am faced with another institution, that of publishing this bloody manuscript! I have been on the internet, and there are so many of them screaming at you: "I am the important one! Not you! If you conform to my rules I might publish your work!"

They are as bad as my wife. If I haven't spelt it right - no sex for an hour! For that reason alone I would take Mark Twain out to dinner.

The Hard Stuff

Beyond my student days and besides the rare occasions when I specifically drink alcohol with the intentions of getting drunk, I cannot stand the taste of the stuff. I am also of the opinion that many other people do not like the stuff. But it certainly is the popular thing to do.

I suspect that it is an excuse for blokes to get together and actually touch each other, slap each other on the back, lean against each other and put their arms around each other.

And wine -people love to show just how fecking well clever they are. What I am getting at here is – do they really, really like the taste of this stuff? I have numerous friends who are vintners and I have been to musical functions at their vineyards. When the wine is flowing and the tables are strewn with endless vintages, I am often asked by the vintner why I am not drinking. I explain that I just don't like wine. This is usually interpreted as an immediate challenge to the vintner, who after several attempts to please me, produces the botryticised wine - you know, the wine that is so sweet that even I can drink it because I cannot taste the alcohol. The bottle is left on the table and the vineyard owner is pleased. I am not a happy chappie, though, because everyone at the table stops drinking what they have previously been drinking and now polish off the rest of the wine that has been brought over specially for me! Soon the vintner is pleased that I have drunk it all, so he replenishes it with another. Again I have one glass, and these wine connoisseur bastards polish off the rest of the second bottle, continually protesting to the vintners that it is much too sweet for them, of course.

A line from a friend's song says it all: "It's the falling over factor and the fact that it gets you drunk!"

The Blues

Time after time in France I have been asked to a Blues concert. The Blues was born out of struggle and toil. Originally it was black music, it has managed to bleed its way to be sung by white folk. There was a time when white folk would only listen to black music played by white folk dressed as black folk, then later to black folk dressed as black folk dressed as white folk. Blues has soul; it's dirty, it's about suppression, anger, passion, sex, drugs, booze, vice: all the great lowlife elements of society. This music is performed in the sleaziest, smoke ridden, alcohol saturated and drug induced state of intoxication to obtain maximum atmosphere and presentation; but this concert I am told will have none of those essential elements. None of that sinful rubbish. This current Blues presentation will be staged at our local tenth century church and the coup de gras is that the performer will be playing on a Steinway, further to boot, the entire production will have the priest's approval. Was that the same priest who forbade the singing of 'The Merry Widow' at a selection of opera arias at last summer's concert? If only that man on the cross could speak! Was it something about throwing the money changers out of the church? Or was it Blues singers?

"But the congregation will be nicely dressed !" I've been assured!
https://www.youtube.com/watch?v=xn50JSI0W-E

This clip on youtube explains it all. Lead Belly performs *Goodnight Irene* to a selected audience of black folks dressed as white folks sipping wine. The white man proudly presents his discovery- Lead Belly. Note the state of Leads guitar, it is held together with sticky tape and hope.

I know there are those among you who believe that this performance should have been played on a Steinway or a Martin guitar. The Klu Klux Klan- the Nazis and the Catholic church would think so (check out the comments below the TV screen).

Its those TRITONES, the very root of the blues and jazz that the Catholic church banned. It certainly is a brave priest and congregation that flies in the face of a papal decree to disallow such music to be performed in a church. (What an absolute load of crap but true!)

The thin edge of the wedge was when the church tried to clean up all those musical instruments. They removed the "Braes" from the harp, the sympathetic strings from the violin (Hardangar), anything that vibrated from the African cora, the buzzing mute on the horn, the grinding bass on the Hurdy Gurdy, the twanging, wining bridge on the sitar, the list goes on and on.

Mostly Ladies

I think that I reared my children with all the understanding of an artist, in that there are two parts to life: the art and the craft. I hope that I have taught them as much as I can about the craft of life, and left them to discover the art of life for themselves. I was going to devote a section of this book to write about my children, but knowing human nature they would be comparing the length and lines of the paragraphs that they have been each allotted. Enough to say that I have loved them all equally.

My own personal religion will die with me. My reward (or punishment) for having enjoyed such a full life are my memories. I rarely view these, though, as there is too much awe to cope with. All my children are there in their entirety in my memories.

If you were to take a peek, you would see:

My son Fintan crying - no, bawling - because his hands are frozen; he didn't know how cold snow was to touch.

Miche sitting in front of a fire knocking over a pile of wooden blocks after her bath and laughing.

Mea asking me why a hammer is a hammer in a Hobart hardware shop, Sunita having a pee in front of our visitors in the garden, her knickers down, straight after she had got off the school bus.

Lena and I laughing our heads off at a ridiculous Greek statue in someone's garden where I dropped her off to school.

I have no use for a god who keeps score. This book is my story and all my children are much too busy to be part of it. However, as a bit of arrogant advice ... many years ago Lena, my youngest daughter, and I became estranged and it took me about a year to discover the reason. All her friends had young parents, she explained, so why should she relate to, or love me when I was about to die on her because I was so old. (I was 50 at the time!) It wasn't fair, she said, that all her older sisters had had a younger Dad and hers was such an old man. I explained that she was the luckier of all the children as she had the advantage of a much wiser Dad. Eventually this pleased her and our life long friendship was renewed.

Children never see it as fair that one child supposedly had what the other was denied, or visa versa. Or how each child travels along a different part of the time line of their parents' wisdom.

My children are mostly girls. In ancient days, when men went off to war for years, when he returned he saw that mostly boys had been born - and people believed that this was the gods way of replenishing the men that had been killed in battle. This myth is alive and well today. Men boast of their manliness when they produce boy children. Statisticians and modern medicine have proven that abstinence produces males, whereas regular sex produces females. When I tell this story to fathers of girls they get embarrassed, and fathers of boys just get angry.

Imagination

I feel people confuse imagination with intimidation. Consider visual imagination. People in the past have often suggested places for me to paint. They go on to describe how it looks, and often that is enough for me to produce a drawing or painting.

Give a child drawing materials – pencils and paper – and they will make marks on the paper. The products of their labours will never make it to the fridge magnet unless there is something recognisable, however. So maybe these early scribbles have nothing to do with the visual; we have six senses. But the intimidation has already started. The closer to reality their drawings are, the more prominent position they get on the fridge. These drawings, they realise, have society's approval, so their imagination is well on the way to be directed.

Soon they will be transferring their skills to interpreting somebody else's imagination. Consider a dragon. Ask any child to draw a dragon and they will relate to any previous references they have seen on TV, in books or in comics, and whatever they produce, the proud parent will declare "What an imagination!" No it's not imagination; it's a re-imagination of something acceptable that they've been indoctrinated with. Imagination is to do with taking two and two and getting five. Every idea owes its birth to what's gone before, but there are those among us who are capable of bringing these originally perceived dragons together, using their own imagination, and coming up with something quite unique and original.

I am cursed by knowing or trying to know how things work. I should have taken my teacher's advice - Mr Smith of Ashfield School and worked at Short's, the aircraft factory. Who knows what I would have done? At first I criticised Quentin Blake, who illustrated a lot of Roald Dahl's books. He seemed not have a clue how things worked, but in later days I envied the bugger.

Once during a dinner party, our conversation turned to TV. One alternate couple - who were almost self-sufficient - declared that they didn't have a TV. They had two children aged six and seven, and last year, they explained, they visited friends who had a television. They went onto say that the two boys were not the slightest bit interested in the TV. "Oh," I said, "they hadn't developed the skills to watch or understand TV." There followed a stunned silence, and slowly the husband, saw an oncoming tunnel at the end of the light. He turned red with confusion and embarrassment. The realisation of having denied his children a skill was devastating, and it brought the evening to an abrupt end.

I don't really know what creativity is, but I certainly know what it isn't: people who when they emerge out of their creative stage as children go on to be awarded a diploma. It solely demonstrates their ability to conform to all our aspirations for them, and nothing else. The diploma is displayed for all to see, kept in place by a magnet … on the fridge door.

I am sure that my attitude to creativity was nurtured by the absence of books, writing and drawing materials as a child.

Playground

The community raised the funds, and the local school commissioned the school of design to manufacture all the necessary equipment for a super-duper new children's playground. Eventually the completed items arrived. They were removed from their crates and installed on the selected sight.

After the initial awed response from everyone concerned - parents and children - things settled down. It was later observed that the children were not playing on the purpose designed and built installations, instead they were playing in, on top of, around, and with the crates that the installations had arrived in. The council eventually removed the crates and the children had no alternative than to play with the those purpose built items, their imagination quashed.

Health and safety arrived one day, and those purpose built items was deemed unsafe and were removed.

Rubbish

A programme on TV showed experts demonstrating how the pyramids must have been built. They were explaining the types of different scaffolding and different ramps that would have to be used for such a mega structure; the ramps obviously having to be bigger than the pyramid itself. I was watching this programme on TV and criticising it.

"Rubbish!" I cried.

"Okay, smart arse, show me how you would do it," Stef said.

At a time like this my interest goes into overdrive. (This was back in the days when I was still trying to impress Stef. I'm still trying to impress her. In my world she's the only one worth impressing.)

Well after some thought, I said, "The pyramid itself is its own ramp. For the first 20 feet build a ramp into the pyramid almost to the other side. From this level all the stones can now be lowered into position all around to the outside. The next 20 feet has its own new ramp at 90 degrees to the first ramp, rather like a spiral staircase. You then continue this until you reach the apex. All stones, including outer white finishing stones can then be lowered, *not lifted*, into position. This ramp staircase would be filled in in during the final stage of the structure. These ramps would also give access to any internal chambers."

As for moving large stone blocks around the continent of Africa, we had done that as kids in Philip's Terrace in Wynberg. Whenever you wanted to move a large item, you turned it into a wheel or a roller, enabling you to roll any massive weight to any location; from Cape Town to Cairo.

Stef insisted that I send a drawing of my idea to the Egyptologist, Philip Adams, for his comments. His reply said that I was 'an extremely smart bugger'. He did not think, however, that they had used this method, and if they had, they would still be building pyramids today.

Look

I was standing in front of the latest high definition TV - which was truly amazing, all bells and whistles, and everything crystal sharp from corner to corner. Then it became impossible to absorb the image as there was just too much information of equal value all over the screen. Perhaps the video they were showing was for demonstration purposes only, and not intended for normal use. Then I realised that all the old rules of how the eyes and brain work together must still apply.

One of my first lessons on the way the eyes work came from Romeo Toogood at Art College. It happened in the still life painting class. If you want to know the influence one object has on another, don't look at it. Look at the object next to it, but concentrate on the object of your interest.

I have done a course in speed reading. The first point of interest was to watch the person in front of you reading and to count the number of pauses they made as they scanned across the page from left to right; it was maybe five times. One of the training purposes of speed reading is to teach you to scan the page in one movement. Another thing is to illustrate how the brain and mind work. Select a small section of three or four words, and try to see just how much of the rest of the page is in focus - it's very little. Turn the page upside down and much, much more comes into focus. This is because we don't know what the words actually say and our brains need more information - so our focus opens up and widens.

When we look at a panorama the eye stays relatively still, but the brain is scanning the entire scene. This is because there is nothing we can discern in detail until we focus on a selected area. Should you switch and change areas or items that are at different distances, again you'll need to re-focus, and the easiest way of re-focusing is to blink. Oddly, we use the same blinking process to punctuate the end of an idea. If you watch someone deep in thought, ask them what they were thinking about. Straight after the thought, they will have blinked.

The peripheral vision is a fantastic concept. We are able to discern movement on the edge of our peripheral vision, yet if we turn our head and look directly at the perceived movement, there is nothing to see. Giving raise to seeing ghosts maybe?

Our eyes contain millions of cones and rods. Towards the centre of the eye they are closer together. Those at the peripheral are fewer and further apart, but are much more sensitive. We are told this is nature's way of being aware of any wild beast in our peripheral vision, for the same reason we can discern more shades of green than any other colour. The less sensitive and more numerous cones in the centre of the eye are more suited to studying detail. The brain is also programmed to detect the whites of the eyes in other people. Walking with a friend across a road, a person might be looking in your general direction, but you can discern if they are looking directly at you or not. There's nothing cosmic about this. We are programmed to detect the slightest movement of the whites of the eyes.

THREE AND A HALF MILLION

What awesome places some churches are! Man's ability to enclose such vast spaces architecturally can be breathtaking. To suspend a roof over such distances has taken much creative imagination and ingenuity. If impressive imagination and awe are what you are after, linger under a magnificent stand of trees when the sunlight is shafting through the leaves. Wander down between the dark hedges in County Down, Ireland. Stand in the entrance to the Jenolan caves in New South Wales, three and a half million years old. Travel down the Colorado River. None of these places are lined with trumpery or gee-gaws. That is for churches and cathedrals. Our economy is charged, and based on that crap. The glitz that we wear, the frills on our dresses, the chrome on our motors. Where do we learn the value of such bad taste? That little man on His opal-encrusted cross would turn in His tomb (if He were still in it) if He saw half the crap that He is hanging around on! Any child in arms being dragged around such values is going to grow up adoring all that trumpery they sell on the jewellery channels.

Those architects and builders certainly had their act together. It was those guys that followed after them with their paints and brushes and their hammers and chisels, including that Michelangelo fellow that did all the harm!

PERPIGNAN

We were wandering around the grand cathedral in Perpignan, past alcove after alcove of religious gee-gaws, each one designed to appeal to certain dimensions in the human psyche. If there is truth that we can be divided into specific characteristic slots, then there was more than one of those for each alcove that would relate to at least one characteristic type.

As we wandered past these icons, I asked, "Does any of this strike you as familiar?"

And at the same time Stef asked, "What sort of people is this supposed to appeal to?"

The night before, while awaiting for the 7.30 restaurant to open, we wandered around the latest, most modern fairground in France. All the booths used the most current electrical technology to solicit our patronage and interest. The fair was crowded, and all attempts to lure us to stop and linger failed. For the same reason we did not linger in that Perpignan cathedral. We were atheists, we had learnt our aesthetics elsewhere.

Craven Images

If you don't drag your babes in arms around those dark, dingy and frightening places, there is no way you are ever going to get them to go to those places of their own accord. If they do, then their minds are already unbalanced – seriously - think about it. What child, teenager or adult is going to choose to enter a dark, poorly lit space with walls covered in images of suffering and agony, with spooky flickering candles everywhere and blokes with hearts on fire? Where 14 images of a bloke dragging a cross across the landscape, having the shit kicked out of him and whipped at every stage of his journey, and spikes stuck in his head - and as a special reward – he is nailed to that cross he brought with him? Even then the cruelty doesn't stop. They go and stick a spear in him after he's dead. The pretty colours coming through the illuminated windows offer some sort of relief, until your mind starts converting the pretty colours into the same pictures that you've just encountered.

Along the walls you will encounter even more of these images, mostly in the forms of statues of people who have supported this lifestyle. Of course, all that trumpery culminates in that naked statue that hovers lifeless above your head - blood oozing around his head. Your brain should be pretty warped by now.

I once took one of my children into one of these spaces at Easter. Christ was there as usual on his cross, and he was surrounded by four tables upon which were the implements of torture that represented the local community. These were covered in pseudo blood, they included whips, animal traps, man traps, pitchforks, spades and swords – but no guns. At times like that, locals can be laughable.

Three young lads sadly killed themselves below our house on the main road after a drunken road accident against the hydro pole that stopped their ambitions. The family erected a monument of beer tinnies bearing the legend: 'There'll be Toranas in Heaven'. Torana is a model of Holden car.

I tried to explain the reasoning behind this sort of thinking to my daughter, but felt perhaps I might be going down a similar but different area of intimidation. I am of the opinion and have argued so, that there are three, maybe four types who support this sort of thinking: the absolute idiot who actually believes it; the power-hungry who exploit it; the person who is hiding behind it all, and the do-gooder.

Clean Up

As this is not a medical journal nor a book of science I shall not refer to the dick as a penis.

I have just looked at the most recent excuses on the web that are given for men peeing on the floor surrounding the toilet. All the excuses are wrong! Even the medical ones are wrong! At best only one of them is half-way right. That excuse went on to explain how men have to milk their dicks to remove those final drops of pee from the channel that leads from the bladder to the opening in the dick. This part is quite accurate, but that is not the problem. The problem occurs at the commencement of peeing, not at the end.

If the foreskin has been pulled back unintentionally, then the opening in the dick is revealed. This is not a predictable aperture, though. No, it is not simply a round opening, it is usually a slit running north to south. It is this aperture that is the cause of the dilemma.

At the first release of pee, the pressure can vary because of the urgency or the age of the male. But where and how this slit will open is totally unpredictable. This opening has a mind of its own, over which you have no control of, it can open in the middle, or either end, or anywhere along that slit. Further to this – if you own one of these instruments where the sheath encases the entire head of the dick and completely covers the eye/slit, then the problems might be two-fold. The chance of lining up that infinite slit in the head of the dick with another unpredictable hole made with the foreskin are nigh impossible. At times of being cold, or when the dick is extremely flaccid, or for those who have an abundance of foreskin, this can create an added tube at the extremity of the dick. This added tube also has a mind of its own; it has an infinite directional ability! To aid understanding for anyone who doesn't own a dick – this is like turning on a floppy garden hose with a pressure nozzle at the end, full bore, and trying to hit a target at first flow holding the hose three feet from the nozzle!

I am 72 and still can't predict in which direction that initial projection will flow. So what to do? Don't ask or expect a man to sit down on a toilet, it is his birthright to point, aim and score, and it is part of his wellbeing. Mothers be careful - you have had your chance to impose your motherly control with sit-down potty training– don't infringe again on a boy's rite of passage. Men piss standing up! And no man can aim correctly in the initial moments! After that we are all brilliant shots!

So men - clean up the floor yourself, use the sink, or sit down on the loo when you are visiting people's houses!

Overdrive

As I mentioned before, in 1966 my libido was zero. And I'd started reading every book that I could get my hands on the subject of sex. One book mentioned how women react at evangelistic meetings, and what happens to them at similarly extreme emotional moments when their imaginations go into overdrive. What I read in the Kinsey report - (the Kinsey Reports are two books on human sexual behavior) - made a lot of sense, and although their findings have been slightly revised all these years later, it is still pretty accurate. I hope I am correct in assuming that a lady's enjoyment of sex is to be found in her own imagination...? What could possibly happen? What's going to happen? What's going to happen next? Why didn't it happen? Will it happen again? All these ideas are in anticipation and with 100 per cent conviction that it will happen. Hopefully,....OVERDRIVE!!!!!!!!.The Clitoris sorry cant help you there, I still don't know where it is ?????????????????????

After the sexual revolution I thought all that the Irish attitude was over (*in out and repeat if necessary!*) but after watching current movies and TV they still don't seem to have got it right. Where is all that ground work, all the fore play? It demands a greater investment and promise. I have only seen a hint of any understanding on TV, were they had the slightest inclination of how it all works. It was in an episode of "Friends". Rachel and Monica explain how sex works for them by drawing a chart of the erogenous zones and how to stimulate these and in which order.

The male role is to be there and appear to look creative and imaginative. Truly enjoyable sex is hours in the planning, the ground work, the foreplay and for me a hasty retreat!

While the unselfish guy is delaying instant gratification, admiring the ladies response and the obvious view, maintaining at all times that erection, he knows that after satisfaction he just wants to *be out of there mate!* Until the scene fades from his memory about one hour later!

Unfortunately the male carries a thermometer to his ego and well being in his pocket. It is a brave and clever woman who has this in her custody. Only a genius can control an item of such fragile temperament. Only a woman is capable of such clever and devious manipulation. Men certainly have a limited use in a relationship. As they say "Man, that useless bit of flesh at the end of a dick!"

The only time I was truly proud of my father was when he died and I discovered hidden in the folds of his wallet a clipping from a medical journal explaining the female orgasm.

Archery cheats

My latest archery magazine from the National Field Archery, challenges me to respond to their photographs on the front cover. "Should I?" I thought. Field archery is not like target archery, it is laid out through woodland areas, usually through undulating terrain, rather like a heavy overgrown golf course. The cover of this magazine showed an archer in camouflage gear. His hat was on back to front. His bow was of the compound variety with attached extended stabilisers, also the image was mirrored, left to right. I felt sure they wanted a light hearted reply but I am a little bit passionate about my archery. This guy was doing everything wrong. He was a danger to all concerned.

1. He was wearing camouflage gear. The target didn't stand a chance with all those bells and whistles but more importantly-
2. The extrusions, stabilisers and high powered sights made him a danger to all and sundry like a stags horns in the thicket.
3. It is claimed that if archery doesn't accept these choices, then the sport will not survive.

If you go on a field archery shoot you can expect traditional longbows, re-curve bows, reflex- de-flex Asian bows, Eskimo bows (basically a bent stick with string and arrows). Then there are the compound bows with wheels, cams, steel cables and 101 different sights. Now we have crossbows, again with 101 different kinds of sights. Among all this toxophilia are an equal number of ways of cheating. There are even one group that go around with cards of each animal, showing the distance to each target and binoculars to locate the kill zone. There are more ways of cheating with your anchor point, that a macramé knitter would envy.

The turnout at these events is phenomenal and yet the organisers claim that if we don't let all these categories compete, the sport will die. "Let it" I say. I don't want to go traipsing through the countryside with a bunch of camouflaged, over-bowed, stabilised, cheating fellows just to keep the sport alive.

Gate Post 52

When we were living in Wynberg, South Africa, a neighbouring man borrowed my father's pincer pliers - so my father had sent me to fetch them back. On the homeward journey, the local lads were having a game of football, so I joined in. I set the pliers on top of a high gate post for safe keeping. But after the game I could not recall where I had left them.

All hell let loose when I returned home without the pliers. The more barging Dad gave me, the more confused I became.

Over 50 years later, long after my father's death, and whilst living in South Hobart, Tasmania, I awoke from a dream recalling where I had left the pliers.

We did return to Wynberg, but the pliers were gone! The gate post was still there, however, but was a lot lower than I remember.

Slainte

There has never been a moment to lose in my life. There must have been a time when I encountered boredom, but it obviously affected me adversely, as I have avoided boredom all my life. I have never travelled in search of happiness or contentment - quite the reverse. Approval from others has never been my goal, except from my family, although I know I am certainly no island.

'Nothing is either good or bad, right or wrong, but thinking makes it so' -

    William Shakespeare (and me!).
   Proud to be Irish? Or ashamed to be human?

Printed in Great Britain
by Amazon